SHAMANS, MYSTICS AND DOCTORS

Sudhir Kakar

SHAMANS, MYSTICS AND DOCTORS

A Psychological Inquiry into India and Its Healing Traditions

BEACON PRESS
BOSTON

First published as a Beacon paperback in 1983 by
arrangement with Alfred A. Knopf, Inc.

Beacon Press books are published under the auspices
of the Unitarian Universalist Association,
25 Beacon Street, Boston, Massachusetts 02108
Published simultaneously in Canada by
Fitzhenry & Whiteside Limited, Toronto

Printed in the United States of America

(paperback) 9 8 7 6 5 4 3 2 1

Library of Congress Cataloging in Publication Data

Kakar, Sudhir.
  Shamans, mystics, and doctors.

  Reprint. Originally published: New York: Knopf, 1982.
  Includes index.
  1. Mentally ill—Care and treatment—India.
2. Healing—India. I. Title.
[RC451.I4K34 1983] 616.89′00954   83-70654
ISBN 0-8070-2903-3 (pbk.)

For my sister, Suleena,
in memory of our parallel
yet shared childhoods.

CONTENTS

ACKNOWLEDGMENTS

The study on which this book is based was made possible by the grant of a Homi Bhabha Fellowship. I am grateful to the Fellowship Council and its honorary director, Narayana Menon, for their generous support. My student and friend Ashok Nagpal, who shared my enthusiasm for the project and worked closely with me through its many phases, was of immense help with the fieldwork, especially with the healers of local and folk traditions. He is the second part of the "we" and the "colleague" referred to in the text, and my debt to him is great.

Parts of the book were presented at the Mind and Society Seminar of the Centre for the Study of Developing Societies, the research seminars of the Department of Indian Studies and the Psychosocial Group at the University of Melbourne, the South-Asian Seminar at the University of Chicago, seminars of the Departments of Psychiatry of the San Francisco Children's Hospital, Parkville Psychiatry Unit, Melbourne, and the Royal Children's Hospital, Melbourne. Without being able to list specific individuals, I am happy to acknowledge my debt to the discussants who helped me to clarify many puzzling issues.

The persons I *can* list, and with great pleasure too, are Wendy O'Flaherty and Kim Marriott of the University of Chicago and Don Miller of the University of Melbourne. They gave much of their time in going through the manuscript, were generous with their praise and delight when they came across something that pleased them and were gently but firmly critical whenever they disagreed. There are indeed very few pleasures in the otherwise lonely work of writing that can match the sharing of its product with such perceptive and concerned friends.

I also wish to express my warm appreciation to Lee Goerner at Knopf, both for his enthusiasm for the book and for his editorial skill which made me realize clearly how sometimes less is more.

And finally, my thanks go to Apeksha, Kamla and my father Sardarilal Kakar, all of whom have been a consistent source of love and encouragement over the years.

SHAMANS,
MYSTICS AND
DOCTORS

1

INTRODUCTION

This book explores the traditions of India that are concerned with the restoration of what is broadly termed "mental health" in the West. Without going into complicated definitional and conceptual issues, I shall only mention that in the context of this exploration, I do not use mental health as a narrow theoretical concept—that would indeed be a dubious undertaking—but as a rubric, a label which covers different perspectives and concerns, such as the absence of incapacitating symptoms, integration of psychological functioning, effective conduct of personal and social life, feelings of ethical and spiritual well-being and so on. Drawing on three years of fieldwork, I have tried to describe, analyze and reflect upon my experiences with gurus of mystical cults, shamans, practitioners of ancient systems of medicine and other indigenous colleagues who are also professionally engaged in the common endeavor which the Oxford English Dictionary, in its third entry under "healing," defines as "to restore (a person, etc.) from some evil condition or affection (as sin, grief, disrepair, unwholesomeness, danger, destruction); to save, purify, cleanse, repair, mend."

The diversity of these traditions in India and the astonishing variety and number of practitioners can make a stranger to the country feel that healing—in its manifold aspects—is a central individual and cultural preoccupation, an impression which may not be far off the mark. Like very few other people, Indians have long been involved in constructing explanatory systems for psychic distress and evolving techniques for its alleviation. Besides the few psychiatrists of modern medicine, there are the traditional physicians—the *vaids* of the Hindu Ayurveda and Siddha systems and the *hakim* of the Islamic *unani* tradition—many of whom also practice what we today call "psychological medicine." In addition, there are palmists, horo-scope specialists, herbalists, diviners, sorcerers and a variety of sha-mans, whose therapeutic efforts combine elements from classical Indian astrology, medicine, alchemy and magic, with beliefs and practices from the folk and popular traditions. And then, of course, we have the ubiquitous *sadhus*, swamis, *maharajs*, *babas*, *matas* and *bhagwans*, who trace their lineage, in some fashion or other, to the mystical-spiritual traditions of Indian antiquity and claim to special-ize (whatever else they might also do) in what in the West in a more religious age used to be called "soul health"—the restoration of moral and spiritual well-being.

While not exhaustive, an attempt to describe this threefold divi-sion of healers does not follow any rigorous categorization, but it does correspond to the general notion that there are three different realms of individual functioning. From the first birth cry to the last breath, an individual exists in his *soma*, his *psyche* and his *polis*; in other words, a person is simultaneously a body, a self and a social being.[1] Of course, the body, the self and the polis do not possess a fixed, immutable meaning across cultures. As we shall see later, the concept of the body and the understanding of its processes are not quite the same in the Hindu Ayurveda as they are in Western medicine. The self too—the Hindu "subtle body"—is not primarily a psychological category in India though it does include something of the Western psyche. According to the Hindus, the disturbances in the order of the self, for instance, are not seen to have their genesis in early family connections, but are related to the notion of the workings of karma over the whole of the individual's life cycle as well as across the cycle of his many lives. When we talk of shamans and other healers of folk traditions correcting disturbances in the individ-ual's social order, then we must remember that for many Indians the polis consists not only of living members of the family and the community, but also of ancestral spirits—the *pitris*—and other spirit beings who populate the Indian cosmos.

The highly diverse activities of Indian healers share a certain family resemblance in that, as compared to Western psychothera-pies, the role of the sacred is more prominent in India. By "sacred" I mean not only the Brahman of the mystics, the Krishna of the devotees or the gods of the rituals, but also the spirits of ancestors and forests, the beings that live in enchanted groves, the specters that haunt cremation grounds and the demons who wait at the next crossing. It is the sacred that links the guru concerned with the malaise of the spirit to the shaman treating illness due to machinations of the spirits. In practice, therefore, there may be a considerable overlap between the three orientations. It is the introduction of the sacred in the assumptive worlds of the healer and his patient and the areas of the patient's *being* that they jointly seek to make *well* which make these healing traditions seem alien to modern man, irrespective of the society he belongs to and the part of the world he lives in—East or West, North or South. For the West, the home of modernism and now a state of mind rather than a geographical region, the connection of health with orders other than that of the body or the mind no longer exists. It is generally forgotten, for instance, that not too long ago, the ministrations of the priest on the deathbed and the doctor on the sickbed were both termed clinical. However, with the irresistible march of scientific naturalism over the last one hundred years, the domain of the clinical has been finally and firmly usurped by the doctor, and the priest forced into exile.

There are many in the West today who regret the disappearance of the sacred from the healing sciences and its removal generally from the world of everyday life. As far as psychotherapy is concerned, these people feel that a psychotherapist in a traditional culture may be greatly aided by the continuing presence of the sacred in his society. The whole weight of the community's religion, myths and history enters sacred therapy as the therapist proceeds to mobilize strong psychic energies inside and outside the patient which are no longer available in modern society.[2] How closely do such views depict reality and how much are they an expression of a Western mourning at the loss of the sacred? How do sacred therapies really work? What are the major differences between sacred and profane psychotherapies? These are some of the questions to which a work on Indian healing traditions must also address itself. A comparison of the form and content of indigenous healing networks with Western assumptions and practices is, then, a second major objective of this book.

The intimate connection between mental illness and society is now widely recognized, though there is a vigorous dispute on the precise nature and the extent of this connection. Foucault, for instance, has pointed out that each age of civilization, from the medieval period to modern times, has had its own view of madness which closely reflects the general social and logical preoccupations of the time.[3] Psychopathology is not independent of social history, for each age draws the split between madness and reason at a different point and in a different fashion. Many anthropologists have complemented Foucault's account of the historical relativity of mental illness by drawing attention to the cultural relativity of psychiatric concepts. Psychotherapy, too, is at least partly a social institution which incorporates many of the values and demands of its surrounding society. Moreover, an understanding of how psychotherapy works in a particular society usually requires an explication of the way psychotherapy is related to the broader cultural context and its symbolic structures. In other words, an exploration of Indian psychotherapeutic tradition not only tells us about certain social values and pressures operating in Indian society but also affords a glimpse into the symbolic universes of Indian culture in which its various healing traditions are embedded. Besides its descriptive and comparative intent, then, a third major aim of this work is an elaboration of the interplay between the individual and his society and culture and an exploration of Indian "cultural psychology," as I like to call this interplay. I have sought to understand the healers and the traditions out of which they operate in their own terms and on their own grounds; however, the identifications needed for this purpose have not always been easy to make. This has only partially to do with the personalities of the various healers, *i.e.*, on the degree of their attractiveness or unpleasantness. The difficulty in maintaining "openness" lay more in the fact that, though we belong to an overarching "Indian culture"—using culture in Clifford Geertz's sense as "an ordered system of meaning and symbols . . . in terms of which individuals define their world, express their feelings and make their judgements"[4]—I was often aware of a substantial historical and cultural distance between myself and some of the healers—the tribal shamans and the *pir*, for instance—and their patients. Often, this gulf made me doubt whether the significance of their healing efforts could ever be fully grasped by the conceptual tools I brought to the task. In such moments of doubt, I generally consoled myself with the thought that, fortunately, a "full and complete" understanding is not a human but a divine prerogative.

In my encounters with Indian healers and healing traditions, I was often aware of a general feeling of ambivalence. One side of this ambivalence ultimately derives from my being a Western-trained psychoanalyst in a culture whose soil is not particularly conducive to psychoanalysis, either as a method of therapy or as a theory of human nature. For instance, to take only one aspect of psychoanalytic practice in India, it is rarely recognized how much a certain kind of introspection—a sine qua non for psychoanalysis—is a peculiarly Western trait, deeply rooted in Western culture. Indeed, as Simon and Weiner have pointed out, the introspective element of Western civilization is ancient and can be traced back to later Greek thought, where the definitions of self and of identity became contingent upon an active process of examining, sorting out and scrutinizing the "events" and "adventures" of one's own life.[5] The activity of introspection became closely connected with the idea of "the true self," as typified by the Socratic use of the phrase "Know thyself." This kind of introspection is simply not a feature of Indian culture and its literary traditions. Even today, in the essentially Western-inspired genre of autobiography, Indian writings often tend to have a curiously flat quality as far as the scrutiny of the life in terms of a ruthless examination of motives and feelings is concerned. The section on childhood, whose ambivalences and ambiguities are the riveting content of a good autobiography, as well as the section on the turmoil of youth, are generally skipped over with driblets of information and conventional pieties such as "Mother was loving," "Father was affectionate," "Brothers were kind." With rare exceptions, Indian autobiographies are evocations of places and accounts of careers, records of events from which the self has been excised. This observation is not meant to be a criticism but to point out the absence of an Indian counterpart to Western-style introspection. The meditative procedures of Indian psychophilosophical schools of "self-realization" to which introspective activity may conceivably be compared, are of a different nature and follow radically different goals. The Indian injunction "Know thyself" *(atmanamvidhi)* is related to a Self other than the one referred to by Socrates. It is a self uncontaminated by time and space and thus without the life-

historical dimension which is the focus of psychoanalysis and of
Western romantic literature. In some of the best of modern Indian
novels, the introspective passages are generally hesitant and unsure,
the look inward often coming to rest upon the self of Indian philosophy rather than the self of a uniquely personal psychology.[6] (Let me
add that I am speaking here in broad cultural-historical terms and
not referring to introspective capacities of particular individuals in
India or, for that matter, in the West, which may vary widely across
the spectrum. My general impression of Indian patients who do not
belong to the Westernized middle classes, however—in the metropolises of Bombay and Calcutta, where the bulk of the small
Indian psychoanalytic community is concentrated—is that introspection in the Western sense may often have to be taught before
the analytical dialogue becomes possible and that an analyst in India
tends to be more didactical than his Western colleague.)

Apart from matters of therapeutic practice, the marginality of
psychoanalysis to Indian culture is also due to its concepts of the
person and the nature of reality, which are radically opposed to the
dominant Indian views on these matters. I elaborate upon these
opposing world views later (chapter 5). Here, I shall only mention
that the Indian psychoanalyst's marginality to his society and culture
is not of the same order as is supposed to have been the case with
the early European analysts. Psychoanalysis, however unacceptable
its ideas may have appeared at the beginning of this century, was still
very much a child of Western culture, with demonstrable and, since
then, demonstrated links to Western philosophical traditions, of
which the echoes of Nietzsche's ideas in Freud's work provide only
one example. Tracing the lineage of psychoanalytic propositions in
the Western cultural tradition is a respected scholarly activity; it
would seem a dubious undertaking at best even to try to establish
such links with the Indian and Japanese cultural traditions, the only
two non-Western societies with a psychoanalytical movement. In
other words, and using an Indian metaphor, the early Western
analysts may have been outcastes of Western society but they were
not the untouchables of its culture, which they subsequently influenced to such a marked degree. Their situation is not comparable
to that of the Indian analyst, whose commitment to his professional
identity may demand if not a rejection of then at least a withdrawal
from much of his cultural tradition.

The other side of the ambivalence I experienced has to do with my being an Indian and, in the study of the Indian healers and healing traditions which are so much informed by the Indian world view, having more than a sneaking sympathy with the healing endeavors, however bizarre their methods and assumptions may appear to a modern psychotherapist. I could therefore identify with John Woodroffe's remarks made more than half a century ago when, in the preface to his studies on tantra, he writes, "When I entered on a study of this Sastra I did so in the belief that India did not contain more fools than exist among other peoples. . . . Behind the unintelligent practice, which doubtless to some extent exists amongst multitude of every faith, I felt sure there must be a rational principle, since men on the whole do not continue throughout the ages to do that which is in itself meaningless and is therefore without result."[7] This does not mean, as Woodroffe also goes on to say, that as an Indian one must accept "what is without worth just because it is Indian," but that the Indianness seems to impose an obligation to understand Indian cultural phenomena as thoroughly as one can, with a critical awareness of the assumptions underlying the methods and sciences with which this understanding is sought to be reached, before evaluative judgments on what is part of one's cultural identity can be made.

Ambivalence and marginality have, of course, their uses; the boundary spaces between cultures are not necessarily bad places to live in, especially if one can call on a few kindred souls for company. A degree of alienation from one's culture, a deep exposure to other world views and even a temporary period of living "as others" may indeed be necessary for heightening one's perceptions about the culture and society one is born into. For this very reason, anthropologists may be eminently qualified for the study not so much of other societies but of their own. ("Marginality," "alienation," "ambivalence," "boundary," are perhaps not the right words to describe what I mean here, since they connote a subjective experience of pain and exclusion without indicating the presence of a corresponding heightening of the self—a knowing of oneself "only in ambiguity" as Merleau-Ponty puts it[8]—and the curious comfort that comes after the first unease has been accommodated.)

Having discussed my appreciation of cultural relativity and the significant role of culture in the study of healing traditions let me

now reverse myself. Very often, one of my most striking impressions
was of enduring human concerns in the Indian psychotherapies and
in the patients' lives where the culture itself seemed to be of little
import. It was the repeated observation of psychological universali-
ties that allowed me to shift from a dialectical mode aimed at
understanding a particular healing phenomenon through an elaboration of its context, to a more categorical mode wherein I sought to
locate the same phenomenon in a wider framework of understanding
provided by psychoanalytic knowledge.

The contradiction in simultaneously pursuing cultural relativity
and psychological universalism, looking at the healing phenomena
first in cultural terms and then in psychoanalytic ones, is evident.
Perhaps it is best to accept this contradiction, as Lionel Trilling does
when he writes of his own response toward literature: "Generally our
awareness of the differences between the moral assumptions of one
culture and those of another is so developed and active that we find
it hard to believe there is any such thing as an essential human
nature; but we all know moments when these differences, as literature attests to them, seem to make no difference, seem scarcely to
exist. We read the *Iliad* or the plays of Sophocles or Shakespeare and
they come so close to our hearts and minds that they put to rout,
or into abeyance, our instructed consciousness of moral life as it is
conditioned by a particular culture—they persuade us that human
nature never varies, that the moral life is unitary and its terms
perennial, and that only a busy intruding pedantry could have suggested otherwise."[9]

The contradiction between a cultural view of the healing traditions and a universalistic psychological approach, the ambivalence in
being an Indian and a psychoanalyst, the experience of living at the
margins of both Indian and Western cultures, are reflected throughout this book. If they sometimes mar its clarity and theoretical
purity, they also provide the work with its impetus. Instead of feeling
uncomfortable about leaving contradictions unresolved and ambivalence "untreated," I have sought to savor cultural differences while
enjoying the recognition of universal human concerns. But, then,
perhaps I am a Hindu after all, who traditionally does not seek a
synthesis of opposites but is content to keep each as it is. As Wendy
O'Flaherty tells us about Hindu myths, ". . . in chemical terms one

might say that the conflicting elements are resolved into a suspension rather than a solution"[10]: the aesthetic satisfaction of a Hindu myth resides in the full savoring of both the extremes rather than seeking a synthesis. The theoretical underpinnings of this book are derived from a psychology of the human mind that originated in the West; its aesthetic inspiration, though, is purely Indian.

I

LOCAL AND
FOLK TRADITIONS

2

SOUL KNOWLEDGE
AND SOUL FORCE

The Pir of Patteshah Dargah

Patteshah's *dargah* is a small, attractive mosque built sometime during the eighteenth century in memory of a Sufi saint. Unlike many other similar mosques and temples in Delhi that have traditional healers practicing on their premises, this shrine has acquired more than a local prominence by the presence of an old *hakim*—the practitioner of the Islamic *unani* system of medicine—whose diagnostic feats through the traditional method of reading the pulse have become widely known and acknowledged all over the metropolis. The *dargah*, however, is a polyclinic in the sense that it has another resident *hakim* who practices in the shade of his famous colleague and, so to speak, picks up the leavings. My interest, however, was directed toward the third specialist of the shrine's trio of healers—the *pir* (wise elder) who, insofar as he also treats what we today call mental disorders, was a professional colleague with whom I could spend some days observing and discussing the practice of his art.

The room in which the *pir* saw his patients and other supplicants was on the right side of the entrance to the mosque. It was small, barely twelve feet in length, the sole window curtained by sackcloth so that even on a bright and sunny day the merest trickle of light filtered through and made only a marginal difference to the room's particular shade of darkness. The gloom was increased by the fact that Baba—as the *pir* is generally addressed—always kept the door closed and switched on the single overhead electric bulb only when it rained or he needed more light to prepare his talismans. In the cold months, Baba kept an old-fashioned room heater constantly switched on, the dull scarlet glow from the heater's filament bathing Baba and a part of the room in a dim, eerie light that seemed to belong to the other, nether worlds where Baba claimed to be at home.

The room was not only dark and dingy but also cluttered with the bric-a-brac of a long professional life. Empty phials and other bottles of all shapes and sizes, covered with layers of dust, were strewn all along the sagging shelves of a wooden cupboard that leaned in a precarious balance against a wall. The whitewash on the walls and the ceiling had peeled off in large unsightly blotches, exposing the red sandstone underneath. On top of the cupboard there was a stone pestle and an oval-shaped mortar used by herbalists and other traditional healers to grind and mix their herbs, while a couple of rusty kerosene stoves that had not worked for many years stood uselessly in the alcove built into one of the walls. Besides the cupboard, there were two other pieces of furniture in the room: the string cot on which Baba sat (and slept) and a sofa in front of the cot on which the patient and his accompanying family members were invited to make themselves comfortable. The sofa was old and sagged in the middle, with springs coming out of the black vinyl cover so that one had to sit with great care to guard against unexpected and painful jabs. At the foot of the cot there was a plastic can that had once contained a well-known brand of cooking oil and was now used as a spittoon. A tin basin full of cigarette stubs and empty packs was pushed under the cot and also served as an ashtray whenever Baba remembered its original purpose. Sometimes a squirrel entered the room together with a patient and headed straight for the basin, where it foraged among the cigarette stubs. Baba told us that five to six months ago the squirrel had given birth to its litter in the basin and since then it had become a frequent visitor; he did not say what had happened to the litter.

The floor was not particularly clean, strewn with burned matchsticks, ash, cigarette and *biri* stubs, and as one sat on the sofa, facing Baba on his bed, there was an unmistakable odor of urine from his direction.

"I cannot always hold my water," Baba said matter-of-factly. "That is why I don't go to the mosque for my prayers but must say them on the bed. It does not matter if one's bed gets soiled but to pollute a pure place like a mosque would be a heinous sin."

Baba's clientele, from all parts of Delhi but also from the neighboring states, was poor and belonged to the lower social strata.

"I try to help people. I am not greedy and am content to pass my days in poverty. Only the poor come to me in the hope that here they will be treated free of charge. No rich man ever comes here," Baba had said once, looking wistfully, I thought, in the direction of his more famous colleague, reclining regally on a cot outside, who was consulted by the wealthy as often as by the poor. In any event, the dinginess and the smell of their surroundings did not seem to bother Baba's patients. It was familiar to them from their own dwellings and in fact, except for a few islands, it is the pervasive ambience of urban India. Whereas the gloomy darkness and the paraphernalia of the magician-healer may have increased the patients' anxiety (and lessened their hope of cure), I felt that the general disorder had a noticeably soothing effect; the combination of the strange and the familiar locating the room therapeutically between "this" and "another" world.

Baba was an old man, "three years less than ninety" as he proudly told us once, the pride lying more in the fact of his longevity than in any illusions about his youthfulness or good health. With his toothless mouth, swollen eyes and protruding underlip, he evoked in me the protective response one feels toward a helpless child. The childlike impression, however, was immediately erased by his scraggly white beard and the profusion of wrinkles etched deeply into his face. In the free time between patients that could sometimes stretch for hours, Baba rested on his bed in a half-sitting, half-reclining posture, an ever-present cigarette in his mouth on which he drew greedily in shuddering deep breaths while he muttered short sentences to himself: "Allah's will. You know it. All is well. Be merciful. . . ."

During the time we saw him, Baba was suffering from sleeplessness. His failing eyesight was also giving him considerable trouble. In preparing talismans, he often lost the thread and had to seek his patients' help. Once, while putting the small plastic pouches (in which the talisman is wrapped) back into the bag, one pouch had stuck to his hand every time he withdrew it. With a troubled mien,

Baba asked my colleague, "Brother, please look if there isn't a demon hovering above me."

Since it is Baba who is the expert on demons, the colleague laughed and said, "Baba, I cannot see demons—you know them much better," and helped him to unstick the plastic pouch.

Baba murmured a blessing and continued, "Ever since I have cataracts in my eyes, it has become very difficult."

On asking why he did not get his eyes treated, Baba said, "I know of many incidents where people have used urine to make the *surma* [a *unani* medicinal powder for the eyes]. Because of the urine the eyes will certainly show an improvement but I don't want my eyes to become impure."

"But if the *surma* cannot be made without urine, how will you ever get your eyes treated?"

"I'll make the *surma* myself, but I'm waiting for Allah's orders. These days are bad for me. They too will pass. In olden times our ancestors had the power where by the mere laying of their hands they could bring light back to the eyes. My own *baba* [his teacher and guru] healed a lot of patients in this way."

As always, his face became soft, even more childlike, when he talked of *his baba*. Lifting up his purblind eyes toward the curtained window he had seemed to be peering into a coming millennium.

"My *baba*, Shah Abdul Wazir Sahib, died twenty years ago and since then my weakness has persisted. At the time of his death, Baba told me that after twenty years he will leave his shrine, my body will get its strength back, my mouth will sprout teeth, light will descend into my eyes."

One of my strongest impressions of the *pir*'s personality was his curious mixture of humility and an evident pride in the conviction that he stood out among the common herd. He traced his lineage back to the seventeenth-century Mughal emperor Shah Jahan though he allowed that his family had fallen on bad days and had been a part of Delhi's poor for two centuries. Nowhere was his conviction that he was a chosen being, selected by God for a special task, more forcefully expressed than in the account of his birth.

"My parents had three children, all of whom died in infancy, before I was born. At my birth my mother told my father to take me away and give me to the mosque so that Allah could protect me. Father took me to the mosque and handed me to the *maulvi.*" Tears were running down Baba's furrowed cheeks as he narrated the story.

"When my uncle came home in the evening he asked where the baby was and on being told what had happened, he went to the mosque and bought me back from the *maulvi* for ten paise. He gave me back to my mother and told her that henceforward I was his son and she should look after me well. From that time onward Mother never let me be separated from Allah."

The account of his birth—whether factual or mythical—reminds us that there is a common tendency all over the world to ascribe unusual characteristics and circumstances of birth to healers. For instance, posthumous children are regarded as born healers in the folklore of North America; unusual curing powers are attributed to seventh sons or to seventh sons of seventh sons in European folk medical tradition; in the British Isles, France and Holland individuals born with the caul are supposed to have the healing gift, while twins enjoy a reputation as healers in Germanic and Romance-language countries.[1]

"I never married," Baba continued, "and at a young age became the *murid* [disciple; apprentice] of my *baba*, who was at that time the manager of Hakim Ajmal Khan's pharmacy. For some years I worked with my *baba* in the pharmacy, making silver and gold leaf used in the preparation of the medicines. Then my *baba*, after taking the permission of *his* guru, left the pharmacy and came to settle down at this *dargah* so that he could serve the world better. I too followed him, to serve and to look after his needs and to continue my apprenticeship. Actually, our line of *pirs* is an old one, starting five hundred years ago with *jenab* [Sir] Abdul Kadri Zilani of Baghdad, who is our *peshwa* [founder] and whose shrine is located in that city." Baba's claim of royal ancestry, dramatic and unusual happenings immediately after birth, renunciation of normal human ties such as marriage, an ancient professional lineage and a long apprenticeship with a distinguished *pir* have all contributed to his own image (confirmed by his clients) as a gifted healer who possesses singular powers.

Idioms of Mental Illness

At our first meeting one cold January morning, Baba, after welcoming me and inquiring as to the purpose of my visit, immediately
plunged into a description of his cases. As a fellow clinician, and like
the rest of our tribe all over the world, I could share his excitement
in the discussion of clinical details and understand his lack of enthusiasm for the more theoretical and abstract matters.

"Many people come to me from long distances," Baba said. "The
first question I put to everyone is, 'What do you see in your dreams?'
Today a woman came who said she was very fearful because she sees
some other man in the guise of her husband who wants to do bad
acts with her."

Here Baba lifted his hands, made a circle with the thumb and
index finger of his left hand, stuck out the index finger of his right
hand, and then moved both hands to and fro in a simulated coitus.

"Thousands of women have told me the same thing; they see
someone in their dreams who wants to do the bad act with them.
And then they become very afraid. I had an interesting case just
before you came. A woman came from Chandigarh. She must have
been very beautiful at one time. She sees a woman in her dream who
does bad acts with her. Now you tell me how can a woman do bad
acts with another woman?"

Here he repeated the copulatory gesture.

"But this dream woman did the bad act with the patient every
night. In reality this woman in the dream is a demon [bala] who
sucks the patient's blood and will gradually suck away the patient's
life. The patient is as thin as a stick now and will die within ten to
fifteen days."

"Did you treat her?"

"There is no cure for this patient. If she had come even a fortnight earlier I could have saved her. Some demons are indeed very
stubborn and do not let go of their victim easily. There was this other
young woman to whom the demon appeared every night in a dream
wanting her to do the bad act. The woman fought with him for two

months and did not let him commit the bad act, although the demon used to hug her so tightly that she could hardly control herself for excitement. Two days before she came to me, the demon again asked her to commit the bad act with him. On her refusing, he spit at her and went away. Next morning, the woman had a big fight with her husband, who left her. Now the fight happened because of the demon's spitting on the woman. He wanted the husband to go away in order to possess the woman. Oh, they cause a lot of trouble to mankind, these wretched *bala*s, trying all kinds of tricks to possess a person.

"There was another young girl," Baba continued, "very beautiful and very innocent-looking, who used to come to me with her father. In her dreams too a man came and incited her to the bad act. The girl did not agree to the man's proposition, but she could not fall asleep at night for the fear that the bad act might be done to her unawares while she slept. I gave her 'holy water' and there was an improvement in her condition. But after a few days some other man started appearing in her dreams and making the same demand. Night after night, the girl lay awake. This time when I asked her what she saw in her dream, she replied that she saw an old tree outside her window. There were animals sitting on each branch of the tree. 'Daughter-fuckers!' I said. 'Now I know why she cannot sleep and falls ill every day. All these demons waiting to enter her house one after another!' I told her father to marry her off immediately. After marriage when she is with a man, the demons will leave her and find someone else. The father followed my advice and now the girl is perfectly all right."

If there were any residual doubts in my mind on our professional affinity and our common endeavor, Baba's description of his last case erased them completely. For I found it a fascinating coincidence that an adolescent Muslim girl in Delhi in 1978 has the same unusual dream that was dreamed by a four-year-old Russian boy at the close of the century. I am of course referring here to the key dream described in what is perhaps the most important and certainly the most elaborate case history in the annals of psychoanalysis—the case of the "Wolf Man."[2] As we may recollect, this patient of Freud had dreamed at the age of four that his bedroom window opened and he saw six or seven wolves sitting on the branches of the walnut tree outside the window. In great terror, the child had screamed and woken up. For the next six months he had suffered from what psychoanalysts call an anxiety hysteria in the form of an animal phobia.

Without going into the fascinating details of the dream's interpretation and Freud's painstaking tracing of its elements to events in the dreamer's early life, a task which lasted for many years, I would only like to mention that in the *psychological idiom* that Freud was creating at the time, he showed that what sprang into activity that night out of the chaos of the dreamer's unconscious memory traces was a picture of his father copulating with his mother. The posture of the wolf was that of his father during the primal scene and the patient's anxiety was the repudiation of his own desire for sexual satisfaction from his father. In other words, the fear of the wolf was the transposition of the boy's wish to copulate with his father—a wish that succumbed to repression (and reappeared as a phobia) because of its unacceptable implications of his being feminine and castrated.

If we continue to look at Baba's last patient in Freud's psychological idiom rather than in Baba's own demonological framework, we would suggest—tentatively and carefully—that the identical dreams of the Russian boy and the Muslim girl may indeed have a similarity in their underlying conditions. Put simply, the girl's fear of going to sleep was her fear of an eruption of her proscribed sexual wishes while she slept, wishes that are perhaps especially threatening because of their strong incestuous coloring, and that her attempts to displace these wishes onto the images of the animals in the trees were not too successful. I would also speculate that Baba unconsciously recognized the incestuous nature of the girl's sexual impulses when he used the (for him) rare expletive "daughter-fuckers" for the demons. It also seems that when Baba's other female patients complained of *dar* (fear) they were complaining of a condition that in various classifications of the psychological idiom is called anxiety neurosis, anxiety state or anxiety reaction. As post-Freudian psychotherapists, we would of course say that the women's condition of anxiety is in response to a threat from within in the form of an instinctual drive—sexual, in the cases described so far—although we would need to know more about a patient's symptoms and her life history to determine exactly the kind of aggression or sexuality involved and the particular quality of patient's anxiety; whether, for instance, the anxiety arises from the fear of being overwhelmed by the impulses, from a fear of punishment by the "superego" or whether it was the revival of a "separation anxiety."

All of this made little sense to Baba, who patiently listened to my exposition.

"You mean this is how Christians see it?" he asked after I had finished.

"Well, no," I stammered. "This is the view of Western science on these matters."

"Yes, yes—but Western science is a Christian product," he said, waving aside my feeble separation of science from culture. And then, like psychotherapists everywhere, he called on the clinical evidence of "thousands of patients I have treated personally"—besides the accumulated evidence, traditions and lore of his thousand-year-old Islamic "school of psychotherapy"—that conclusively "proved" the role played by demons in the etiology of his patients' illness. His manner conveyed that if this was how I understood *dar* and other forms of mental distress then Allah help me if I thought I could help any of *his* patients! I must confess that I tended to concur in this silent judgment. For if your world view is demonological and peopled with "ghoulies and ghosties and long-leggety beasties and things that go bump in the night," then any task of buried feelings toward fathers is irrelevant and certainly very irreverent. Conversely, if one's framework is psychological, with unconscious wishes and fears swirling around in a subterranean cavern filled with the childhood images of parents and siblings, then a talk of *bala*s and other demons is patently absurd and, well, a little "crazy." It is evident that before we can analyze Baba's healing methods and consider such questions as to which idiom—the psychological or the demonological—is therapeutically more effective, and under what individual, social and cultural conditions, we need to understand Baba's idiom of demon possession better.

It is difficult for me to subscribe to a widespread Western attitude which would summarily dismiss Baba's beliefs as erroneous and characterize them as a residual mode of thought long outgrown in the West. Such an "evolutionist" view will condescendingly look at

Baba's ideas as incipient and less adequate stages in the development
of Western psychiatric understanding.[3] On the other hand, as a
psychoanalyst, it is equally difficult for me to adopt the "relativist"
position of many anthropologists, who would regard Baba's ideas
about mental illness as a coherent system derived from different
premises and related to different goals which I cannot appreciate but
which are as valid and valuable as Freud's contributions. My preferred way, then, is to search for common understandings lying
behind the psychological and demonological frameworks which may
be masked by superficial idiomatic differences. Besides this "universalism," I must also admit subscribing to a fourth model which the
psychologist-anthropologist Richard Scheweder has called confu-
sionism,[4] namely the honest confession that many of Baba's ideas
leave me baffled.

   In most parts of the world, the belief in possession by spirits and
demons has been historically the dominant theory of illness and
especially of conditions that we call mental illness. The Arabs and
the Chinese, the Hebrews and the Greeks, have all believed in some
form of spirit possession and the monumental study of Oesterreich,
with its hundreds of examples, from all parts of the world and
historical eras, attests to the universality of such beliefs.[5] The indications of spirit possession have traditionally covered a wide range—
from an alteration in the possessed person's state of mental and
physical well-being to such florid manifestations as trances and other
dramatic states of altered consciousness. The latter, of course, have
always exercised a powerful hold on man's imagination. We also
know from ethnographic literature that belief in possession is widespread in most human societies even today. Erika Bourguignon, for
instance, in her analysis of 488 societies from the *Ethnographic
Atlas,* has shown that these beliefs were present in 388 societies, or
nearly four fifths of her sample.[6]

   As a devout Muslim, Baba believed that his own theory of demon
possession could be ultimately traced back to the Koran, although
he was somewhat fuzzy on the details of the exact connection. Islam
recognizes three classes of living beings "higher" than men: *farishta*
(angels), *shaitans* (satanic beings) and jinn (demons or spirits).
Among the nonhuman spiritual beings the jinn are the most common and likely to be encountered in daily life. The common charac-

teristic of these disembodied beings is that they are made from one substance rather than from a combination of substances that constitute a human being. The jinn, for instance, who are Baba's chief antagonists, the *balas* he deals with daily in his healing encounters, are said to be made of fire. We need not go deeper into the whole sweep of esoteric lore on the jinn—the different accounts of their origin, their various classifications, the magical rites by which they can be exorcised and practices through which they can be enslaved —that is found in the Islamic literature on the subject, especially in the *Tafsirs*, the commentaries on the Koran, and the *Hadis*, the Traditions of the Prophet.[7] Here we'll restrict ourselves to a brief presentation of the Muslim belief on the essential nature of the jinn.

The word *jinn* comes from the Arabic *jann*, signifying covering and covertness, veiling and darkness, but also something that lies hidden in the womb like an embryo. The extent of a jinn's power and knowledge is great indeed, although these too are hidden from humans. While a few jinn (who are "believers") are benevolent, many of them are destructive and highly amoral beings. It does not take a great feat of deduction to arrive at the conclusion that, psychologically speaking, something that is powerful and has "knowledge" beyond the limits of human rationality, something that is fiery and fiercely amoral, and lies veiled in darkness, refers to our unconscious impulses. Jinn, we would say, though having a logic of their own in the religious idiom, also belong to that covered part of the human nature psychoanalysts call the *id*. For like the jinn, the id too is an unbeliever in "laws"—its alienness from human consciousness being vividly expressed in its original German name of *das Es*, the "It."

"Each human being has its own jinn," Baba said, "who is born with him and stays with him till he dies. When the angels come to take away the soul of a good man, they kill the jinn. This is the reason why we Muslims bury a dead body and you Hindus cremate it—to ensure the death of a man's jinn. Sometimes, however, especially in the case of a sinful man, it happens that the jinn escapes by hiding in the organs of elimination, which are impure and cannot be reached by the angels. He then becomes a demon [*bala*] and is on the lookout for a victim in whose body he can find a home and whose blood he can drink."

These demons, Baba went on to say, are all around us, on the ground, flying in the air, invisible to everyone except to men of "knowledge" *(ilm),* among whom Baba humbly counted his own teacher but not himself. No human being is entirely safe from the demons' unwelcome and decidedly unpleasant attentions. Baba made this point clear when one day I had complained of a persistent swelling on the lips. Baba broke off our conversation to ask with great concern.

"What do you see in your dreams?"

I almost burst out in laughter. "Don't worry, Baba, no demon has overpowered me."

Baba was patient. "Why do you feel that you cannot be possessed by a demon?" he asked.

"Because I don't feel that I have committed any such sin to deserve this kind of punishment from Allah," I replied.

"Look, it's not that demons possess only a sinner," Baba explained patiently. "What sin has a nursing infant committed that it should be possessed by a demon? A demon possesses a person for two reasons: either because a sorcerer who has a demon in his power lets him loose against his own enemy, or against the enemy of someone who has bribed him; or, a demon while roaming around in the firmaments espies someone whom he fancies as a victim."

Attributing possession to accident and pure waywardness on the part of the demons and not to any wrongdoing by the patient of course absolves the patient of responsibility for any of his own "sinful" desires. But demons, as we would expect, are not strictly consistent even in their capriciousness. As I pointed out to Baba, *balas* did seem to prefer young unmarried girls, who formed the bulk of Baba's clientele. Baba thought for a moment and then qualified his earlier statement.

"Demons can possess everyone, yes, but the taste of fresh blood is of course the best and the blood of virgins is especially fresh."

"Why does the blood become stale after marriage, Baba?" I asked.

"When the man pours his strength into the woman then the strength mixes with her blood and makes it stale," Baba answered.

"And how does the man's strength get mixed with the blood?" I asked.

"You know that forty drops of blood make one drop of semen.

When this drop of semen goes into the woman's body it mixes with the blood."

On another occasion, Baba had talked of the way demons enter the human body. "Almost invariably the demon will get into some item of food or drink like milk, curd and cream. When a person eats one of these the demon gets into the body. It will then start sucking blood and after it has drained off the blood it will go on to the marrow and the meat, stopping only when the person dies."

I had often asked Baba to describe the various kinds of *balas* but had generally received a curt answer. "They may be of many kinds but the wretches have all the same function—to suck a human being's blood!"

Evidently, Baba felt that a discrimination between the *balas*—or a differential diagnosis, as we would call it—was not an important factor in his healing ministrations. As we shall see later, this was due to the selection of the patients he received where the crucial decision to be made was between possession and nonpossession and not between the varieties of possession. One day, however, when he was in an especially good mood, reminiscing about his childhood and his training under his beloved teacher, the subject of various *balas* had come up again and he had spontaneously embarked on a description of the different kinds.

"One is the *jaljogini* who takes the form of a beautiful woman and approaches men with the sound of tinkling bells that are tied around her ankles. Once I had a disciple who was very fond of wrestling. Every evening he would go to Ferozeshah Kotla with a friend for wrestling practice."

Here Baba paused to warn me that I should be careful when I go to Ferozeshah since the *jaljogini*s still roam around in the ruins of this fort.

"The wrestlers had just finished their practice session," Baba continued, "when a *jaljogini* in the form of a beautiful young woman walked past them, swaying her hips invitingly. My disciple's friend wanted to follow the woman immediately. My disciple warned him that she was a *jaljogini* as well as a *pichalpairi* [one whose feet point backward] and he said, 'Please stay here, don't go after her.' But the man was mad with lust and followed the woman down the steps into one of the cellars. When he did not return for a long time, my disciple went looking for him. What does he see when he comes to the cellar? His friend is lying dead, the corpse chalky white and drained of every drop of blood, with the penis slit through the middle. This is what the *jaljogini* did: first she let the wrestler do the bad act with her and then, when he was exhausted, she slit open his penis and drank his blood."

Fascinated, I had listened to Baba describe one of the core fantasies of Indian culture (common, it now seems, to both the Hindus and the Muslims), namely the horrific vision of an overpowering feminine sexuality that exhausts, sucks and drains even the most powerful male to death. I have described this fantasy in detail elsewhere,[8] relating it to the Indian male child's dread of the mother's "demonic" eroticism so that later for many who fall ill and suffer from acute anxiety—become possessed by the *jaljogini,* as Baba would say—the orgasmic act of love can become a fearful affair, transformed from a normal "little death" into the dread of a permanent annihilation and emptying of the self. Here it seems that in the notions of *jaljogini* and *pichalpairi,* the Muslim *bala* has merged with the Hindu *churel,* the feminine spirit who appears as a seductively beautiful woman, recognizable from the fact that her feet point backward, and who strikes impotent any man who has intercourse with her.

"Another type is the *sirkata* [headless]. There was once a policeman who was drinking water from a well near Jama Masjid one night when someone addressed him from behind: 'Brother, give me some water too.' The policeman turned around with a full bucket and said, 'Here, drink.' To his surprise, what does he see but the torso of a headless man standing next to him! So he says, 'Brother, you have no head. How will you drink the water?' 'Just pour it down the neck,' the *sirkata* replied. The policeman poured a bucket of water down the neck, but the *sirkata* was still thirsty. The policeman went on pouring one bucket after another till he was tired and threw away the bucket in disgust. 'Aren't you afraid of my anger?' the *sirkata* asked. 'Listen,' the policeman said, 'I keep order the whole day by knocking heads together. Why should I be afraid of someone who doesn't even have a head?' The *sirkata* ran away but the policeman fell ill the same night. He was later cured by my *baba.*

"Yet another type is the *bhutna,* which is often seen in the form of fire. Once when I was fourteen years old I was playing with my friends on top of the roof of our house when I saw a whirlpool of fire rising toward me from the ground. I did not know about demons at that time and was scared. But before the fire reached me it suddenly disappeared. At night, however, we heard strange sounds coming from my grandfather's room as if he was being strangled. We rushed to his room and asked him what had happened. He pooh-poohed the whole matter but gave me five iron nails and said, 'Run to Akhim Sahib'—he was a *sayana* [sorcerer] in our neighborhood—'and ask him to blow on the nails. Then hammer a nail at each corner and the fifth one in the middle of the room. If there is any demon here it'll leave.' Much later, he told me that he had seen a fire in his dream and then suddenly felt someone strangling him. Actually, the *bhutna* was after me but right from the beginning the Merciful One had chosen me for this work [of the *pir*] and I have been protected from the demons."

The tenor of my observations so far, implied in the report of conversations with the *pir* and explicitly in my own commentary on these conversations, is of a correspondence—though of course not a complete identity—between the (Freudian) psychological and the (Muslim) demonological approaches to the understanding of mental illness. To me, the *bala*s are the reification of certain unconscious fantasies of men and women which provoke strong anxiety in the Indian cultural setting. To Baba, on the other hand, "unconscious fantasies" and "repressed impulses" would seem to be abstractions for the corporeal *bala*s with whom he lives in such close proximity though in a state of perpetual confrontation. In spite of the vast difference in the richness of their vocabularies, Western psychoanalysis and northern Indian exorcism can then be seen as two different languages of psychic disturbance and healing which can be translated into each other, though this translation can in fact be very complicated since the *bala* is not a simple reflex of the id. Because of the cultural and historical distance between the two languages, there may be many concepts and idioms in one language that can only be translated imperfectly into another while a few may be well-nigh untranslatable.

Take, for instance, Baba's statements that demons enter a person through his mouth when he is engaged in the act of drinking and

eating—chiefly, milk and milk products. Given a knowledge of the
language of psychoanalysis, one would say that Baba is referring here
to what Melanie Klein calls the archaic fantasies of devouring and
incorporating the mother's breast and to the accompanying fears of
retaliation. This translation is not the application of mechanical
formulas but is validated by clinical experience which shows that
"oral" fantasies are indeed prominent in the Indian setting—in
contrast, say, to the dominance of Oedipal fantasies in another
culture. Similarly, as we saw earlier, *jaljogini* can be easily comprehended and almost precisely translated; *sirkata* cannot. On the
other hand, *bhutna* seems less an individual childhood anxiety than
a collective fear of Indian Muslims. *Bhutna*, of course, refers to the
bhuta, the Hindu spirit of the dead. Together with other Hindu
superhuman beings, the *devis* and *devatas*, the *bhutas* are looked
upon by Muslims as part of a numerous, powerful host. A *bhuta* can
be warded off by sorcery—the driving in of nails, for instance—or
by taking the help of a *pir*. Best of all, as Katherine Ewing points
out in her study of *pirs* and their followers in Pakistan, one can
protect oneself from the *bhuta* by being a pious Muslim and by
constant proclamations of the faith.[9] Indeed, if someone dies a bad
Muslim, he may become a *bhuta* himself. This, it seems, expresses
the primary fear of the Indian Muslim—of somehow lapsing from
the faith and becoming reabsorbed by the insidious Hindu society
surrounding him.

The difficulty in comprehending a different idiom of mental illness cannot always be attributed to a matter of cultural gulf and
historical distance. This was vividly brought home to me one day
when Baba was not in his room and I spent some time with the
famous old *hakim* whose "clinic" consists of a simple cot placed
under the dense foliage of two overlapping pipal trees next to the
entrance to the mosque. While marveling at his diagnostic feats
through reading of the pulse—among others he diagnosed a thyroid
malfunctioning, a malformed uterus and damage to heart valves,
later confirmed by specific medical investigations—we also talked of
mental illness. I asked him about possession by demons in the *unani*
system of medicine, in which he is widely recognized as an adept.

"They [the demons] are products of false imagination," the *hakim*
scoffed. "Why doesn't a demon possess *me?* I am blind and can't

even protect myself against a demon's onslaught. And if the *balas* like to drink blood they should be licking their chops at the sight of my strong healthy body. Some people's imagination becomes over-heated and operates beyond all rational bounds. What has happened in these cases is that certain nerves in their brain have become stretched, and I can generally treat these patients successfully with my medicines."

These remarks of the old *hakim* reminded me, if a reminder was needed, that the line of cleavage in the healing professions and among different healers is not simply between "traditional" and "modern" or between "Western" and "Asian," or between healers belonging to different cultures. The real line of cleavage, cutting across cultures and historical eras, seems to be between those whose ideological orientation is more toward the biomedical paradigm of illness, who strictly insist on empiricism and rational therapeutics and whose self-image is close to that of a technician, and others whose paradigm of illness is metaphysical, psychological or social, who accord a greater recognition to *arationality* in their therapeutics, and who see themselves (and are seen by others) as nearer to the priest. Such a line of demarcation may indeed by an expression of an immemorial dialectic in the healing professions; we know, for instance, that the development of Ayurvedic medicine in ancient India was characterized and greatly influenced by this very dialectical process.[10] I can also easily imagine that a Western psychoanalyst would feel professionally much closer to the *pir* of Patteshah Dargah than to a neurophysician colleague whose model of mental illness is based exclusively on changes in the electric activity and chemistry of the brain.

The Basis of Healing:
Soul Knowledge and Soul Force

Before we look at Baba's particular healing techniques more closely, we should note here that his therapy system has its source in (and is part of) a much larger system of knowledge which the Muslims call *ilm-i-ruhani,* or soul knowledge. Though the mystical practices of the Sufis, the philosophical and religious answers in Islam to the riddles of birth, death and human suffering can all be seen as the legitimate domain of soul knowledge, *ilm-i-ruhani* also refers to spiritualism and especially to its branches of white *(ulwi, rahmani)* magic and the black arts *(silfa, shaitani, sihr, jadu).* In spite of the Koranic condemnation of these magical arts—"whoever goes to a magician and asks about mysteries and believes what he says, verily is displeased with Muhammad and his religion"[11]—there are many practicing sorcerers called *sayanas* (wise; cunning) who cater to a large clientele. These *sayanas* perform the healing function of casting out demons in addition to going about their "proper" occult tasks—"to command the presence of the Jinn and demons who, when it is required of them, cause anything to take place; to establish friendship or enmity between two persons; to cause the death of an enemy; to increase wealth or salary; to gain income gratuitously or mysteriously; to secure the accomplishment of wishes, temporal or spiritual."[12] The therapeutic practices of Baba and other *pirs* embrace only a small part of the vast spectrum of *ilm-i-ruhani* where at one end we find the "higher," mystical disciplines of the Sufis, while assorted practitioners of the occult ply their trade at the other end. *Ilm-i-ruhani,* then, is a continuum that connects the *sayanas,* the *pirs* and the Sufi mystics. We can see this connection clearly when, for instance, we look at the sorcery ritual that is designed to summon jinn and demons to carry out the sorcerer's commands.[13]

The preconditions for this ritual, as for many others, are that the sorcerer should be pure in mind and body, honest and always truthful. Before commencing the main ritual, the sorcerer closets himself in his room for a week of purification. The closet is smeared with red ochre and the sorcerer spreads a red prayer mat on which he repeats the mighty names of God *(ism-i-asam).* His diet is strictly controlled, its various items depending upon whether he is repeating the terrible *(jalali)* or the amiable *(jamali)* names of Allah. After this he shuts himself up for forty days in some secluded spot where he is not likely to be disturbed and repeats the specific invocation for summoning the jinn, the Tashkir-i-Jinn, 137,613 times, dividing it into forty parts, one for each day. During this *chilla,* "after he has

begun the recital of the spell every night or week, some new phenomenon will appear, and in the last week the demons and the jinn,
attended by their legions, will arrive."[14] The stress on purity of body
and mind, the specific dietary instructions, the temporary seclusion
and reduction of all sensory stimuli, the hypnotic chanting of an
invocation over and over again—very much like the repetition of a
mantra in mantra yoga—all show the affinity of sorcery ritual to the
"higher," mystical practices that lead to altered states of consciousness.

In his opposition to magic and sorcery, Baba was as implacable as
in his respect for the mystical. As a devout Muslim, he regarded
sorcery as an abomination in the eyes of Allah.

"Personally, I have never had the wish to go to a graveyard and
learn the sorcerer's craft," he said. "My *baba* taught me to fight the
*bala*s and other forces of evil, not to be allied with them. Whenever
someone asked me to call a jinn, I always replied that I was Allah's
humble devotee who kept himself far away from such practices. The
part of soul knowledge I practice is what you Hindus call *Jantar* and
what we Muslims call *Santar*. Basically *Santar* is very simple, invoking Allah to rid a person of the *bala* if he is possessed by one or to
protect him if he is threatened by one."

Baba's self-image as a healer was of being a conduit to Allah and
a channel for the Divine Force that did the actual work of healing.
He saw himself merely as a go-between and neither accepted praise
for his successes nor blamed himself for his failures. Many times,
when asked by an anxious patient about the prospects of a quick
recovery, Baba conveyed this self-image with simple yet striking
metaphors. "I only knock at Allah's door on your behalf," he would
say. "Whether he lets you in or not is a matter between you and
him."

Or, "My job is to carry your voice to Allah. If he hears you then
that is *your* good fortune."

Or, "I just play the notes. Whether Allah will make music out of
my efforts, only he knows."

To Baba himself and the simple, God-fearing souls who constituted his clientele, he was not the possessor of any powerful
science or technology of healing. What he had was the *ilm*—the
knowledge—of communicating with the Deity to intervene on be-

half of an afflicted soul. Whether God heeded this appeal and sent
out even a fraction of his legions to combat the forces of evil had
of course nothing to do with the quality of Baba's transmission. In
any event the dramatic imagery pervading the healing process—the
mise-en-scène of Baba's therapy—was not of a prosaic conflict between impulses derived from man's biological nature and his psychological defenses against the impulses, but of a vastly more impressive
battle between cosmic forces of good and evil that had chosen the
afflicted person as a battlefield.

I could imagine that for a majority of Baba's patients who were
lost in the anonymity of an urban mass society and constantly struggled against a crippling sense of their own insignificance, such a
conception of what was happening to them could be a very heady
experience. It seemed to me that in contrast to much of Western
psychotherapy which is organized around increasing a man's sense
of *freedom of choice*, the Muslim and many other non-Western
therapies are organized around another central human need: the
restoration of a sense of *centrality* in time and space which in the
Western world view has been almost destroyed by the Copernician
and Darwinian revolutions. *Santar*, the *pir*'s knowledge of invoking
the Deity, consists of many parts. First, he has to know the appropriate Koranic verses *(ayat)* and the particular name of Allah (out of
his ninety-nine names) to be used for a specific affliction; for instance, the name Al-Hefiz, "the Guardian," is invoked to relieve
fear, Al-Muhyi, "the Quickener," to ward off demons and fairies,
Al-Qadri, "Lord of Power," to remove distress and anxiety and so
on. Second, in the preparation of talismans, he has to know the
proper "packaging" of the invocation by a thorough familiarity with
the many kinds of mystical squares—binary, ternary, quaternary, the
squares of Eve, of fire, of water, of air, etc.; the numerical values of
the different names of Allah, which are derived from a complicated
system that links the twenty-eight letters of the Arabic alphabet to
the twelve signs of the zodiac, the seven planets and the four elements, and the proper combination of a particular invocation with
a particular mystical square. Third, he has to know the most effective
way a talisman should be used: whether it needs to be worn as a
charm around the neck *(tabiz)* or tied as an amulet *(ganda)*; whether
it is to be burned and the patient fumigated with its smoke; or the

writing is to be dissolved in water and drunk; whether it needs to be bound up in cotton soaked in perfumed oil and burned as the wick of a lamp. Moreover, if a *pir* also treats patients who are in a possession trance and does not restrict himself to healing cases of "simple" possession, then he may need to know the art (and the significance) of controlling the jinn by drawing various magical circles and other geometrical figures in the middle of which the patient is seated, the properties of various perfumed herbs that are burned in the ritual exorcism and the text of other special invocations.

In spite of the detailed differentiations and the almost obsessive classifications of *ilm-i-ruhani*, all its practitioners agree that Soul Knowledge is inert without the living breath of the healer's soul force, his *ruhani-takat*. More precisely, the soul force is not the possession of a healer but, in effect, is the divine force that is transmitted to the healer (after he becomes ready to receive it) through the grace and agency of what the Muslims call the *murshid* and the Hindus call the guru. Without this soul force, conveyed personally by a living teacher, the knowledge can be neither "really" understood nor practiced with any profit. A hundred and fifty years ago, Ja'far Sharif, one of Baba's predecessors, who had been asked by a surgeon of the East India Company to write down the customs of the Muslims in India, had also reflected on the problem of what made *ilm-i-ruhani* effective:

"I have always been accustomed from my youth up to study the practice of exorcism or incantations, the writing of amulets and charms, the consulting of horoscopes and the prognostication of the future," he writes. "Many a time have persons possessed by the devil consulted this humble student, and either by the recital of supplications, or by some wise contrivance of my own, they have been cured. I used to feel much doubt regarding the effects produced, and I frequently said to myself, 'O God! What relation or connection can possibly exist between the Jinn and men, that the former should possess such powerful influence over the latter, or that by the recital of incantations they should be cast out?' With these doubts in my mind I continued studying the subject, consulting learned men and divines and reading standard works on the subject, like the Tafsir, or Commentary on the Koran, the Hadis or Traditions of the Prophet, and others, in order that I might acquire knowledge of these matters."[15] One of the conclusions reached by Ja'far Sharif is that though one can learn to recite the mighty names of Allah, the attributes of the Deity, and the special verses of the Koran, yet ". . . to gain *knowledge* of them you must humbly supplicate the great adepts in the art, and they communicate them only privately, breast to breast, hand to hand, ear to ear. If they are described in books it is never with sufficient minuteness to make them intelligible."[16]

Baba too attributes the power of healing to the soul force which, so to speak, is the *knowledge* of knowledge.

"One gets soul force after years and years of service to the guru and devotion to God," he said. "It requires many years of training. But once a man receives the soul force he starts running toward Allah and Allah too starts pulling him toward him. Once their connection gets established then he only needs to concentrate to get the soul force flowing through him. Now, before treating the patients I take Allah's name, close my eyes and try to see my *baba*. After some effort, the *pir* becomes visible and he tells me what to do."

"What does your *pir* tell you, Baba?" I asked.

"I can't reveal those things, for they are a secret between the guru and the disciple."

"But did he give you any special instructions before he died?" I persisted.

Baba looked at me pityingly.

"We people do not die. I told you that he had the soul force which keeps him alive even after death.

"Actually," Baba continued, suddenly humble again, "my knowledge is very little. Twenty years ago, my *baba* gave me this seat, told me what to do, and I have continued to follow his instructions ever since. He of course was a reservoir of soul force, possessing *raaz-i-fanah* [lit. the secret of annihilation]." Intrigued, I had inquired what this *raaz-i-fanah* was that made his *baba* and the other *pirs* such embodiments of the soul force. "It is the secret of dying while living," Baba answered. "Listen to a story. There was once a man who went looking for someone who possessed the *raaz-i-fanah* and was directed to an old *pir*. The *pir* told him to come the next morning. When he came back the next day, he found that the *pir* had died during the night and his corpse was being prepared for the funeral. 'How could the *pir* tell an untruth?' the man wondered, his faith shaken, when he saw a masked horseman coming toward the funeral cortege. The horseman dismounted and read the *namaaz* [prayer] over the corpse and then rode away, motioning the seeker to follow him. When they reached a lonely spot, the horseman took off his mask and, to the astonishment of the seeker, he found that it was the *pir* himself. This is what having the *raaz-i-fanah* means —to read the *namaaz* at your own funeral.

"There was another *pir* called Firad who lived in Chandni Chowk in Delhi. One day people saw him outside his house, frantically searching for something. 'What are you looking for?' they asked him. 'It seems Firad is lost,' he said. 'I am searching for him.' This too is *raaz-i-fanah*—to lose oneself."

Baba was now full of enthusiasm, speaking rapidly, visibly delighted at having the opportunity to explain to me through his preferred medium of fables and stories what kind of a person a healer needed to be.

"Soul force requires many years of internal preparation. I have already told you about the necessary service to teacher and devotion to God." Here he used a Hindi word, *bhagwan-bhakti*. "Together with these you need purity, truthfulness and to develop selflessness and detachment. Listen to another story.

"There was once a *pir* who was married and possessed both the 'knowledge' and the 'force.' A young man came to him one day to become his disciple and asked him: 'Tell me, how may I serve you?' The *pir* said, 'Go and get lunch for one person from my home.' The man did so. The *pir* said, 'Now go and give this lunch to my colleague who is sitting at such and such a place.' The disciple asked, 'Guruji, there is a river on the way on which there is neither a bridge nor arrangements for a boat. How will I cross the river?' The guru replied, 'Tell the river that you have been sent by a man who has never been close to a woman in his life and you will get your way.' The young man thought to himself that he was being made a fool of since the *pir* had both a wife and children. Anyway, he carried out his instructions and on reaching the river repeated what his teacher had told him. To his surprise the river parted and he walked across to the other bank where the other *pir* was sitting. After the old man had eaten, the disciple collected the utensils for his return trip but became worried as to how he would cross the river again. On inquiring the cause of his apprehension and hearing the answer, the *pir* said, 'This is really a small matter to get so upset about. Just tell the river that you have been sent by a man who has never eaten in his life.' The young man of course doubted the *pir*'s sanity! Here was a man who had just finished his lunch asserting that he had never eaten in his life! But let me test his words too, the disciple said to himself. On reaching the river he repeated the *pir*'s message and the river parted once again to let him through. When he came back to his guru, the young man confessed his bewilderment at the strange happenings and demanded an explanation. 'It is not the act but the spirit in which it is done,' the guru said. 'I cohabit with my wife not because of my needs but because of hers; the *pir* eats not because he wants to but because of others who wish to keep him alive.' This is our ideal of *fakiri*, of detachment, in which both Allah and world-liness walk arm in arm."

"Every sickness is a musical problem," Novalis once said, "and every cure a musical solution."[17] The musical metaphor is indeed much more apt for Muslim psychotherapy than the scientific meta-phors of biology, psychology or information processing that govern contemporary Western psychotherapy. With his self as the musical instrument whose many strings have been tuned to the required pitch, when Baba plays the healing raga he is not practicing a science but what Auden called "the intuitive art of wooing Nature."[18] The success of the "wooing" depends much more on the person of the healer than on the depth of his knowledge or the technique he employs. In Baba's world view, shared by his patients, a *pir* must develop certain essential qualities if he is to be a successful wooer of nature and a musician of healing. First, he must cultivate certain virtues of character—purity of mind and body, truthfulness, a defi-nite detachment. Second, he must be what we may call a "boundary man"—someone who chooses to live at the margin of his society, where he is in the world but not of it. Third, he needs to pass through an inner transformation that would connect him with and make him receptive to what the Sufi mystical tradition calls the soul force. Needless to say, none of these requirements can hope to find a place in the graduate training of a clinical psychologist or in the medical education of a psychiatrist. In fact, the only counterpart of "inner transformation of the healer" in the Western psychotherapeutic tradition, namely the meditative procedures of a long personal analysis that every aspiring psychoanalyst must go through, has now become an old-fashioned rarity among the burgeoning number of Western psychotherapists and psychiatrists who are crusaders for one or more "techniques" of mental healing.

The belief that it is the person of the healer and not his conceptual system or his particular techniques that are of decisive importance for the healing process is also an unquestioned article of faith for most Indian patients. One of Baba's patients, who had successively consulted an Ayurvedic physician, a psychiatrist, a *sayana,* a tantrik, a *bhakta* and a *pir* (*i.e.,* Baba) before he had settled on the choice of his therapist, looked at me uncomprehendingly when I asked him as to how he reconciled in his own mind the different explanations on the cause of his illness. It had seemed to me that his selection of a therapy from those being offered by the various healers—whose conceptual systems derived from traditions as diverse as ancient Indian medicine, Western psychological medicine, Muslim sorcery, Hindu shamanism, Hindu devotional mysticism and Sufi spiritualism—must have been especially difficult. "It is the *vishwas* a healer inspires which is crucial," he had said, using a Hindi word that denotes both trust and confidence. And how did a healer inspire the *vishwas?* From his groping attempts at putting into words what is clearly a matter of feeling, he conveyed that whereas one level of a patient's interaction with the healer is the talk about symptoms, their etiology, the possible therapy and the prognosis, there is another and perhaps more significant exchange taking place simultaneously. In this other conversation carried out without words and below the threshold of consciousness, the patient is busy registering whether and how well the doctor opposite him fits into his culturally determined image of the ideal healer. The choice of the therapist is then determined by the fit between the actual man and the ideal image whose main features I have sketched above. It was also obvious that not only the healer but the healing process too is located at the edge of the society, in the sense that religious restrictions and social taboos tend to be suspended for the duration of the healing encounter. For instance, it did not seem to disturb Baba's

many Hindu patients (high-caste Brahmins among them), who
scrupulously observed the caste taboos on pollution in their daily life,
that the healing water they received from Baba and drank with
apparent gratefulness came from the hands of a Muslim and had
been made "potent" by a recitation of Allah's names and verses from
the Koran. The brotherhood of sickness indeed seems infinitely more
inclusive than that of health.

Patients and Supplicants

From my conversations with him, I think I can divide the people
who approach Baba for help into two main classes: patients and
supplicants. By patients, I mean primarily persons with distinct
neurotic symptoms as well as what handbooks of psychiatry call cases
of "marital maladjustment." In the class of supplicants, I include
those who come in the hope of receiving divine help for a favorable
outcome of such uncertain situations as court cases, pending applica-
tions for employment insurance and so on; as well as those who
wish to have the healing power of medicines prescribed by various
vaids, hakim and doctors increased through Baba's prayerful intervention with the Deity.

Baba's classification, though never stated explicitly, is somewhat
different and follows logically from *his* theoretical premises. It seems
to me that Baba would divide the seekers for help into three main
groups: those who are possessed by a *bala,* those who are merely
threatened by one, and those who seek his spiritual offices rather
than his healing services. The possession category would comprise
all who show obvious symptoms of possession (neurotic symptoms
in our idiom). In Baba's framework, cases of marital disharmony and
maladjustment are excluded from the possession category since he
attributes these to the machinations and the threat posed by a
particular demon *(chalawa)* who creates conflicts within families in
general and between married couples in particular. Such family
quarrels, including cases of court litigation among family members,
belong to the second category of "threat by the *balas,*" while the

third group would consist of the remaining supplicants. According to my reading of Baba's classification, then, the twenty persons who came to him for help during the time I spent with him would be distributed as follows: *bala* possession, ten; *bala* threat, six; and supplicants, four. In my own psychological/psychiatric framework, the distribution would be as follows: anxiety neurosis, eight; hysterical conversion, two; marital maladjustment, five; and other supplicants, five. As I have mentioned at the beginning of the study, all of Baba's patients belonged to the lower economic and social strata and had little or no formal education.

Categorical differentiations—whether psychological or demonological—are rarely ever so clear cut in practice as they appear in theory, the illness of an individual patient invariably containing some gray areas, not to speak of a few opaque ones. Consider the case of a couple who had come to consult the *hakim* for the husband's asthmatic attacks and then come to Baba to have the prescribed medicines blessed. They told Baba that the man's asthma had started after a serious scooter accident and that curiously, to the couple's great consternation, these accidents kept on occurring at regular intervals. Baba had unhesitatingly ascribed the man's accident proneness to the work of *bala*s.

"Hakim Sahib must have recommended a treatment for your asthma," Baba had said in a tone that subtly conveyed doubt in the correctness of his colleague's diagnosis and therapy, "but *bala*s too are active here. As long as the *bala*'s influence prevails, no medicine can help."

He had then given a short exposition on the *bala*s to which the couple had listened with an increasing sense of conviction in Baba's diagnosis of the case, and the man who had come as a supplicant became an enthusiastic patient.

Considering the whole spectrum of mental illness, Baba is a relatively more specialized healer than a Western psychiatrist or psychotherapist who ranges over a bigger segment of mental disorders. On the other hand, Baba's practice explicitly covers a part of "disorders" in the religious-spiritual spectrum which are generally hidden and unavowed in psychotherapy. Baba's reputation—as a specialist healer of "possession illness"—has been spread by satisfied patients through word of mouth. This naturally draws to him "matching" patients who, in turn, are in a particular state of expectancy and readiness to be cured, thus contributing mightily to the therapeutic outcome.[19] In such cases, as Erna Hoch's work with traditional healers in Kashmir and Obeyesekere's study of exorcists in Sri Lanka show, both the healer and his patients are quite aware of the healer's special capabilities and limitations and the qualitative differences that are involved in various forms of possession-related illnesses.[20] For a serious disorder that involves more elaborate and expensive rituals, a patient and his relatives will not approach Baba at all but go directly to the relevant specialist or to a famous healing shrine, such as the Balaji temple of Mehndipur that I describe in the following chapter.

The sharing of the demonological framework by the whole culture, where the patient, his relatives and friends are all united on the etiology of the illness and the means of curing it, certainly makes the process of therapy more efficient. In the first place everyone concerned easily grasps the meaning of a patient's illness, can make a rough diagnosis and reach a quick consensus on the kind of healer to be consulted—giving the patient the reassuring feeling that matters are well under control. Second, the common, *public* idiom of illness greatly facilitates the communication between the patient, his family, the larger community and the healer, thus considerably enhancing the cooperation that is required from each for a therapy to be optimally effective.[21] In contrast, treatment in the psychological idiom is relatively more private and exclusive and, perhaps, also more mystifying. Since the psychological idiom is largely confined to and shared by the highly educated classes in the urbanized centers of the West, one would suspect that the therapeutic effectiveness too would be highest among these groups.

Healing Encounters

In my many asides so far, I have compared the psychological and demonological frameworks of mental illness and healing in more or less abstract terms. We can also see the concrete operation of these two approaches by considering the case of Sundar, a twenty-six-year-old man who tried out both kinds of "doctor." I was the psychotherapist concerned and Baba the religious healer I recommended to the patient after he had expressed his intention to discontinue with me. After a few difficult sessions (for both of us), this young man had stated his determination to go to a traditional healer who, he felt, would be better able to deal with his possessing spirit. As far as a quick cure of this particular patient's symptoms is concerned, I must admit that the score stands: demonology, 1; psychology, o.

Since the seeking out of a therapist in case of mental illness in India is generally a family and collective affair, the therapist very often has to listen to the family members of the patient recount their version of the illness before he gets a direct access to the patient. This happened in the case of Sundar, whose father came to consult me one day on his son's quasi-epileptic attacks. Such an attack was generally heralded by a tic in the underlip, followed by a heavy, numbing sensation in the lower jaw. The feeling of numbness gradually spread down through his arms to the whole body and Sundar would keel over into semiconsciousness. In the first attack that occurred three months before the father met me, Sundar had convulsions in his body and was unconscious for a few minutes. The later attacks never reached the intensity of the first one and Sundar could generally control them if he lay down immediately and held his jaws together with some force. The fear of these attacks occurring in the street had confined Sundar to the house and made an invalid out of a young man who loved to be outdoors with his friends.

After the first attack, Sundar's father, suspecting the involvement of evil spirits, took his son to the neighborhood exorcist who performed *jhar-phook*, a minor ritual of exorcism. However, to make sure that no organic factors of the brain—the "devils" of Western medicine—were involved in the illness, he also took his son to the hospital for a series of skull X-rays and EEGs. These and other neurological investigations had ruled out brain damage. Confirmed in his initial diagnosis and since the *jhar-phook* did not have the desired effect, the father took Sundar to a tantrik who enjoyed considerable reputation as a healer of demonological disorders. The tantrik's diagnosis was that an enemy, either of Sundar or of his father, had by magical means caused a nerve in Sundar's brain to be pulled. After going through his dramatic ritual, the tantrik gave Sundar three small packets of "holy ash." He was to keep one packet on his person, the second was to be kept in a safe place at the house and the third was to be mixed with water and drunk. The tantrik also forbade Sundar to drink milk or eat milk products and instructed him to stay at home for the next six weeks except for the weekly visit to the tantrik to collect fresh packets of the "holy ash." There had been a marked improvement in Sundar's condition, his father told me, but occasionally he would still get an attack. And since my office was in the same building where Sundar's father worked as a janitor and since he had heard that I was a "brain doctor," the father thought there was no harm in having another opinion on his son's illness.

Sundar's family, high-caste Brahmins, had been forced by economic deprivation to move from their village in the hills of Garhwal to Delhi many years ago when Sundar was still an infant. Working at a low-paid job, Sundar's father had experienced great financial difficulty in looking after his family, which, besides Sundar, included Sundar's mother, a brother five years younger and a sister seven years younger. Right from Sundar's childhood, his father was determined that come what may he would put his son through school and college. Education, he felt, was the only raft that could save the family from the ever-present possibility of sinking back into the abysmal poverty from which they had barely emerged. In this chilling fear, Sundar's father was not alone. Surrounded by a vast sea of poverty and the visible evidence of human degradation that it leads to, the unspoken and unacknowledged fear that one may someday sink into this sea is a specter that haunts almost everyone in urban India.

Sundar was an intelligent boy but even as a child he was stubborn in his refusal to take his studies as seriously as his father would have liked. There were frequent recriminations, threats, occasional beatings, all of which Sundar bore with sullen resignation—and his mother's silent support. Driven by his father's vision of having an educated man in the family, Sundar reached the bachelor level in college but could not pass his final examinations. Twice his father borrowed money for the examination fees so that he could make another attempt at passing the final hurdle but both times Sundar spent the money in "eating and drinking with his friends," an activity that he preferred to poring over textbooks. If he had passed the examinations, the father remarked wistfully, Sundar would have been the first one in their village with a college degree. Sundar now went to work but somehow he always got into a fight with his employers and was asked to leave. He had held four jobs in the last five years, ranging in duration from a few weeks to a few months. There was constant tension in the house on this account. Not that Sundar lacked respect for his father. He never argued back whenever the father berated him (which was frequent) for his habit of staying away from home at all times of day and night and taking neither his work nor his responsibilities toward the family seriously. He was at an age when he should have been married long ago and made proud grandparents out of his father and mother. But of course all this was now irrelevant, his father felt, and his only concern was that his son should get well. In spite of the many complaints against his son, I could sense the father's concern and his pride in the educated son who was still the family's only hope of someday rising out of their lower-middle-class status.

When I met Sundar the next week, he confirmed his father's account of his illness. He did not seem overly concerned with his symptoms, discussing them as if they belonged to someone else and we were both colleagues (though he a very junior and deferential one) reaching a diagnosis together. He was a handsome young man, dressed fashionably in Western-style clothes, and obviously took considerable interest in his appearance. Yes, he was always respectful toward his father even when he was being scolded for not pulling his weight in the family, he told me with the mien of a "well-brought-up" and obedient boy. He knew that his father shouted at him only because he had his (Sundar's) welfare at heart. Sometimes his father had lost his "balance" (here Sundar used the English word) and since he did not want to lose *his* balance too, the only choice for Sundar was to walk out of the house whenever the father lost his temper. He had had bad luck with his employers, he felt, since they held some sort of grudge against him. Just before his attacks started, his last employer had wanted to send him as a salesman to the villages of Uttar Pradesh. He did not want to go since he felt he was doing well as a salesman in Delhi and in any case an epidemic of deadly encephalitis was reported to be raging in these villages. Now, of course, because of his illness he had been compelled to give up his job, though his employer had told him to take a long leave and rest as much as was necessary to regain his health.

Speaking of himself, Sundar felt that he too was ambitious and wanted to better his lot. In fact, he had been thinking of finally taking his examinations this summer but again the illness had thwarted his plans, at least for this year. Sundar could also understand his father's wish that he should get married and settle down but again all these plans had to be temporarily shelved. Moreover, he hinted, though girls often approached him, he kept himself away from their advances and only wanted platonic relationships with the other sex.

Some months before the attacks started, Sundar was involved in a serious truck accident. Two of his close friends died in this accident and Sundar was lucky that he escaped without serious injury, though he lost his right thumb. Following the narration of this accident, Sundar told me of a recurrent dream that he has had since childhood. "I am sleeping on my bed when a shadow attacks me. I fight against the shadow but fall down from the bed. My mother picks me up. When I wake up I feel tense, as if I have been in a fight." On my pressing him for further details of the dream Sundar suddenly turned pale, his breathing became shallow and he cupped the lower jaw with both his hands. "I am getting an attack," he told me, his voice curiously calm, "please get me some water." He then got up from the chair and lay down on the couch, holding his jaws tightly together with his hands. I went out to get the water and his father, who was waiting outside, came back with me. Solicitiously, he held his son's head in his arms and lifted up the glass of water to his lips. "See, this is what happens, Doctor," he said. "Perhaps it was a mistake for Sundar to come here against the express instructions of the tantrik." After a few minutes Sundar recovered enough to come back to the chair, his face wan but composed. "I am all right again," he said in a tone intended to reassure me. "You can ask me anything you wish." Both of us knew, however, that the interview had effectively come to an end. By arousing a mixed feeling of guilt and protectiveness in me similar, I imagine, to the one he must have evoked in his father (and perhaps in his employer), Sundar had checkmated any further probings on my part as effectively as he had checkmated his father's pressures or his employer's wishes.

It will be evident to all who share the psychological idiom of illness that Sundar's symptoms enabled him to be relieved of onerous responsibilities and to receive protection, help and attention. His symptoms, including *"la belle indifférence"* toward them, their appearance and disappearance in response to changes in the environmental stress, his distaste for sexuality and so on, point toward a case of hysterical conversion. We can also get some feeling for the latent psychodynamic factors involved, especially as they come through in his attitude toward the father (and toward me in the interview): an outer deference marking an inner rage that takes dramatic form in the dream of the shadow attacking him. The jaws become numb, we would speculate, so that the rage does not spill out in a torrent of abuse; the arms go limp so that they may not strike. The guilt and anxiety at these feelings of hostility, compounded by an intense, Oedipal attachment to the mother, we would say, constitute the core factor in his illness.

Baba neither asked for nor did Sundar volunteer any information on his feelings or his life history, contenting himself with a bald narration of the symptoms when he went to see him.

"What do you see in your dreams?" Baba asked his standard opening question.

Sundar hesitated for a moment before replying that he had many kinds of dreams.

"Do you see a woman, a man, a child, a snake or a monkey or any wild animal in your dreams?" Baba clarified. This is the sequence Baba normally uses and if the patient answers that he does have a recurrent dream involving a human or an animal figure, Baba further asks what the dream figure was doing. Normally, the first question is sufficient (especially for women patients) to break the dam of reserve and for the patient to describe the dream figure and its actions in detail. Baba generally listens with an air of concern, nodding occasionally to convey that the patient was only confirming what he had suspected all along, and at the end of the narration delivers his judgment with finality: "You are possessed by a *bala.*"

This opening exchange, however stereotyped it appears at first glance, nevertheless gives a patient the opportunity to communicate his or her central conflict through (dream) symbolism—a means of communication that throughout history has found acceptance in literature, art, ritual, mythology and folklore as well as in everyday life. Although the *range* of symbols "offered" by Baba—man, woman, child, snake, monkey, wild animals—and their *context* ("What are they doing in the dream?") are rather limited, it appears that this range is sufficiently wide to convey the central conflicts of those patients who approach Baba. Consider the dream of a large number of women in which a strange man is being persistent in his demands for sexual intercourse. I would relate the cropping up of this specific dream in so many cases and with such monotonous regularity to two cultural facts: one, the strict taboo on the expression of a young woman's sexuality in urban India—a taboo which is equally strong (if not more so) among Muslim as among Hindu women; and, two, whatever sexuality that escapes the operation of this taboo generally gets expressed within the family (in contrast to aggression, which must always be expressed *outside* the family[22])—a situation that can evoke considerable feelings of guilt. In the well-known fashion of dreams, the woman's dream then ensures that her guilt-provoking sexual wishes are made bearable by being displaced to the man who, "naturally," must be a complete stranger.

We must also remember that the communication of psychic events, including mental distress, through the narration of dreams is a well-known device on the Indian subcontinent. Both Hinduism and Islam have always believed that dreams convey important messages and have a correspondingly active tradition of dream interpretation. Popular manuals of dream interpretation are avidly consulted by millions. In the case of Muslims, these manuals ultimately derive from the oldest Arabic treatise on the subject, *al-Qadiri fi't ta'bir*, written down in 1006 A.D. These manuals list thousands of objects and hundreds of situations occurring in dreams and ascribe each a standard meaning. However, as Katherine Ewing has pointed out in the case of Punjabi Muslims, it is widely accepted that the standard meaning given to dream "symbols" is only indicative.[23] The proper interpretation of a dream is a complex affair that requires a knowledge of the dreamer's impressions about the dream, the combination of symbols occurring in the dream, and the personal characteristics of the dreamer—his age, sex, profession, habits, preoccupations and so on. A dream regarded as significant by the dreamer is accordingly often taken to an expert—usually a *pir*—for an interpretation. Skilled *pirs* strive to elicit from the dreamer himself the source of tension that may have initiated the dream, often inquiring about his marital relations and family problems. The point is, there exists a great deal of culturally instilled confidence in the patient that the *pir* will understand his problems as communicated through his dream.

In his method of dealing with dreams, Baba does not proceed quite as other *pirs* do. To him, the man, woman and child, the snake and the monkey in the dreams, are all wretched *balas* that suck a patient's blood. To some extent his purpose in asking for *the* dream is diagnostic—deciding between possession and nonpossession. But more than that, the narration of the dream acts as a therapeutic lever, enabling the patient to communicate a symbolized account of his conflict and thus to "abreact" his strong emotions, reducing the intensity of their affect.

I cannot be categorical, but my impression is that Baba often has an intuitive, unconscious awareness of a dream's symbolic significance and actually possesses a greater knowledge of dream divination than he revealed during our sessions together. Thus once when a patient told Baba his dream of a clear lake, Baba remarked to me that dreaming of clear water was a good prognostic sign, while to dream of being mired in mud or slush was a bad augury. My nod of agreement was of vigorous appreciation and did not spring from any reflexive politeness. For water symbolism in many cultures is indeed an expression of the vital potential of the psyche that can renew a person. This is what the Hindus mean when they compare the unconscious *chitta* to a lake of muddy water which needs to be clear for self-realization; or what Buddha meant when, in his Assapuram sermon, he regarded the mountain lake—whose transparent waters reveal at the bottom sand, shells, snails and fishes—as the path of redemption.[24] In psychotherapy (as in the ritual of baptism), water is then often a symbol of birth into a new life, expressing the hope of a renewal and rebirth through the therapeutic process that makes the depths transparent.

Sundar's particular dream of struggling with a shadow did not fit in neatly with the general pattern of most other dreams.

"Aha, the shadow is a *bala* that is attacking you," Baba pronounced confidently.

He then asked for the bottle of water that Sundar had brought with him and closed his eyes for some meditative moments. His lips moved soundlessly as he silently recited the required Koranic verses while he held the bottle in his hands. Intermittently, he opened his eyes, blew forcefully on the water, and then continued his silent recitation. "Drink a little water from this daily," he said after he had finished the ritual. "Come back next week when I'll 'read' another bottle for you."

Sundar thanked him, put a two-rupee note on the cot—Baba never asks for fees—and left. Since Baba acts as an emissary of a higher, divine power, it is assumed that the effect of his priestly healing would be obviated by the demand of fees. However, he accepts gifts of money when they are offered voluntarily.

Although Baba sometimes "reads" sugar, the "reading" of water is his preferred therapy in cases of possession illness. Occasionally, in addition, he may also do *jhara*, which involves a similar ritual except that instead of blowing on water he blows his breath onto the patient's face. After a patient leaves, and if Baba remembers, he often says a short prayer with the tenor, "God, do not disappoint these poor souls. Keep them safe and in good cheer."

Baba's explanation for the power of "holy water" to drive a demon away is uncomplicated. The water, he says, washes the patient's blood clean so that the *bala* cannot drink it anymore and is forced to leave. Water, as well as talismans and other objects given to a patient at a Sufi saint's shrine, is believed to contain some of the saint's own essence and thus possess the same divine blessing *(barakat)* as was received by the saint himself. The symbolic suggestion involved here is that the water is a potent cleansing agent, charged with purifying energies that come from God. "Keep the bottle in a pure place," Baba often tells a patient. "With the grace of *Allah-pak* ["Allah the Pure"] the water will wash your insides clean." The pure *barakat*-laden water may not be thrown on the ground or down the drain but must always be drunk.

Since, as I have observed earlier, we would tend to see the anxiety of Baba's patients as being caused by an unconscious sense of guilt over their sexual and aggressive wishes (especially involving family members), Baba's suggestion to the patient that holy water will cleanse and purify his "insides" makes eminent psychodynamic sense. The effectiveness of his therapy in ridding a person of *balas* also suggests that Indian patients often experience guilt as a feeling of being dirty and polluted *inside*. Speculatively, this postulated difference in the Indian and Western ways of experiencing guilt can also partly explain why Indians—at both the individual and the social level—have been traditionally obsessed with matters of pollution and purity, in contrast, say, to the Judeo-Christian societies where the preoccupation has been with sin and morality.

I have earlier mentioned that Baba generally gives talismans in cases of "threat by *balas*," mostly involving family quarrels or strife among married couples. In the latter case, the talisman may be given together with some sugar which has been "read" over and which the aggrieved partner is supposed to mix in the spouse's tea. "Marital maladjustment" is a prime cause for many who seek professional help in the West. It is no different in India: the number of men and women who seek Baba's help to deal with an actual or threatened break-up of their marriages, wife beatings and the problem of runaway wives or husbands, constitutes the second largest category among his patients. As in the West, a married couple's sessions with the therapist are sometimes both tragic and farcical.

One day, Baba was approached by a thirty-year-old man who told him that a few months ago his wife had run away from home but had recently returned. She had, however, brought a twenty-year-old boy along with her who, she insisted, must remain in their house. She loved the boy but, she claimed, they were not lovers. Baba told the man that he did not think there was a *bala* involved in the case and asked him to come back together with his wife the next day, when he would prepare amulets for the couple and also try to "talk some sense into her." "But you must do something about your virility," Baba cautioned the man, "for almost always a woman runs away from home when the man cannot satisfy her sexually."

The man insisted that he was fine as far as *that* was concerned, but Baba continued to look doubtful. When they had left, Baba said, "I don't believe him! Look at him—as dried up as a blade of straw! I once had a case where a man had two wives whom he thrashed every day. On hearing of the bad treatment meted to their daughters, the parents wanted to take them away. The girls insisted on staying with their husband, saying that they were happy in spite of the beatings since the man could satisfy them. As you know, sexual satisfaction is absolutely essential for a woman's well-being, far more than it ever is for a man." My nod was noncommittal.

When the couple came back the next morning Baba was happy to find his diagnosis confirmed by the wife. In the presence of her husband the woman told Baba plainly that her husband did not satisfy her sexual needs and she was very unhappy. To be quite certain that *balas* were not involved, Baba asked his question about what she saw in her dreams. Giving her husband a venomous look, the woman replied spiritedly that she saw herself breaking her husband's head and did not feel afraid at all. She also told Baba that her husband wanted to bed the boy she had brought with her and this was another reason for their fights. The husband contested the wife's version and there was a heated quarrel. Baba pacified them both, prepared a talisman, "read" over some sugar and exhorted them to be God-fearing and not indulge in perverse sexual practices.

After the couple left, Baba seemed disappointed and pessimistic with regard to the outcome of his efforts. Although the talisman and the sugar would mobilize the pure, godly energies on behalf of the couple, I had the impression that Baba thought the grip of sensuality on both the man and the woman to be too strong to be loosened easily. It seems that success in the resolution of marriage conflicts also depends on the "innate character" of the woman. These character types, in order of their obdurateness to therapy, Baba enumerated as follows:

"First, there is *yar-marani*. Whatever the husband may be and however badly he treats her, this woman never looks at another man as a possible lover. Second, there is the *pet-marani*. She has great hunger in her stomach and will go to bed with anyone who can fulfill her love for food. Third, we have the *hirs-harani*, who follows whatever her neighbor is doing, in matters of clothes, fashion or taking lovers. And fourth, there is the *kus-marani*, who needs three or four men all the time. For her to feel satisfied, her vagina must be stuffed with a penis." The woman who had just left was a *kus-marani*, Baba felt, as he explained his doubtful prognosis. Both of us were silent for a while as we sat there companionably, contemplating the limits to our respective healing traditions.

3

LORD OF THE
SPIRIT WORLD

Two hundred and fifty miles south of Delhi, the Balaji temple is best reached by taking a bus from the nearest town of Bharatpur, a town described in tourist brochures as "the eastern gateway to Rajasthan." Founded by the Jat chieftain Suraj Mal, who carved out a kingdom of his own in the eighteenth century in the twilight of the Moghul empire, Bharatpur is not unlike other north Indian towns. Except for the presence of Suraj Mal's dilapidated fort and a group of palaces, cannily turned by his descendants into a luxury hotel for tourists, the ecology of Bharatpur's bazaars is universal. In summer, there are the usual flies in dense clusters on the overripe fruit and sweets and the dust that steams and not infrequently smells of horse urine once the monsoon comes. There are the irate tonga drivers cursing their scrawny horses, apparently lifeless but for their running sores; the placid oxcarts plodding unhurriedly through crowded bazaars, overloaded with everything from hay to steel girders; the Sikh drivers, strands of hair defying the purpose of their dirty turbans, two feet on the accelerator and two hands on the horns of their ancient trucks. There are the dank eating places with grime-covered clay ovens, radios blaring the latest film songs and the all-pervasive smell of frying onions and hot curries.

If the impression I have given of Bharatpur is one of sweltering discomfort, an unrelieved drabness, then I should hasten to correct it. For during the four or five months of cold weather at least, Bharatpur is transformed. These months are a feast of brilliant color and sharp smells, patches of wild bougainvillaea and strings of red chillies drying under the wintry sun. It is the season for fresh spices and the bazaars abound in heaps of gnarled turmeric roots and rich brown tamarind stocked in front of the shops. The air is crisp and the intervening haze of dust no longer dulls the clear sky, which has only a few wisps of gray to mar its blinding blue symmetry. The Ghana bird sanctuary, three miles from the town, lies on the great migratory route to the warm south and is a resting place for the birds from north and central Asia, the Siberian cranes, the gray-legged geese and countless others that are the ornithologist's delight. In fact, on our first trip to the Balaji temple in the middle of November, it was the variety of birds in the countryside outside Bharatpur that made the strongest impression on me. Families of peacocks pecking their way through the plowed furrows, sleek blue kingfishers swooping down gracefully to find a sure perch on the telegraph wires that run parallel to the road, flights of parrots and flamingos, were a common sight.

At least for the first few miles outside Bharatpur, the visual impressions one receives as the bus clatters past the villages lining the road are ones that are familiar from the rest of the Indo-Gangetic plain. They are registered as a succession of snapshots: a buffalo, immersed up to its neck in a pond thickly carpeted with green slime, motionless except for the occasional movement of its primeval head; a little girl, wrapped up in a yellow *chudder*, trying to move a recalcitrant ox by pulling at the string that runs through the animal's nose; the deeply pitted mud wall of a hut, plastered with flat cow-dung cakes drying in the sun. Gradually, however, as we move deeper into Rajasthan and approach Balaji, the landscape begins to change. Squat hills, with thorny bushes and eroded topsoil that exposes the underlying rock, become more frequent. Some of the hills are crowned by the ruins of equally squat fortresses that loom above the road and once guarded this old invasion route to the medieval Rajput kingdoms to the south. The countryside is sparsely populated. Miles and miles of barren land, dotted with olive-green scrub and scarred by dried-out gullies and narrow ravines, stretch out on either side of the road. It is as if the vast Rajasthan desert, still hundreds of miles to the south, is sending out intimations of its inexorable existence, an impression enhanced by the increasing number of camel carts coming from that direction.

The temple of Balaji lies between two hills in the middle of just such a desolate landscape, three miles off the main road to Jaipur. After a twenty-minute tonga ride through a sun-drugged silence, broken only by the sound of the horse's hooves rhythmically striking against the metaled road, the sudden din on reaching the lane that leads up to the temple comes as something of a shock. In fantasy, I had envisioned the temple having been built in the tradition of the classical Hindu temples—those of Bhubaneshwar or Puri, for instance. I had pictured it being lovingly hewn out of rock by ancient guilds of anonymous craftsmen, strong in their simple faith and devotion. I had thought of it standing in a solitary if somewhat decayed splendor in the middle of jungle scrub and rocky hills. Except for the scrub and the hills, the reality does not bear the faintest resemblance to the imaginary product. Flat-roofed, the temple is a simple two-storied structure at the end of a long lane which is lined on both sides by shops and a number of *dharmashalas*, the free boardinghouses for pilgrims erected by the pious. The temple can be distinguished from its neighbors only by the fact that its façade has been painted a bilious green. In spite of the fluted columns, small arched windows and stone latticed balconies typical of the Rajasthani style of architecture, the building still manages to convey a general impression of shabbiness, enhanced by the patches of green paint peeling off the underlying stucco. There is a total absence of any atmosphere of sanctity both in and around the temple premises. The space in front of the steps that lead into the temple (as also the steps themselves) are littered with banana skins, orange peels, crushed marigolds and other assorted refuse. The sides of the temple are crowded by eating places, small provision stores and hawkers selling fruit, vegetables, gaudy posters and painted clay images of the temple deities as well as prayer books and other holy bric-a-brac. The shop on the right side of the temple displays the signboard of an R.M.P.—registered medical practitioner—and the good doctor, a stout unshaven man with a roll of fat bulging out between the end of his undervest and the top string of his pajamas, can be seen reclining on a cot, thoughtfully paring his nails as he waits for customers who might have cause to be disappointed with the healing powers of the gods inside the great temple. In Balaji at least, medicine exists as a poor relation to religion, obsequious and faintly disreputable.

Like the ancient Greek temples of Asclepius at Epidaurus, Pergamon and Cos, the temple of Balaji at Mehndipur has acquired more

than local prominence as a shrine of healing. To the large number
of patients from all over northern India who approach it in "a spirit
of service, faith and devotion," the temple promises a quick relief
from many afflictions, including "obstacles raised by *bhuta-preta*
[malignant spirits], madness, epilepsy, tuberculosis, barrenness and
other diseases." The overwhelming number of patients I interviewed
had come to Balaji because of certain bodily symptoms and altera-
tions in behavior that were diagnosed, by their neighborhood exorcist *(sayana)* or by knowledgeable elders in the family and community, as manifestations of a mental illness caused by spirit possession.
It is its promise of cure from mental illness caused by malignant
spirits, illness that has proved intractable to the best efforts of modern doctors and traditional shamanic healers, which gives the temple
its distinctive reputation.

The malignant spirits of which I speak here are collectively known
as *bhuta-preta*, though Hindu demonology distinguishes between
the various classes of these supernatural beings. The *bhuta*, for
instance, originates from the souls of those who meet an untimely
and violent death, while a *preta* is the spirit of a child who died in
infancy or was born deformed.[1] A third class, that of *pishacha*,
derives from the mental characteristics of the dead person: a *pishacha* being generally the ghost of a man who was either mad, dissolute
or violent-tempered. In addition, to complete the malignant pantheon, there are a few female spirits of which the best known is the
churel—the ghost of an unhappy widow, a childless woman or, more
generally, of any woman who lived and died with her desires grossly
unsatisfied. It is emphasized by both laymen and experts alike that
a common characteristic of most malignant spirits is the fact that
they are souls of persons who could not live out their full life and
potential. In other words, they are all *atripta* spirits—*ghosts of unsatisfied desires*--and this of course makes them of professional
interest not only to the exorcist but also to the psychoanalyst.

The *bhuta-preta* are said to exist in a halfway house between the
human world and the world of ancestral spirits *(pitri-lok)*. Until they
have been judged, have paid their Karmic debts and are allowed into
the world of ancestral spirits, the *bhuta-preta* continue to yearn for
a human body which they can enter and contrive to make sick
through their nefarious activity. I was, however, struck by the fact

that both the individual's guarded apprehensiveness in relation to the malignant spirits and his longing for guidance from the benign ancestral spirits had an underlying tone of easy familiarity. In his relationship with these spirits, the person did not seem to feel the terror and the awe often evoked by the village and local deities; nor did he have the feelings of reverence that are due to the major gods such as Ganesha and Hanuman, and he certainly had none of the distant devotion with which the great gods and goddesses (and their incarnations) are apt to be regarded. Perhaps this psychological proximity is due to the fact that these spirits, occupying the lowest rungs in the Hindu hierarchy of supernatural beings, are closest to the human state. Whatever the reason, both the *bhuta-preta* and the *pitri* are a tangible, living presence for most people. They seem to populate a mental region that is contiguous and has open borders with the land of ordinary consciousness in which normal everyday life takes place. Persons may occasionally have encounters with the spirit world without these encounters being necessarily regarded as auditory or visual hallucinations of the pathological kind.

The Legend of the Divine Healer

Balaji, the chief deity of the temple, is better known throughout India as Hanuman, the monkey god who was Rama's main assistant in his epic battle against Ravana. The myth goes that Balaji was born of Anjana, a heavenly nymph who married a noble monkey and was cursed by the gods with a simian form. One day, while standing on top of a mountain, lost in a pleasant reverie, Anjana was ravished by Vayu, the god of the winds. Balaji was the offspring of this forced union. Like Bhima, the mighty warrior of the *Mahabharata* and another son of Vayu, Balaji was distinguished right from the start by great strength and gargantuan appetites. As an infant, he was perpetually hungry. Once he ran after the sun with all intentions of swallowing the orb to appease his hunger pangs. This caused great consternation among the gods and elicited vociferous protests from Rahu, whose right to periodically swallow the sun and cause the solar

eclipse was being so insolently violated. In anger, Indra, the king of
gods, hurled his thunderbolt at the greedy infant, who fell down on
a mountain top, breaking his jaw or *hanu*; hence also his name of
Hanuman. The father Vayu picked up his unconscious son, retired
into a cave and in sorrow and protest over the treatment meted to
his offspring refused to carry out his assigned tasks. With Vayu on
strike, there was a sudden absence of the ten forms of wind (*prana,
apana, samana, udana,* etc.) and thus a stoppage of such functions
as breathing, elimination, digestion, sleep and so on, with the result
that creation ground to an abrupt halt. Thrown into a panic, the
gods came rushing to the grieving Vayu's cave, begging for forgiveness and offering to make the necessary amends. As a first step, each
god blessed Balaji with a special power. At the end of this process,
Balaji had not only become immortal and invulnerable but also the
very personification of all the powers—mental and physical—of the
gods. Perhaps the most important blessing given to him, at least
from our viewpoint of tracing his status as a divine healer for those
afflicted with possession by malignant spirits, was Brahma the Crea-
tor's blessing of total *fearlessness.* Indeed these are the two qualities
—power and freedom from fear—that Balaji displayed in abundance
in his later exploits on behalf of Rama.

From this point onward, the all-India myth of Balaji gets diverted
into a local channel to become the legend of the temple at Mehndipur.[2] In the local legend the Vedic gods and the masculine preoccupations with power and fearlessness are given short shrift as the
legend chooses to focus on Balaji's mother. For while the father gods
are fighting the infant, grudgingly relinquishing their powers to him
and otherwise acting out the unconscious script of an immemorial
paternal fantasy toward sons, the mother is longing to reclaim her
darling boy. As the local legend has it, the mother waited at a spot
between two hills (yes, the spot where the present temple is located)
and was beside herself with joy when she could finally take Balaji in
her lap. She "kissed his face repeatedly, gave him both her breasts
to drink from and then after seating him in her lap, both mother
and son were soon absorbed in their spiritual practices."[3] Here, it
seems to us, the local additions and elaborations of the original myth
intuitively recognize the fact that the worship of Balaji as a god of
power and fearlessness alone makes him much too masculine and

distant to fulfill ideally the role of the divine healer. Like the female members of Asclepius's family to whom prayers for cure could be addressed,[4] the local legend recognizes the need to surround Balaji with the feminine-maternal principle and the "feminine" powers of nurturance, warmth, concern, intuitive understanding and relatedness which, many psychotherapists claim, are essential in every healing encounter and for the success of the healing process.[5]

For millions of years and many world ages, the legend goes on, Balaji sat here in the lap of his mother, accessible only to the gods who approached him for removal of their troubles. Then one day, a thousand years ago, a young prince was murdered at the spot where the temple now stands. His soul, taking the form of a *preta*, cried out for justice and clamored for liberation into the world of ancestral spirits. Moved by the *preta*-prince's plight and seeing that the *bhuta-preta* were a source of such misery to mankind, Balaji decided to make his "court" *(darbar)* accessible to troubled human beings. He sent a vision to a young priest of Mehndipur village, intimating this decision and requiring that a temple be built. The descendants of this priest are even today the priests of the Balaji temple.

To help him in his task of bringing order in the chaos of the spirit world and in regulating the relations between humans and the *bhuta-preta*, Balaji invited two other deities to take up their abode in the temple. The first god who accepted the invitation and moved to the Balaji temple with his own court was Preta-raja ("lord of the *preta*"), which is another name of Dharma-raja, the god of death and the guardian of *dharma*. As lord of the *pretas*, Preta-raja is expected to consider the problems and difficulties of a *preta* before deciding upon his fate, determine the *preta*'s proper quantum of punishment and decide the time when its soul is to be liberated from the *preta* order into the next order of the spirit world. The second deity to take up his residence within the temple was Mahakal Bhairav, an incarnation of Shiva, who was entrusted with the task of administering the punishments.

Following the inexorable laws of bureaucracy which seem to apply impartially to both the human and the divine worlds, the original trio of gods has since then mushroomed into a whole department of spirits. The three chief gods have added on assistants who specialize in different functions relating to the *bhuta-preta* and some of whom

have further acquired assistants of their own. The origins of these
minor gods and how they became a part of the temple are unknown,
even to the temple priest, who expressed his frank bafflement at the
proliferation of deities. It is, however, indisputable that people have
allotted these minor gods temple space and rituals of their own and
that these deities take a vigorous part in the healing process and in
the life of the temple: in fact, there are many patients whose cures
would not be complete without the full collaboration of these suprahuman functionaries. Here, I am specifically thinking of *bhangiwara*, a minor god in the court of Preta-raja who specializes in
dealing with the Muslim *bhuta* and those belonging to the untouchable castes. When a patient comes out of the *bhangiwara* enclosure
after having exorcised one of these *bhutas*, it is imperative that he
take a ritual bath to rid himself of the pollution. Otherwise it is held
that if the patient touches someone else after his *bhangiwara* so-
journ, it is almost certain that his *bhuta* will be transferred to the
other person.

The Temple and the Healing Rituals

The shabbiness of the temple's surroundings and its unimpressive
architecture become of minor importance once we enter the temple
premises. The moment one steps inside the halls and courtyards of
Balaji there is little time and even less inclination for contemplating
aesthetic issues. The senses are taken hold of violently and wrenched
out of their normal grooves by strange sights and unfamiliar sounds
and smells, embedded in a whirling crowd of pilgrims, patients and
their families in various stages of self-absorption. If I look back to
my own first impressions before the bizarre became the familiar, I
am struck by the wide gulf in the range of behavior permitted and
encouraged in a healing space—in this case, the court of the Lord
of the Spirit World—as compared to rooms and spaces where everyday life is carried on.

Passages from the journal of a colleague describing his first visit
to the temple vividly illustrate the drama of the healing process

and the colorfulness of the surroundings in which it takes place.
"Climbing up the temple steps to enter the outer courtyard, I am
greeted by an unfamiliar aroma. It takes me a few seconds to identify
the sweet, smoky smell coming from the direction of the main hall
as being produced by burning rice, grain, sugar crystals, coconut and
other offerings that the patients are required to make to Balaji. The
courtyard is crowded, mostly by young women, many of them sitting
or lying on the floor in odd, contorted postures. A young girl, perhaps
eighteen years old, quite attractive despite the unnatural pallor of
her face, is lying on her back. Her loose hair is spread around her
head which is violently jerking from one side to another as expressions of pain flit across her face. Her lips move in an inaudible
murmur, interspersed by full-throated shouts of 'Baba, Baba, I won't
go, I won't go!'—the *bhuta* (a male to judge by the timbre of his
voice and the gender he uses in the verbs) expressing his refusal to
vacate her body. My attention is caught by another young girl. She
is crouching on her knees, her hips thrust back, the pelvis moving
provocatively to both invite and repel an unseen violator. 'Get away!
Get away from me, leave me!' she is crying out in a strong voice. She
then bursts into deep moans of 'Oh, Baba! Oh, Baba!' her tightly
closed eyes shutting out the world from her private struggles with
the possessing spirit. I look around but no one else seems to be
noticing the girl and my gaze slides off incurious eyes. Another girl,
barely into her teens, is standing on her head against the wall. I hear
a swishing movement and a shoulder brushes against the back of my
legs. I turn around to see a girl bounding away in high, leaping
somersaults; the acrobatic somersaults taking her from one end of
the courtyard to another and then back again.
"From the outer courtyard, I step into the main hall. This room
is much larger, squarer in shape, and the grilled roof at the top makes
it bright and airy. On the left side, beyond the columns of the
temple, there is a narrow, dark corridor from where I get a good view
of what is happening in the main hall. As my eyes get accustomed
to the darkness I notice that I am not alone. An old woman is
squatting next to me, surrounded by the paraphernalia needed for
the ritual worship. There are two copper pots in front of her, both
of them filled with water. She is counting beads from a rosary in her
lap and with every count she dips a spoon into one of the pots, takes

out a spoonful of water and pours it into the second pot. I suddenly notice the presence of yet another person. This is another old woman, with a dark-complexioned face that almost merges into the surrounding darkness. As I move nearer, I am startled to see an unusually long and purple tongue protruding out of her mouth. She is being Kali, I tell myself, and reflexively bow to her. The woman raises a withered hand in benediction and I could almost swear that she has pushed her tongue out a little more for my benefit. Feeling somewhat uneasy I quickly move back into the main hall and step into the path of a dog who swerves to avoid me. The dog is hurrying toward the front of the hall to the dense crowd pressing against an iron grill behind which lie the food offerings heaped into a mound. A part of the offerings is being burned by a priest in a large brass lamp, producing sacred ash and the thick acrid smoke which I had smelled at the temple entrance. Through the smoke, the squares of the iron grill and over the heads of people clamoring to get nearer, I can see the idol of Balaji, which is in fact a triangular piece of stone, vaguely reminiscent of the shape of a human head, painted in ocher and silver colors and with two large black eyes painted on it to give it the appearance of a face.

"On the right side of the main hall, there is another corridor in which the temple of Mahakal Bhairav is located. The god of punish- ment is again represented by a large round stone, enclosed in a protective grill, painted the same ocher and silver colors and with eyes drawn on the surface of the stone. Next to the grill there is a circular cavity in the floor, barely six inches deep and little bigger than a man's head in circumference. An old man, noticing my show of interest, enlightens me as to the cavity's purpose. 'This is where the hangings take place. If you are here for some days you must see a hanging.' Later in the evening I would indeed get a chance to witness a 'hanging.' In fact it was the old Kali woman of my earlier encounter. She had put her head in the cavity and with the help of a female companion who held up her legs, she stood on her head for a full thirty minutes. Her muffled groans of pain indicated both the *bhuta*'s distress and her own physical discomfort, which must have been considerable indeed: 'It's enough, Baba,' she kept on repeating during her ordeal. 'Forgive me now!' 'Don't let him go, Baba,' her companion would shout back. 'Leave him only after you have choked him to death.'

"In the open courtyard I join a group of five women and a boy sitting around an elderly man. The man's eyes are closed, a faint smile plays around the corners of his mouth, and the whole atmosphere is charged with a suppressed merriment that is very different from the solemnity of a modern psychotherapist's office. The elderly man, whom they call 'Panditji,' is supposedly in a trance and the women seem to be enjoying themselves as they engage his *bhuta* in an animated conversation. 'O *re* Mussulman!' one of them says. 'Tell us quickly from where you have come.' Panditji murmurs something in reply and the woman repeats it aloud for our benefit. 'He says he is a Sayyad [a particularly strong Muslim *bhuta*],' and then turning to Panditji she says, 'Just now you were telling us that you want to eat kababs. Don't you know that you won't get any kababs as long as you are on this pandit? Do you understand? Run along now!'

"Panditji is now distinctly agitated. His head moves up and down vigorously and his voice is stronger, though it has the quality of a stubborn child, 'I'll eat kababs; I'll eat kababs! I'll certainly eat kababs! I have been hungry for three years. This idiot pandit has neither eaten kababs himself nor has he given me some to eat.' Panditji's wife, who is sitting next to him, takes umbrage at the *bhuta*'s rude tone and starts scolding him, but I'm more interested in the women's conversation. 'These Mussulmans! They have ruined our dharma,' says one of the women, referring to the *bhuta*. 'I don't know where they all come from!' 'First check up whether he is a Mussulman at all,' the second woman retorts, and she is supported by another one: 'Perhaps he is trying to fool us. Sometimes he says he is a Rajput, sometimes he says he is a Mussulman.' As I muse over the fact that Muslim *bhuta*s are considered to be the strongest and the most malignant of evil spirits, indicating perhaps the psychological depths of the antipathy between Hindus and Muslims, I hear Panditji speak: 'I *am* a Mussulman. My home is the shrine of Islaudin. Burn an oil lamp for me there every day or I won't leave.' I ask one of the women about Panditji's problems. 'Panditji stays at our boardinghouse,' she confides in me without hesitation. 'His whole family has the *sankat* [lit. stress, predicament]. Sometimes Panditji also gets possessed by a Mussulman who asks to be fed kababs and then we bring him here.' *Sankat* or distress, I have gathered by now, is the word used in Balaji to describe possession by a malignant spirit.

"It's almost three in the afternoon when I leave the group and climb up the staircase to the second floor where the 'court' of Preta-raja is being held. Since the 'King of the Spirits' is most intimately involved in the affairs of *bhuta-preta,* the second-floor hall is crowded and humming with a suppressed energy. Most people are sitting in an orderly fashion, their prayer books open in front of them, singing hymns in praise of Preta-raja's miracles. The singing is led by a boy of fifteen. under the approving eyes of the priest sitting in front of Preta-raja's stone representation and enclosed by the inevitable iron fence that prevents the patients from touching the stone. The singing is full of devotional excitement, punctuated by the sound of dull thuds produced by patients who are hitting their backs rhythmically against the walls. I go up to the back of the hall, which has three iron gates, similar in appearance to those that bar prison cells. I lean back against one of the gates and notice that the space in front of the other two is already occupied by two girls whose legs are chained to the iron bars. A couple of yards to my right, a woman is lying on her face with heavy stones piled on her back. She lifts up her head and calls me in a pleading voice, asking me to shift one of the stones, which is hurting her. With some effort I lift the heavy stone and put it down on the floor. 'Who told you to remove that stone?' she asks angrily. 'Put it back at once!' A couple of men and a woman—her family, I presume—loudly reproach me at my effrontery and the older of the two men seems very annoyed. I try to explain my action but he is shaking his head angrily muttering abuses against 'good-for-nothing interferers.' Noticing my consternation, a kindly man explains the situation. 'Actually when the girl called you, her *bhuta* was in considerable pain. If you had not lifted the stone he might have perhaps confessed his origin and his wishes. The family has been waiting here for three months for the *bhuta's* confession.' I sulkily retire to my place, warning myself never to interfere again and to be on my guard against expressing any human impulse of sympathy and fellow feeling.

"The chained girl beside me, whom I have studiously ignored so far, is getting noisier. She is rattling her chains loudly and occasionally she starts shouting in a hoarse voice, 'Stop it! Shut up and stop this nonsense or I'll reduce you all to ashes.' Some people in the crowd who hear her turn their heads but hurriedly look away as she grimaces at them and makes obscene gestures. She then calls her husband, a young man who is desperately trying to ignore her and concentrate on his hymn singing. She loudly asks him to have intercourse with her right away and then attempts to lift up her *sari*. This produces the desired result since the husband rushes to her side to stop her. As if she had been waiting for this, the girl catches hold of her husband's arm and sinks her teeth into his forearm. The husband gives her a hard slap which sends her sprawling against the gate. 'I am fed up,' the young man is saying, addressing no one in particular. 'I don't know what happens to her. Rot here for all I care! Show everyone your dramas, I am going home!' The girl, recovered from the blow, is sitting up and laughing delightedly.

"Looking out of the gate, I see the high cliffs against which the temple nestles. In fact it has been carved out of the hillside. There are big stone steps leading to the top of the cliffs. Names of *preta*s who have been exorcised and have joined Preta-raja's court as his servants and helpers are chiseled in these stone slabs. Next to the first step there is a raised platform, on which boiled rice, dhal and other edibles from the offerings made by the devout are heaped. Stray dogs and street urchins are gathered around the heap, rushing in to snatch the delicacies—*burfi*s or *laddoo*s—when a fresh offering is added to the growing mound. Dogs, I learn, are Mahakal Bhairav's mount and are thus sacrosanct within the temple precincts. Slightly higher than the platform and toward its left, there is a small water cistern which is supposed to be the home of another god known as Kundi Wale Baba. The dirty water of the cistern (it is a favorite bathing place of the dogs) is drunk by those whose spirit proves to be particularly stubborn."

The direct attack on the possessing spirit takes place through a series of temple rituals that seem to be patterned after judicial procedures. The first step is called the "application" *(darkhwast)*, in which a patient makes an offering of rice and dhal worth one and a quarter rupees and gives two *laddoo*s to an attendant every morning and evening before the start of the temple service. During these services, a priest touches the *laddoo*s to a part of Balaji's idol and then gives them back to the patient to eat. It is believed that with the eating of the *laddoo*s the power of Balaji goes into the patient and forces the *bhuta* to make his "appearance" in the court *(peshi)*

—the dramatic high point of the healing rituals. If the application is unsuccessful and the spirit does not appear, then the patient can make a "petition" *(arzi)* in which the "court costs" are seventeen and a quarter rupees' worth of *laddoo*s for Balaji, boiled rice for Preta-raja and boiled *urad* for Mahakal Bhairav. If the *bhuta* proves to be stubborn and does not appear even once during the morning and evening services for Balaji or in the afternoon service for Preta-raja, then the petition money is raised to twenty-one and a quarter rupees *(badi arzi).** In addition, the patient may be asked to make offerings of sweets to various minor deities such as *bhangiwara*. Meanwhile, the family members too have been active. Many of them are asked by the priest to chant specific mantras or to read aloud certain passages from the Ramayana and the Hanuman-Chalisa. Others are found in the temple halls, chanting mantras over spoonfuls of water that they keep transferring from one pot to another. The mantras supposedly impart divine energy to the water, which is later drunk by the patient, presumably to the further dismay of the possessing spirit. It is quite understandable that the *bhuta* is rarely able to withstand the concerted onslaught of so many "divine energies." In secular language we would say that the application and petition rituals incorporate the awesome authority of the gods in their demand that the patient go into the trancelike state of *peshi*. The demand is reinforced by the expectations of the priests and family members and is encouraged by the contagious effect of observing other patients having their *peshi* in the midst of approving groups.

The start of a *peshi* is marked by well-defined signs of which the rhythmic swaying of the upper half of the body and the violent sideways shaking of the head are the surest evidence of the *bhuta*'s "appearance." Beating of the floor with hands, hitting the back against the wall, lying down on the floor with heavy stones piled on the back, and other acts of self-punishment are further signs of *peshi*. In essence, *peshi* is a trancelike, altered state of consciousness (not of unconsciousness) where the focus of the patient's awareness of the environment is radically narrowed but not completely erased. In this

*In Hindu ritual, the number of quantities ending in quarters, *i.e.*, broken numbers, denotes the magnitudes of misfortunes transferred to the gods.

state, technically known as dissociation, the patient can generally carry out a conversation with members of the audience, though the conversation is often subject to later amnesia. He is careful not to cause himself serious injury in his acts of self-punishment and the *peshi* stops automatically with the end of the temple service. If the *peshi* is interrupted for any reason, patients report a fullness in their chests and a choking sensation in their throats "as if something wanted to come out."

In many patients, the next phase of *peshi* is marked by a struggle between the patient's *bhuta* and one of the temple's presiding deities. "You have called me here," the spirit may challenge the god, "but if you had any courage you should have come to me and then I'd have shown you my strength!" The people around the patient try to provoke the spirit by shouting slogans in praise of the god. Excited, the spirit often becomes angry and abusive, hurling obscenities at the god and mocking the piety of the onlookers. The torrent of aggressive abuse, especially when it is issuing out of the otherwise demure mouths of frail young girls and women, leaves little doubt that we are witnessing a convulsive release of pent-up aggression and a rare rebellion against the inhibiting norms and mores of a conservative Hindu society of which its gods are the most obvious representatives. Temporarily, some of the patients even opt out of the Hindu fold by their *bhuta* claiming that it is a Muslim, a *Sayyad* in fact, who is as powerful as Balaji and would never admit defeat. The excitement crescendoes as the community now brings its full weight to bear upon the rebellious and wayward spirit, "You'd fight Baba, will you?" the audience shouts. "Baba, give it a good thrashing, otherwise this villain will not listen!" Indeed the patient begins to hit himself, which simultaneously increases the volume of his spirit's protesting screams, "I shall not submit! I'll see you and all of them [the audience] in hell first!" After some time, the patient, patently tired, stops beating himself and the spirit admits defeat: "Fine, you have won. You starved me and you thrashed me, but after all you are my father. I'll obey you." There is obvious relief among the onlookers at the reestablishment of the normal cosmic order and the patient's acceptance of old values and old authorities. Many begin to laugh, "Baba, this is a clever one! Just because you thrashed him, he recognizes you as his father." The ritual now goes into its next phase of "statement" *(bayan)*, where the spirit begs for forgiveness and, at the urging of the crowd, identifies itself. The spirit then promises to leave the patient alone and to throw itself at the mercy of the god. Sometimes the god might send a reformed, benign spirit —the *duta*—to protect the patient against the onslaught of other malignant spirits; the coming of the *duta* is signaled by a short trancelike state in which the patient repeatedly prostrates himself before the idol.

The Patients and Their Illnesses

As I attempted to enter the inner world of the patients, reflecting on their life histories and observing the possessing spirits at close quarters, many of the *bhutas* turned out to be familiar acquaintances from clinical psychoanalytic work; the happenings that seemed so mysterious on the first visit gradually lost their sense of the strange and the uncanny. Perhaps a few case histories will not only add to our understanding of possession illness from a dynamic psychoanalytic viewpoint—as distinguished from the more psychiatric, sociological and cultural contributions of other writers[6]—but also highlight certain kinds of culturally unacceptable behavior and make vivid the psychic stresses to which the individual is subjected in Indian society.

1 SHAKUN'S AUNT

Shakun was a nineteen-year-old girl from a small town in Bihar who came to Balaji with her mother and her three brothers. A shy and pretty girl, Shakun was sixteen when she was first possessed by a *bhuta*. One afternoon she had gone out to the courtyard to urinate and had called to her mother to help her with her underwear since she had freshly dyed her hands with henna, a cosmetic primarily used by girls on the eve of their wedding. On the same night, after everyone had gone to bed, the family heard Shakun's frightened screams. It seems that in the hypnogogic state before falling asleep, Shakun "saw" a laughing woman come up to her. The girl was frightened and claimed that the woman then danced on her head, giving her a violent headache. The dancing woman's visitations and Shakun's consequent headaches and severe anxiety states occurred at regular intervals for the next three years. The diagnosis of the family and the exorcists brought in for consultation was unanimous in attributing Shakun's state to possession by a female *bhuta*. Since the local exorcist's efforts at exorcism proved fruitless (though in one of the rituals the *bhuta* had identified herself as the spirit of Shakun's father's brother's wife), it was decided that the girl be taken to Balaji.

In contrast to Shakun, who was painfully self-conscious and reticent, her mother willingly provided details of her daughter's illness. The dead aunt—Shakun's possessing spirit—the mother said with an air of conspiratorial secrecy, had committed suicide when Shakun was only three years old. "Surely Shakun was too young to remember her," the mother said. The suicide of the aunt, who was married to the elder brother of Shakun's father and who lived in the same household, had taken place in scandalous circumstances and the mother's salacious delight was unmistakable as she went on to describe the exciting details. The aunt, it seemed, was quite promiscuous and took her lovers indiscriminately from among all comers, including the low-caste laborers who worked in the family's small cigar-making enterprise. Though everyone else in the family knew and strongly disapproved of the aunt's affairs—Shakun's father had forbidden his wife even to talk to the woman—the husband had proverbially remained unaware of his wife's amorous adventures to the very end. One day, however, he caught his wife *in flagrante delicto* with one of his laborers and there was a violent quarrel between the couple. The aunt committed suicide on the same night. "But, of course, Shakun doesn't know anything about her aunt. We haven't even mentioned her name in Shakun's presence," the mother repeated.

Here, I am afraid, I must disagree with Shakun's mother. I cannot imagine that the three-year-old child, at a stage of life when curiosity is at its highest, remained unaware and unaffected by an exciting yet also violently disapproved-of aunt who died in such mysterious circumstances. At that time (and even later), there must have been

whispered conversations between her parents and other family elders
—conversations that simultaneously reflected their condemnation
and vicarious sexual excitement—and which would suddenly cease
when the child came within hearing distance of the adults. There
must have been many references to the family tragedy, which Shakun overheard, and explicit taunts by other children which left
Shakun in little doubt about the aunt's promiscuity and its disastrous
fate. For Shakun, the memory of her aunt must have remained
vividly alive in the unconscious, becoming involved with all that is
both strongly forbidden and overwhelmingly exciting, harboring
that "secret of life" which every child yearns to unravel.

The aunt, I am suggesting, gradually became the personification
of the growing girl's *negative identity*[7]—all that Shakun "knew" she
should never be but feared she might become, especially when her
sexual impulses started asserting themselves during the tumult of
adolescence. Changing from the Eriksonian to the Jungian idiom,
one would say the aunt is the *shadow*, the inferior, dark part of the
personality which is repressed to the unconscious and consists of all
those forbidden desires that are incompatible with the values and
strivings of the conscious persona. Shakun's *bhuta* is, then, a figure
of her unconscious, an iconic representation (in the form of the
aunt) of the girl's own sexual (even homosexual?) wishes. Because of
the social standards of her community but especially because of the
horrible fate of the aunt who gave in to *her* sexual wishes, Shakun,
I believe, has struggled desperately to keep these desires from
becoming conscious. At sixteen, a time of heightened sexual impulses, the repression failed for the first time, resulting in a psychological possession that led to great anxiety as this inhibited girl's ego
fought desperately against being overwhelmed by the feared unconscious content.

2 ASHA AND HER SPIRITS

Asha was a twenty-six-year-old woman from a lower-middle-class
family in Delhi who had come to Balaji accompanied by her mother
and her uncle. A thin, attractive woman with sharply chiseled features and a dusky complexion, Asha had a slight, girlish figure that

made her look younger than her age. She had suffered from periodic headaches ever since she could remember, though her acute distress began two and a half years ago when a number of baffling symptoms made their first appearance. Among these were violent stomachaches that would convulse her with pain and leave her weak and drained of energy. Periodically, she had the sensation of ants crawling over her body, a sensation that would gradually concentrate on her head and produce such discomfort that she could not bear even to touch her head. There were bouts of gluttony and fits of rage in which she would break objects and physically lash out at anyone who happened to be near her. "Once I even slapped my father during such a rage," Asha told us. "Can you imagine a daughter hitting her father, especially a father who I have loved more than anyone else in this world?"

Treatment with drugs (her uncle was a medical doctor) and consultations with an exorcist did not make any appreciable difference to her condition, but what really moved Asha to come to Balaji was her discovery, six months after her father's death, that her skin had suddenly turned dark. This caused her intense mental anguish, since she had always prided herself on her fair complexion. Asha now felt that she had become very unattractive and toyed with the idea of suicide.

After coming to Balaji, Asha's *peshi* was immediate. She had barely finished eating the two *laddoo*s in Balaji's "court" when she fell down on the floor and revealed that she was possessed by two spirits. The first spirit, who caused the stomachaches, stated that it was sent by Asha's brother's wife. Its name was Masan, it said, a ghost that inhabits cemeteries and cremation grounds and whose "specialty" is the eating of unborn babies in the womb. The second spirit admitted its responsibility for the sensation of crawling ants and for Asha's rages, and further revealed that it had been sent by the elder brother of Asha's fiancé. After their first confession, both the spirits were silent and did not make any further statements. On subsequent occasions Asha's *peshi* was a gentler affair consisting of a dreamy swaying of the body from which Asha emerged with a feeling of heightened well-being and the conviction that her skin had become lighter. Asha, it seems, had become addicted to *peshi*. She was not overly concerned with the punishment of her *bhuta* and indeed seemed indifferent to the prospects of her cure. If for any reason the *peshi* did not take place for more than two to three days, Asha's eyes screwed up into narrow slits, her headaches became worse and she inevitably had one of her fits of rage. In a more theoretical formulation, Asha was attempting to exchange her possession symptoms, a pathological reaction to individual conflict, for the ritual trance of *peshi*, a socially sanctioned psychological defense.[8]

Though Asha was anything but secretive and talked animatedly about her life and her problems, the talk was mostly diffused and scattered. She flitted from one experience to another, from the present to the past and back to the present again so that a chronological piecing together of her life history became a difficult task. Dramatic impressions and nostalgic memories, described with elaborate gestures and in a theatrical voice, succeeded each other with bewildering rapidity, making it difficult to sift facts from impressions, reality from fantasy.

As the youngest child in the family and the only daughter after a succession of five boys, Asha had always been her father's favorite. The memories of her childhood were pervaded by images of a father-daughter closeness and of their delight in each other that had excluded other members of the family from their charmed circle. The first thing the father did on coming home from the office every evening was to ask for his beloved daughter and play with her till it was time for dinner. Even when she was twenty, Asha remembers that her father inevitably brought her sweets in the evening, and then, lifting the now not-so-little girl upon his shoulders, he would romp around the house, often exclaiming, "O my darling daughter, what would I do when you get married and leave this house! My life would be ever so emtpy!"

The only discordant note in the "idyllic" father-daughter relationship occurred when Asha was fifteen. She fell in love with a young college student who had been engaged as her tutor. When her father came to know of their budding romance, he was furious and packed Asha off to her aunt in Saharanpur. Here she was so closely watched that she could neither write nor receive letters. For one year the girl pined away in virtual imprisonment and came back to Delhi only when her father fell sick and refused to be nursed by anyone except his favorite daughter. Asha devotedly nursed him back to health and the subject of the young tutor was never mentioned by either one of them; in fact, the episode seemed to have brought the father and daughter even closer.

The sequence of events that led to Asha's possession by the two spirits seems to have been as follows. Three years before, Asha's favorite brother had got married, and according to Asha, under the influence of his wife he became quite indifferent to his sister. Asha felt very unhappy at her brother's "betrayal" but continued to perform all her sisterly duties. Once, when she had gone to her brother's house for a short stay—her sister-in-law was pregnant—Asha found some of her own clothes in her sister-in-law's cupboard, which made her very upset at her "thieving" sister-in-law. Her stomachaches started shortly afterward.

It was during this time that a young man from the neighborhood began to take a pronounced romantic interest in Asha. Every day the man dropped in at the clinic where Asha helped her uncle in his work and would talk to her for hours. Asha was uninterested in her ardent suitor, she claims, but this did not faze the young man in the least. In their long and frequent conversations the man openly declared his love for the girl. When Asha's father came to know of the young man's pursuit of his daughter, he was, once again, furious. Accompanied by two of his sons, the father went to the man's house to remonstrate with his family. The man's mother persuaded Asha's father and her brothers that Asha should be married into their family and it was decided (it was not clear how and by whom) that Asha would marry not her suitor but his younger brother instead. Asha felt very unhappy at this arrangement but her father fell sick and she could not give vent to her feelings as that might have worsened his cardiac condition. Once again she devotedly nursed her father through his illness, even "holding and cleaning the organ which a girl never holds in her hand."

The elder brother of her fiancé had now become bolder and even more insistent in his sexual advances toward the girl. He seemed unmoved by Asha's repeated plea that since she would soon become the wife of his younger brother he should, like a good Hindu, begin to look upon her as his daughter. It was during this period that Asha was attacked by her second spirit for the first time. She had gone to her mother-in-law's house for a visit but found that everyone was out except her lovelorn admirer. He had asked her to come up to his room and Asha had fainted. Her rages, the sensation of crawling ants and the headaches began soon afterward.

As a psychoanalyst, trying for the moment to understand the basic underlying psychic processes rather than the cultural significance of Asha's behavior and symptoms, I would say that apart from its Indian stage and Punjabi middle-class setting, Asha's case seems to be a part of the same genre that is often encountered in the early psychoanalytic literature on young women who fell ill while caring for an older, sick relative. Torn between her duty and her love for her father and her own unacknowledged sexual wishes toward another man, Asha's conflict is similar to that of many girls in the European bourgeoise society of the late nineteenth century—that of Freud's patient Elisabeth von R., for instance.[9] With her need for intense closeness to her father, Asha seems to have had little choice but to deny the hostile component of her feelings toward him—as she must have denied her rage during her first, abortive love affair with the tutor. Given the present stressful circumstances—her father's illness, her engagement and the man's importunate demands —Asha's defense of denying her aggressive and sexual wishes was no longer sufficient but needed to be supplemented by having these wishes split off from consciousness and attributed to the machinations of a *bhuta*. Naturally, the spirit was "sent" by the lovelorn swain who is unconsciously held to be responsible for the conflicting emotions that constantly threaten to overwhelm her. Asha's other distressful symptom of a darkening of her skin, I would say, springs from her identification with her father, since we learn that just before the father died, *his* skin had turned blue-black in color. Such an identification is not only intended as a compensation for the loss of the beloved father but can also be the expression of Asha's vain attempt to free herself from him. Asha's other *bhuta*—the embryo-eater Masan—too represents a similar symbiosis of destructive and sexual wishes. Her stomachaches, I would suggest, are an expression of her unconscious pregnancy fantasy, created by means of an identification with the "fortunate rival," the sister-in-law. The ghost killer of unborn babies then symbolizes the idea, "It is not I who would like to destroy my sister-in-law's unborn baby but she who wants to kill my [fantasied] baby." Asha's bouts of gluttony would seem to reinforce this interpretation. As many creative writers have also known, neurotic greed is the reflection not of the need for food but of unconscious wishes that cannot be satisfied, and thus can never be assuaged by eating. In his novel *Two Women*, for instance, Balzac in describing a pregnant woman's passion for rotten oranges intuitively recognizes the cannibalistic nature of her wishes directed against the child in her body.

I have suggested above that Asha (but also Shakun) has much in common with Freud's women patients from the Viennese bourgeoisie. The similarity does not lie in their symptoms but in the underlying *hysteric personality* which they share. The elements of this "ideal type" hysteric personality are well known: an intense, erotic attachment to the father and an unresolved Oedipal conflict, a fear of sexuality accompanied often by a strong but hidden interest in it, overly great concern with conventional values and social proprieties, an impressionistic way of experiencing the world, dramatized and exaggerated behavior, a capacity for multiple identifications and so on. Indeed, a majority of the patients interviewed at Balaji—fifteen out of twenty-eight, eleven of whom were women—evidenced such a core hysteric personality. Significantly, though many of the other patients did not have a *peshi* in the temple, nor did their *bhuta* appear to make a "statement," in the case of all the fifteen hysterical patients the possessing *bhutas* appeared without exception to give their "statements." Although possession is more than hysteria, the hysterical personality seems to make the best use of possession states.

Where Asha and other Indian hysterical personalities differ from their European counterparts is in the display of a rich, dramatic and concrete imagery of the *bhutas*, this kind of visual imagery being diffuse, if not completely absent, in the recorded cases of *la grande hystérie* in the West. Here, the culture comes in. The rich mythological world, peopled by many gods, goddesses and other supernatural beings, in which the Indian child grows up, his early experiences of multiple caretakers, all contribute to the imagery of possessing spirits. Hysteria, as Alan Krohn has pointed out, is uniquely a neurosis that takes on the coloring of a specific historical and cultural setting.[10] "Vapors," fainting fits, inexplicable paralyses and convulsions in the Victorian era, the devil or a witch wresting control of the body to use it for its own purposes in the Middle Ages, are some of the many costumes that the hysterical personality has worn in its time in the West. In fact, the hysterical personality is probably unique in aligning itself with what Krohn calls the prevailing "myth of passivity" of its culture. I am the "passive" vehicle of gods, or of the devil, of my twitchings, or my *bhutas*, which make me do these things, not my own desires.

It may well be that the hysterical personality has not largely disappeared in the West but has merely adapted itself to the culture's present myth of passivity. "To be the helpless victim of one's society, the stars, one's unconscious, or mental disease," Krohn writes, "are now our culturally sponsored myths of passivity and this forms the basis of current hysterical alternatives."[11] In any event, for an Indian psychoanalyst, Freud's libido theory, derived from his studies of hysteria, which often tends to be relegated these days to the realm of an aesthetic metaphor, is still central to much of his clinical work. In spite of the newer theoretical developments, such as Heinz Kohut's "psychology of the self," which may preoccupy his colleagues in the West, for the Indian analyst psychoanalysis remains preeminently the child of a hysterical woman.

We saw above that the single largest category of patients, comprised mostly of young women who come to Balaji in search of healing, are suffering from a hysterical disorder; or, if one prefers to use the traditional idiom, they are possessed by the ghosts of forbidden sexual and aggressive wishes. Though the individual variations in all these cases are of great interest from the clinical angle, the wide prevalence of hysterical personality among Indian women and their use of this particular cultural myth of passivity, are also reflections of certain social conditions prevailing in the society. In other words, there is no individual anxiety that does not also reflect a latent concern common to the group, a fact that Erik Erikson pointed out long ago but which we clinicians often tend to underplay in our pursuit of the uniquely individual in case history.[12] For in going through my Balaji case histories, especially of rural women, I am struck by their accumulated and repressed rage, the helpless anger of young women at the lack of their social emancipation being the canvas on which the individual picture of hysterical illness is painted.[13] Let us look at another case which illustrates this clearly.

3 URMILLA'S RAGE

Urmilla is an attractive eighteen-year-old from a village in Rajasthan who had come to Balaji with her husband. A couple of years ago, immediately after her marriage, she started complaining of body aches accompanied by difficulties in breathing. Shortly thereafter she began to get into uncontrollable fits of rage. During these fits of rage she would heap abuse on everyone who came near her, though reserving her choicest epithets for her husband, toward whom she often became physically violent. "She gets such strength at these times that it takes two or three strong men to restrain her," the husband reported with grudging admiration. "She also gets so hungry that she'd eat up the food cooked for the whole family and so thirsty that she'd drink up a full bucket of water." "Yes, Doctor Sahib," Urmilla confirmed her young husband's account. "Before marriage I did not get angry even once. But when the *bhuta* comes I don't remember what happens to me. Later, they tell me the filthy abuses I have used against my husband but I have no memory of such a shameful act."

Urmilla was possessed not only by a malignant *bhuta* but also by a benign spirit—that of her dead father—who would come to protect her when her *bhuta*-inspired rages threatened to cause grievous injury. The father had died when Urmilla was five years old and had the reputation of being a short-tempered man. The father's spirit, though also hot-tempered, was perceived by Urmilla as a guiding and benevolent *pitri* and it was at *his* advice that the couple had made the pilgrimage to Balaji. The couple had been in Balaji for some time now and though the *bhuta* came often he had yet to confess his origins and his wishes. The husband was getting impatient to go home but Urmilla insisted that she would not go back till her father's spirit instructed her to do so. When the husband insisted, Urmilla became possessed by her father's spirit and roundly abused her husband, threatening to break his legs for even daring to think of leaving his daughter behind. The spirit also told everyone in the boardinghouse where the couple was staying that the man was perhaps planning to take a second wife and that he (Urmilla's father) would see to it that he was severely punished. Occasionally, Urmilla also got possessed by another benevolent spirit—that of her dead mother-in-law—who complained of the family's neglect in carrying out the proper rituals for the welfare of her soul and ordered them to make up the deficiencies.

For the past few days, Urmilla had increasingly got the feeling that her *bhuta* was leaving her. One day she announced that they would all go to a nearby temple of the Mother Goddess Vaishno Devi—two miles from Balaji—where the Mother (the goddess) would come to possess her and tell them whether the *bhuta* had really left or whether he was playing one of his tricks for which the *bhutas* are so notorious. Next morning, a small group consisting of Urmilla, her husband and another couple from a neighboring village went up to the temple and waited for the Mother in the small room where the idol was kept. Urmilla went on staring at the Mother's face while the others kept up a rhythmical shouting of "Victory to the Mother!" Urmilla's breathing was becoming faster and expressions of pain and anger flitted across her face in quick succession. Suddenly we noticed a transformation on her face, which became quite still and devoid of all expression; the Mother had come. In a loud and confident voice, Urmilla began to speak rapidly. Urmilla: "What do you want? Speak. What do you want? Why have you called me?"

The husband (in a low, respectful tone): "Please tell us if we should leave on Saturday."

Urmilla: "Yes, go away. Leave."

The husband: "Please also tell us whether her distress is over. Sometimes she is fine but sometimes she starts getting angry again."

Urmilla (in an excited tone): "Haven't I told you to leave? We'll look after the girl there. Have faith. We are with her."

The husband: "One more favor . . . the *bhuta*'s name—" This sentence was left incomplete since Urmilla thundered back angrily: "Why do you want to know the name, you villain? We'll tell the names when we go back. The whole family is torturing this poor girl! How many names do you want?"

The husband was intimidated and mumbled his assent. Urmilla sought to confirm her domination by ordering him to rub his nose on the floor, the sign of abject surrender. The husband caught the lobes of his ears with his hands and bowing down before the idol rubbed his nose three times on the ground. The other woman who was sitting with folded hands now addressed Urmilla, "Mother, tell me something about myself too."

Urmilla (speaking very rapidly): "The villain eats babies in the womb. Has ruined this poor woman. But everything will be fine. Say 'Victory to the Mother.' I'll take care of the Mussulman."

The woman bowed to her and after a couple of minutes Urmilla came to herself. She looked exhausted but at the same time her face glowed with satisfaction at her recent experience. As they walked back to the boardinghouse, Urmilla told us that they would leave Balaji this Saturday. There was no fear of the *bhuta* returning, she said, since the Mother had decided to be with her and she could protect Urmilla even better than the spirit of her father.

The evidence is strong that Urmilla harbored within her a violent rage, which she suppressed till her marriage, until finally her inability to control the rage provoked the mysterious aches and the motor discharge in possession states. In these states, assured of the protection afforded by the clouding of consciousness and the subsequent amnesia, Urmilla was able to give an otherwise forbidden satisfaction to her pent-up fury. Under the pretext that she herself was not the subject of the rages, she could refuse to acknowledge them as her own and split herself off from her other "selves"—the *bhuta,* the father spirit, the mother-in-law spirit and the Mother Goddess. The question then arises: what was the cause of Urmilla's rage and against whom was it aimed, since such rages can be directed not only against actual persons but also against parental images and other inner figures from childhood? As I do not have enough information on Urmilla's past, I can only look at her present circumstances and suggest that Urmilla's expression of rage against her husband and his family is also a rage against her feelings of powerlessness. It is indeed a striking fact that her identifications are with the powerful figures of the father, the mother-in-law and the Mother Goddess. In a Rajput village community where the young daughter-in-law is expected to be completely subservient and not even think angry thoughts about her husband's family and especially about her "lord and master," possession by spirits who behave otherwise seems to be one way for a young girl to express and yet not acknowledge the resentment against the powerlessness of her condition. Anger against "superior" family members seems to be particularly difficult to express. Even "She hates me," as in the case of Asha and her sister-in-law, is not easy to acknowledge, while one has to be terribly ill and possessed by all manners of spirits to be able to express "I hate him [or her]." The coin that depicts the *Bharatiya nari*—the "Indian woman"—in all her sentimentalized chasteness and calm fortitude on one side, shows the same woman engaged in a desperate struggle with her inner demons on the other.

4 SUSHIL'S POSSESSION

Whereas powerlessness is the social denominator of female hysteria—the cumulative trauma of Indian women, so to speak—the demands of autonomous functioning and anxiety at the prospect of individuation seem to be the social correlates of male hysteria. Instead of reproducing detailed individual case histories in support of this contention, perhaps a vignette will serve the purposes of illustration.

Sushil was a twenty-seven-year-old man who was possessed by a spirit when he was twenty-two. A year earlier, after Sushil graduated from his college in Agra, his father had set him up in a small pharmaceutical business which he expected his son to manage on his own. Things had gone well for a couple of months till Sushil was married. A few days after the marriage, Sushil found that he had lost all interest in business. Instead of going to the shop in the mornings, Sushil would wander around in the bazaar in a daze. Then one day, in this dazed state, Sushil "saw" his younger brother—who had died in an accident when Sushil was ten—walk toward him, his school bag swinging from a thin, jaunty shoulder. From that day onward Sushil frequently became possessed by his younger brother's spirit. In these possession states, which he did not find unpleasant, Sushil's voice changed into a childish treble, his vocabulary dwindled to that of an eight-year-old and his whole demeanor took on a pronounced childish cast in which his renunciation of independent adulthood was complete.

In the *timing* of his illness, Sushil's case was identical with that of other male hysterics who also had invariably suffered their first attack of possession a few days after their marriage. It was as if they had experienced the sexual activity and the demand of establishing a close emotional bond with a strange woman as the first truly individual act of their lives in which the family could not participate and which had threatened to isolate them from the web of their familial and group emotional ties.

Healing at Balaji:
Psychotherapeutic Perspectives

In the West, a big step in the treatment of mental disorders was taken at the end of the last century with the realization—primarily attributed to Charcot and Freud—that hysterical "illnesses" were the symbolic expression of a definite emotional content; that the person's bodily symptoms could be seen as bits of behavior intended to convey a message. In other words, the essential and distinctive feature of a hysterical disorder was the substitution of a bodily state for a personal problem which enabled the individual to ignore and escape the anxiety caused by the personal problem. Moreover, Freud demonstrated that the roots of the personal, emotional problem lay in the individual's past of which he or she was normally unconscious. The psychoanalyst's task was to foster a self-reflective attitude in the patient toward his bodily signs or symptoms so as to facilitate their translation into ordinary language. As Thomas Szasz has aptly put it, those who want to deal with so-called hysterical patients must therefore learn not how to diagnose or treat them but how to understand their special idiom and how to translate it into ordinary language.[14] The assumption of psychoanalysis is that by helping a person to decode his symptoms and become explicitly aware of past events that have influenced their genesis, the persistent effects of these events in his future can be mitigated and indeed radically modified.

This approach to the cure of hysteria later became the dominant psychoanalytic paradigm for dealing with other types of mental illness. In short, psychoanalysis and Western psychotherapies influenced by psychoanalysis concentrate on what I would call the *text* of the mental illness—on its understanding, translation and genesis. In contrast, as we shall see below, the healing rituals of the Balaji temple follow radically different principles of therapy. They seem to be more concerned with the *context* of the illness. In traditional therapy, the special idiom underlying the visitations of Shakun's aunt, Asha's spirits and Urmilla's rages is left at the symbolic level without any attempt at translation. Instead, the healing efforts seem to be directed more toward changing the context of the problem by changing the person's feelings about himself or herself. Basically, the healing rituals seek to connect (or reconnect) the individual with sources of psychological strength available in his or her life situation and thus counteract the more or less conscious feelings of despair, shame, guilt, inferiority, confusion and isolation in which the "illness" is embedded. Let me illustrate the essentials of the contextual approach to healing through an analysis of the healing process at Balaji.

Typically, a patient whose illness started with disturbing bodily and mental symptoms has exhausted all the local resources before he makes the decision to come to Balaji. He has tried out home remedies, consulted doctors—both of traditional and of modern medicine —and has perhaps undergone the exorcism rituals of one or more exorcists. The decision to go to Balaji is then an admission, both by the patient and by his family, that things are seriously wrong and that the temple represents perhaps the last chance of a cure. The journey to Balaji then acquires an added emotional significance and given the considerable distance a patient and his family must travel, with all the attendant inconvenience and hardship, the long trip to Balaji becomes a sacred journey, a pilgrimage in search of healing. From the medical metaphor of illness, the patient has shifted to a religious-spiritual metaphor of the pilgrim's progress toward wholeness. All of this represents a strong emotional investment by both the patient and the family in the success of the pilgrimage. We find this increased investment in dreams that some patients had before they came to Balaji. The dreams typically involved a personal summons from the divine healer, either through the god speaking directly in the dream or through the dream image of one or more monkeys—the symbol of Hanuman. Thus even before they embarked on the healing journey, some patients had begun to send themselves messages of reassurance from the unconscious depths, increasing their hope and confidence in the success of the healing mission. Many other patients reported that once the decision was made, their *bhuta,* knowing of his imminent demise, began to raise obstacles which the patient had to overcome before he could come to Balaji. Obviously such a patient no longer feels himself as a passive recipient of healing ministrations—whether the doctor's medicines or the exorcist's incantations—but has become a more active participant in the process of his own cure.

Expectations and hope are greatly strengthened by the culture prevailing in the Balaji community. Patients and their relatives constantly extoll the powers of the divine healer and describe to each other (and especially to the newcomers) the details of miraculous cures that have taken place over the years. The fact that these cures are neither ephemeral nor hearsay is underlined by the presence of a large class of ex-patients. Many of these ex-patients come to Balaji at periodic intervals or on special festive occasions in order to sustain their link with the healing temple and to remain free from distress. Others come to fulfill their commitment of *sava-mani* in which a patient promises to feed the poor with food weighing fifty kilograms after he has been cured. All these former sufferers are living witnesses and reinforcers of the patient's growing faith that the temple healing really "works."

A second important characteristic of the temple's healing culture is the involvement and integration of the patient's relatives in the healing process. According to the temple rules a patient can stay in a boardinghouse only if he is escorted by at least one caretaker. In practice there are often three or four family members who accompany the "sick" person on his pilgrimage. Many rituals that need to be carried out in the temple require the active participation of these family members. Accompanying the patient from morning till late in the evening through the various healing rituals and living in an environment where *sankat* (and its vicissitudes) is the central theme of community life, the distinction between a "sick" and a "normal" member of the family is gradually eroded. There were many cases where a person who had come to Balaji with a possessed relative soon discovered that he too was in distress from a *bhuta* and in need of healing. Another bridge between the "normal" and the "sick" is through the concept of *sankat* transfer. According to this belief, if a close relative of the patient prays to Balaji that he is ready to take on the distress then the *bhuta* often leaves the patient and possesses the supplicant. However, in the three cases of *sankat* transfer that I observed, the family member began to show signs of *bhuta* possession without any corresponding relief for the original sufferer.

The importance of the wall between "sickness" and "health" becoming porous and the blurring of the distinctions between "normal" and "possessed" lies in the fact that it helps the patient considerably to overcome his feelings of isolation and moral worthlessness. Even though possession by a *bhuta* is not culturally alien to the patient, who has seen and heard of many others who have been similarly afflicted, possession by a malignant spirit nevertheless isolates and bars the individual from sources of collective strength residing in his or her group and community. The feeling of isolation is attributable to the fact that possession is also seen as a stigma, a kind of leprosy of the character that cuts off the individual from members of his immediate and extended community. This becomes evident when we read of the kinds of people that Hindu culture considers especially susceptible to possession by *bhuta-preta*. These are "the impotent, the lustful, the lately widowed, bankrupts, sons and brothers of whores, convicts, the idle, the brooders on the unknowable, gluttons and starvers. . . . Intelligent and educated men and healthy intelligent women are free from spirit attacks."[15]

The temple regulations, verbally communicated to the patient by the priest and available in a printed brochure, lay considerable stress on the patient's achieving a state of purity before any appeal to the deities can be made. These rules enjoin a strict observation of celibacy during the whole of his or her stay at Balaji, prohibit the use of spices, onion, garlic and other impure foods and require daily morning baths and a fresh change of clothes every time the patient enters the temple precincts. Elsewhere, I have suggested that the feeling of being dirty and polluted is the Indian form of experiencing guilt.[16] The purification rituals, then, with their washing and cleansing the inner "filth," seem to be directed toward a symbolic expiation of the patient's feeling of guilt, while at the conscious level they prepare the patient to receive the superior power of the god.

Yet another quality of Balaji's communal culture is the openness with which *sankats* are discussed. Patients (and their families) exchange detailed case histories within and outside the temple premises and when two patients encounter each other in the street, "How is your *sankat* doing?" is both an acceptable greeting and a mode of inquiry about the other's well-being. The possible responses to such an inquiry—"There is no change," "It is turning out well"—are very much like the matter-of-fact exchanges between two graduate students in physics on the progress of their experiment. The point is that possession illness and the presence of *bhuta-preta* are accepted in a plain, uncomplicated way. In the boardinghouses, after their gates are closed for the night, patients and their families spontaneously form into small groups to discuss each other's distress. In such therapeutic group sessions, the most intimate details of the individual's distress are revealed, speculations on the probable origins of the spirit are advanced and the possible outcome of a particular healing ritual debated. Besides lessening any residual feelings of shame, the public sharing of the illness certainly makes the malignant spirits lose their private terrors. Anxious and fearful emotions that we would normally expect to be associated with the *bhuta-preta* are quite conspicuous by their absence as the patients begin to address their possessing spirits derisively with the diminutive *"bhutra."* What one's *bhutra* did on a particular day during the healing ritual in the temple is related to others in an indulgent manner, as if the *bhuta* were a naughty child whose antics had to be suffered patiently. This marks a distinct change in the individual's attitude toward the illness, for it is no longer the *bhuta* who is possessing the patient but the patient who has to bear with the *bhuta*. From our own clinical experience, we can appreciate the difference it makes (and the big step it constitutes toward cure) when a person begins to feel he has the neurosis instead of the earlier feeling that the neurosis has him. We can now understand better how a "standard ritual"—as Obeyesekere in his excellent study of exorcism in Sri Lanka has called such healing practices[17]—can help patients who are suffering from various kinds of mental illnesses. Ignoring the different texts of the illness, the standard ritual works chiefly through the context in which the feelings aroused by the illness are embedded. This approach "works" since the context is also the nexus for those universal human strengths whose restoration in the individual makes for his wholeness.

Of the multiple perspectives on mental illness—illness as an expression of alienation from the bodily order, illness as an alienation from the self and illness as alienation from the social order—we see from the above description that healing at Balaji lays an emphasis on ending the patient's alienation from his social (and cosmic) order. The judicial court of the god recognizes two parties who are clamoring for the possession of the individual: his or her cut-off "selves" (the *bhutas*) and the representatives of the family and community. The judicial (and therapeutic) task, in the judgment of the court, is not only, or even primarily, the reintegration of the cut-off parts of the self, as in Western psychotherapy, which therefore demands that an isolated neurotic be put into an isolated setting under a treatment dominated by a scientific theory. Instead, the "court" also sees as its task the reintegration of the individual with his community. This requires a polyphonic social drama that attempts a ritual restoration of the dialogue, not only within the patient but with the family. By participating in rituals together with the patient, and especially by having the patient's *sankat* transferred onto themselves, the family members too seem to be accepting their share of the blame for the patient's problems.

As far as the cut-off parts of the self are concerned, the therapy proceeds along two separate lines. One, the individual's tolerance of the *bhuta* is sought to be increased by lessening the spirit's fearsomeness. The spirit's potentially benign nature—the *bhuta* being replaced by a *duta*, the god's "messenger"—is pointed out and it is reemphasized that malignant spirits are only unfortunate *pitris* or ancestral spirits deserving compassion rather than anxious reactions. In other, psychoanalytic words, the unconscious content of the psyche is considered neither fixed and immutable nor malignant and threatening, as in the notion of the psychoanalytic id, but as fundamentally capable of a benign transformation. And we must remember that the *bhuta-preta* are only defendants in Balaji's court and not outside the pale of society. Preta-raja, after all, is as much a defense lawyer who must look after the *bhuta-preta*'s interests, as a judge who must punish them.

Second, *peshi* ritual attempts to transform the patient's belief into a conviction that his bad traits and impulses are not within but without; that they are not his own but belong to the *bhuta*. The fact that fifteen out of twenty-eight patients were possessed by a Muslim spirit indicates the extent of this projection in the sense that the Muslim seems to be *the* symbolic representation of the alien in the Hindu unconscious. Possession by a Muslim *bhuta* reflects the patient's desperate efforts to convince himself and others that his hungers for forbidden foods, tumultuous sexuality and uncontrollable rage belong to the Muslim destroyer of taboos and are farthest away from his "good" Hindu self.

Like every other system of therapy—Western or Eastern—which can help some but not all of its clients, the temple healing finds reasons for not being as universally effective as it would like or as its adherents might claim.[18] In cases where a patient has successfully gone through the complete course of "application," "appearance" and "statement" and yet retains many of his original symptoms, he is declared to have multiple *sankats*, with more than one possessing spirit being involved. In such cases, the patient is expected to go through the complete ritual all over again and to repeat it as many times as the number of *bhutas* that possess him. The record is held by a man who had twenty-one possessing spirits! In other cases, where the patient is obviously relieved of his symptoms but falls ill soon after he gets back home, the relapse is attributed to the inherently deceitful nature of the *bhuta*, who has sneakily reneged on its solemn promise to Balaji. For more severe disorders where in spite of all efforts the *peshi* is at best limited to a swaying of the body, without the dramatic struggles between Good and Evil and without the *bhuta* making the "statement," the solution offered is "imprisonment" of the spirit for a year at the temple. The patient may then go about his normal affairs, but must return to Balaji before the end of the year to once again go through the healing rituals. As a direct suggestion to the patient to remain well for at least a year, the *sankat* imprisonment seems like a last desperate measure and has correspondingly little success.

In conclusion, without going into a comparison of the effectiveness of the temple healing vis-à-vis modern psychotherapy in the treatment of the various classes of mental disorder, I would only like to underline their radically different assumptions. The assumptions underlying Western psychotherapy are also the highest values of modern individualism. They are epitomized in psychoanalysis (in Kenneth Keniston's words) as "its almost limitless respect for the individual, faith that understanding is better than illusion, insistence that our psyches harbour darker secrets than we care to confess, refusal to promise too much, and a sense of the complexity, tragedy and wonder of human life."[19] The underlying values of the traditional temple healing, on the other hand, stress that faith and surrender to a power beyond the individual are better than individual effort and struggle, that the source of human strengths lies in a harmonious integration with one's group, in the individual's affirmation of the community's values and its given order, in his obedience to the community's gods and in his cherishing of its traditions.

4

OTHER SHAMANS

In much of popular Western literature, the non-Western professional who attends to the relief of distress and alleviation of anxiety in his society is known by many names, none of them exactly respectful. He is a medicine man or a witch doctor, native healer or voodoo sorcerer—the "quack," so to speak, never the "doctor." Of the many epithets for an institution that is found all over the world, the term shaman—of Northeast Asian origin from the Tungusic šaman and the Manchu saman ("one who is excited, moved, raised")—has found global acceptance. Shamans generally specialize in "spirit illness" and a salient characteristic of many shamans is their ability to go into a voluntary and controlled trance during their diagnostic or healing efforts.

Summarizing the literature on a subject which has fascinated anthropologists since the beginnings of this century, Jilek has succinctly shown that the Western image of the shaman is full of contradictions.[1] On the one hand, he is seen as a mentally ill person to whom a wide variety of psychiatric labels have been attached. When he is not a "veritable idiot," as proposed by Wissler in the case of American Indian tribes,[2] or a "trickster" and of the "neurotic-epileptoid type," as maintained by Radin in the case of the Eskimo and the Arunta,[3] then he may be—as in the case of shamans of the circumpolar cultures—suffering from severe maladjustments, anxiety hysteria, arctic hysteria and other mental abnormalities.[4] Psychoanalytically trained anthropologists too have subscribed to this notion of the shaman as a genuinely ill person. George Devereux, for instance, states categorically that "the Mohave shaman of either sex is an outright psychotic,"[5] while L. Bryce Boyer, who interviewed the Mescalero Apache shaman Black Eyes, diagnosed him as afflicted with a "personality disorder with impulsive hysterical traits" and as a person who "lacked clear masculine identity and suffered from problems resulting from latent homosexuality."[6]

The other side of the picture portrays the shaman as a religious specialist who connects his community with everything that is sacred and gives meaning to life.[7] He is the mediator between the supernatural and the community who makes the desires of one known to the other.[8] Recent anthropological literature mentions the shaman's social and political influence, recognizes his considerable psychotherapeutic acumen, praises his intellectual qualities and is admiring of his creative and innovative capacities.[9]

As Jilek, among others, has pointed out, the negative picture of the shaman, primarily (though not exclusively) found in the earlier anthropological literature, is the expression of a Zeitgeist, the spirit of the times, wherein the Western rationalistic-positive ideology was considered the norm against which other cultures and institutions were judged. Non-Western systems of explanation, where they deviated from these Eurocentric positivistic norms, were considered abnormal, a product of ignorance and error or, in psychopathological terms, an expression of "poor reality testing." This Zeitgeist has had a powerful effect on anthropology and especially on psychiatry. Psychiatrists were certainly quite late in recognizing that "What in shamanistic behaviour may appear hysterical or psychotic to the Western psychiatrist is, to the people concerned, a time honoured ritual through which practitioners heal sick people or divine the future. Hence the 'symptoms' of the shaman may in fact be the result of learning and practice."[10]

Our contemporary understanding of the shaman owes much to the influential work of Claude Lévi-Strauss, who pointed out that the shaman provides the sick member of his society with a language by means of which unexpressed and otherwise inexpressible psychic states can be immediately expressed.[11] Lévi-Strauss further delineated the parallels between the roles of the shaman and the psychoanalyst, though, given their respective collective and individual orientations, the role performed by each is different. Both the shaman and the analyst establish a direct relationship with the patient's conscious and an indirect relationship with his unconscious—the analyst through listening, the shaman through oratory.

Both become objects of transference for the patient and, through the representations induced in the patient's mind, the protagonists of his conflict. When the transference is established, the patient puts words into the mouth of the analyst by attributing to him alleged feelings and intentions; in the shaman's incarnation, on the other hand, the shaman speaks for the patient, putting into his mouth answers to questions that correspond to the interpretation of the patient's condition and with which he must become imbued. Lévi-Strauss thought the parallels important enough to note that "psychoanalysis can draw confirmation of its validity, as well as hope of strengthening its theoretical formulations and understanding better the reasons for its effectiveness, by comparing its methods and goals with those of its precursors, the shamans and the sorcerers."[12]

The more positive image of the shaman is a relatively recent phenomenon which could gain a measure of acceptance only in the context of decolonialization and the accompanying changes that have led to an upgrading of the Western image of non-Western cultures. An expanded notion of science that goes beyond positivism, the injection of some humility into an otherwise glorified Western self-image, have all tended to contribute to a reconsideration of the shaman and to redefinition of shamanism. Indeed, in the so-called counterculture movement of the sixties and the seventies that produced a radical cultural self-examination in a large sections of Western youth, the shaman tended to acquire a romanticized image as an exceptionally wise man who was the knower of another, "separate reality." Similar to the political utopias of the counterculture which were believed to be on the way to realization in far-off lands such as China (this was before Coca-Cola made its appearance in Peking), the psychiatric utopias over which the shaman presided were also believed to exist in the more remote corners of the world—for instance, in Dahomey.[13] To someone belonging to a culture where the shaman is a part of everyday life and shamanism is as exotic as dentistry, however, the romantic image of the shaman that emerges from the Western search for utopias is as incomprehensible as his earlier ethnocentric denigration. The shamanic reality I am familiar with bears little resemblance to its portrayal in much of Western literature; the shaman, it seems, continues to be invented and reinvented according to the changing needs of Western culture and its restless Zeitgeist.

The Oraon Shamans

The Oraon are a Dravidian tribe of about a million people who are concentrated mainly in the Chota Nagpur plateau of eastern India.[14] Lying at an average height of two thousand feet above sea level, the Oraon country is studded with low hills and isolated peaks of bare igneous rock, and is crisscrossed by small streams that are dry during most of the year but become impassable torrents in the rainy season. The plateau was earlier covered by a thick sal forest. The forest has gradually receded toward the west, where the hills are steeper and the land wilder. Here, ranges of jungle-covered hills stretch from north to south in one unbroken line after another, making access to the plateau difficult. Indeed, though the Oraon came under the nominal rule of the Mughal emperor in the seventeenth century, it was only during the nineteenth century that Hindus and Muslims from the plains—traders and adventurers, mainly —began settling down in Oraon country in any large numbers.

The Oraon are an agricultural tribe, with both men and women sharing the tasks of farming—the men doing the heavier work of plowing, sowing, repairing ridges, threshing and winnowing, while the women plant, weed, husk the rice and help in harvesting. The many hunting festivals of the Oraon, however, are witness to a bygone age when the forest, with its abundant game and its profusion of forest spirits, constituted the dominant reality of tribal life. The forest in the central part of the plateau has been cleared for cultivation but its laterite soil is infertile. There are a few wells and some tanks but generally an Oraon farmer depends on the vagaries of an uncertain monsoon for his irrigation needs. Farming is at subsistence level, with little surplus left over after the needs of bare existence are met, and the Oraon are poor even by the standards of a poor country. Their houses, built of mud, with tiled roofs and with narrow rectangular slots for windows, huddle together in a disorderly fashion on the high ground preferred as the site for a village. The household goods of an Oraon family are meager, consisting of a couple of string cots, mats from woven grass, earth pitchers and—the family's prized possession—a few brass pots that are cleaned with mud after every meal and frequently and lovingly polished with ash to keep them gleaming. In spite of the many changes in tribal life that have taken place over the years, an Oraon village still distinguishes itself from an Indian village of the plains. In an Oraon village, there would be a grove sacred to the village deity (generally female), where sacrifices are offered during village festivals. There would be a sacred pool or stream where the bones of dead members of the tribe are ceremoniously immersed at certain times of the year. Each village will have a distinctive flag and an emblem which is believed to bring it luck. There will be a part of the village set apart as the dancing arena, which will be frequently used for communal dancing as well as for the periodic *jatra* festivals, when the songs and dances of the outgoing season are ceremoniously exchanged for the songs and dances appropriate to the incoming one. Thrice a year, there may be hunting excursions in which all male members participate and which serve to bring together different villages in shared tribal activity. As compared to the plainsmen, the Oraon take great pleasure in drinking and feasting, and their free and easy sexual ways are secretly envied by their Hindu neighbors even when these neighbors hypocritically decry "tribal immorality." The distinctive feature of an Oraon village, however, is the *dhumkuria*—the youth dormitory—where an Oraon boy is admitted around the age of eight. Until he gets married in his late teens, an Oraon boy will spend all his nights in the *dhumkuria* (there is a corresponding institution for girls), going back to his home only in the morning. Here, in the *dhumkuria,* he will learn the essentials of the male role in tribal life, go through various rites, and pass many tests before he is granted adult status. Instruction in folklore, traditions, magical beliefs and practices, music and dancing are given by the older members of the *dhumkuria* and prepare the Oraon child for the intensely group-oriented life of the tribe.

Ayata is a shaman, or *bhagat,* as the Oraon call their shamans, in the village of Palamu twenty miles from Ranchi, the district headquarters. Ayata's house, larger than others and testifying to his relative prosperity, is easily identified as a *bhagat*'s dwelling by the multicolored flags that flutter on bamboo poles outside the entrance. The flags represent the gods and goddesses worshiped by the *bhagat* and include the flag of his own special deity, who "mounts" him *(sawari)* and sends him into a trancelike state when he is divining or treating the illness of a patient. Of Ayata's six deities, I am familiar only with Rama, one of the "great gods" of the Hindu tradition. The other five are female goddesses of the tribe, one of them being Mandari Maharani, who is the goddess of Ayata's particular village. In a small, dimly lit room just off the inner courtyard that serves as his consultation and treatment room, Ayata has installed terra-cotta representations of three other deities of which again I recognize only the ubiquitous *linga* of Shiva. The profusion of divinities in Ayata's house reminds me of the changes taking place in some urban Hindu temples which too are moving away from being the home of one particular god to become supermarkets of the divine.

A short, dark man now in his mid-thirties, Ayata has been a *bhagat* for twelve years. Ayata's father was a *bhagat* before him and Ayata in fact took over the practice after his father's death. Ayata is the youngest of four brothers and two sisters, of whom two brothers and a sister died during his childhood. Since only one child, male or female, has the right to become a *bhagat,* Ayata is not quite certain why his father chose him in preference to his brothers and sisters. He suspects, though, that the father's choice had something to do with Ayata's shadow. In the selection of an apprentice, an Oraon *bhagat* pays special attention to the candidate's shadow—whether it is "fat" or "thin." Someone with a fat shadow is automatically rejected since he is thought to have "a bad temper" and is believed to be "stubborn and domineering"—traits which are inimical to the practice of the shaman's profession. As one might suspect, fat and thin shadows have little to do with bodily size but pertain to the whole person. "A *bhagat* can *see* such a shadow" was all that Ayata would say and, sounding positively Jungian, he added that the "shadow is joined to the person and is the other side of his 'power' [*shakti*]." Ayata has two assistants but he has not yet seen the shadows of his own three sons and two daughters and must still decide which one of them will be a *bhagat* after him.

Before he was apprenticed to his father, Ayata remembers that he was very fond of eating meat (whenever it was available), and especially of drinking *hadi*—the local rice beer, which he consumed in enormous quantities. Once he was selected by his father for the shaman's profession, Ayata's life-style changed radically. Now he had to live according to the prescribed conduct (dharma) and the rules *(niyam)* that govern shamanic training. For instance, Ayata daily performed the ritual worship of the family deities and underwent regular periods of fasting. Indeed, the Oraon shaman differs strikingly from his fellow tribesmen in his attitudes toward eating and drinking. Perhaps because he must often go hungry throughout his life, food is extremely important to the Oraon villager. An Oraon approaches eating and drinking—and their excesses—with an abandon and a seriousness that are incomprehensible to those who have not known hunger. A *bhagat*'s periodic and voluntary renunciation of food and drink even when they are available marks him out as a heroic being who has transcended one of the basic preoccupations of his compatriots. Abjuring the eating of meat and refusing to eat all food that is cooked outside the home, a *bhagat* is someone who has successfully struggled with what may be called "the gluttonous passions." In the economic and social context of an Oraon village, the gluttonous passions are of as great import as the sexual passions that are said to plague the well-fed.

Ayata's pride in being the chosen son of his father comes through clearly in his general air of self-confidence and calm authority. With an approving and applauding father as his permanent inner audience, Ayata could live on the margin of his society without needing the confirmation provided by others, doggedly following his self-chosen path despite obstacles and the opposition he encountered on his way. "After my father died, we went through some very hard days. At times, I have gone hungry for a fortnight or more. My brothers quarreled with me and wanted me to leave the house. 'You'll starve,' they warned me. 'Stop this business of being a *bhagat*; there is nothing in it.' I tried to make them understand that I was following the tradition of our father; I could not just throw away the knowledge that was my patrimony. But they refused to listen. Today, thanks to the One-Who-Is-Above-All-of-Us, I am very well off. I possess a bicycle, a cow and some goats. I am in a position to give away food to others who are in need. Anyone who comes to my house will be fed. God tells us that we should treat the body of another like our very own."

To be chosen by the father (as with Ayata) or by Allah (as in the case of the *pir*) seems to be a common theme in the life of many shamans. Among the Oraon, to be selected by a parent (there are a few female shamans, too) who is a *bhagat* is only one way of becoming a shaman; the other way to *bhagat*hood lies in being directly chosen by a god *(devata)* without the help of human intermediaries. Budha, who lives in a village about ten miles away from Ayata, became a *bhagat* through one such direct intervention. Budha's *sawari*—the possession by a god—began with a vivid dream of Shiva one night when he was twelve years old. On the following days, his legs would suddenly start trembling and then thrash about uncontrollably while the rest of the body was relatively still. "The god then told me"—Budha does not say "in a dream," as if such distinctions are unimportant—"to go to the temple of Khambha Maharaj and take some rice and bamboos with me for the worship. The temple is thirty-five miles away and I walked for two days to reach it, fasting the whole way. There were people inside the temple when I arrived and I hesitated outside, uncertain whether the god wanted to speak to me alone or in front of others. Later in the evening, when the other devotees had left, I went in and performed the required *puja* [prayer ritual]. He [the god] told me to take the *linga* from the sanctum and go home, since he wanted to live with me in my house. I was scared that if someone saw me I'd be accused of theft. Without taking the *linga,* I returned home. What a mistake I had made! Such an opportunity only comes once in a lifetime! For six weeks, I stayed inside my house, refusing food and begging the god for another chance. Finally, he relented and told me that I'll have to do *bhakti* for eleven years and he will then give me the 'power.' If I had only brought home the *linga* that day, I would have been spared so much hard work."

Besides being shamans, Ayata and the other *bhagat*s are also hardworking farmers. Normally, Ayata sees his patients at home between seven and twelve in the morning. In the planting and harvesting seasons, however, when he is often away working in the fields before dawn, returning home only late in the afternoon, a patient may be first seen by his assistant and only the more serious cases will come up to the fields for a personal consultation or to fix an appointment. Fortunately, most *shaitani* (lit. "satanic") illnesses which are due to the work of demonic spirits, and in which the *bhagats* specialize, occur either in the summer or in the months after the monsoon rains, when agricultural operations are at a relative standstill. None of the *bhagats* could offer an explanation for this phenomenon, though Ayata came closest to an answer when, grinning broadly, he remarked, "Perhaps the *shaitan* [Satan] too looks after our welfare just as God does."

An Oraon *bhagat* distinguishes between two kinds of mental illness: *apropi*, or endogenous madness, occurring because of excessive worrying, anxiety or some physical illness, and *shaitani* disorders, which are the work of demonic spirits—our familiar *bhuta-preta*. In the case of the endogenous madness, the patient is held responsible for his affliction and the *bhagat* does not offer any treatment except advice with the general tenor of "Stop worrying. Don't be afraid." In *shaitani* disorders, on the other hand, the patient is considered blameless. These illnesses, the *bhagat* say, do not last long if the afflicted person comes to a *bhagat* straightaway for diagnosis and treatment. The diagnosis of *shaitani* is not lightly arrived at and may be called a product of careful divination. Thus a woman who brought her one-year-old child to Ayata with the complaint that the child had difficulties in eating and further voiced the suspicion that it was probably a *shaitani* problem, was promptly told that the child had worms in its stomach and should be taken to the local *vaid*, the practitioner of the Indian system of medicine. "I never give false assurances regarding a sickness which I cannot treat" was Ayata's comment on the case. "When it is clearly a stomach disease, why should I make up a story that it is the doing of a *shaitan*?" In fact, in such cases, Ayata is not averse to using his prestige as a shaman to help his medical colleagues. "A patient came the other day complaining of a persistent and strong pain in the stomach. Immediately I told him that he had an ulcer that was about to perforate. The patient however insisted on a *jhar-phook* [a ritual to drive away demonic spirits]. I acceded to his wish but warned him that the *shaitan* will go on troubling him if he did not see a doctor immediately."

On the other hand, when a spirit *is* involved and where a *jhar-phook* or other shamanic healing rituals are called for, Ayata is unrelenting in his insistence that the patient undergo the ritual even if the patient himself is wavering in his commitment to the *bhagat's* view of his illness and its causation. Like any other people, not all the Oraon are equally convinced by the claims made by their medicine men. One of Ayata's former patients, who flew into uncontrollable fits of rage and picked fights at the slightest pretext, related that though the *bhagat* had told him that his problems were due to the mischief of a *shaitan,* he personally did not believe in demonic spirits and had also got himself treated at the mental hospital in Ranchi. "They [the doctors] gave medicines. The *bhagat* read mantra. I am all right now but don't know whether I was cured by the medicine or the mantra." Ayata ascribes to the machinations of the possessing *bhuta* the doubts and resistances created in the mind of a patient which tempt him to go to a doctor rather than consulting a *bhagat* straightaway. In such cases (as well as in cases of snakebite) he tolerantly lets the patient also take the doctor's medicine but is firmly convinced that the therapeutic agent in the cure is the *jhar-phook, puja, bali* or one of the other healing rituals he has employed, while the drug was, at best, a harmless placebo. In mental illness, of both the *apropi* and the *shaitani* types, Ayata believes that the cures achieved by a psychiatrist's drugs are placebo cures, hence temporary and symptomatic, and have not touched the roots of the patient's problem.

Shaitans are of many kinds. One type is the *bhula-bhuta* ("lost spirit"), an order of demonic spirits entered by those who meet accidental death. Another way of entering the *bhula-bhuta* order arises when someone promises a feast to an ancestor and then fails to keep the promise. The offended ancestral spirit temporarily becomes a *bhula-bhuta* to afflict the remiss individual and remind him unpleasantly of his broken promise. Midnight and dusk are generally the times when possession by a *bhula-bhuta* takes place. Another type is the *aner-shaitan,* the *shaitan* "without an order" who is a spirit of a lower order; while yet another type is the *dayan,* the female spirit who comes into existence at the death of a pregnant women. The *bhagat's* task during divination, which he does by "reading" the sal tree leaves brought by the patient for this purpose, is to identify the possessing spirit. If a spirit of a lower order is involved, it can generally be put to flight by the mantra or power of the *jhar-phook* ritual. If the possessing spirit is a stronger *shaitan* belonging to a high order, one seeks to mollify him by asking him his wishes—whether he wants a full ritual worship *(puja)*, an animal sacrifice *(bali)*, or any other ritual—and then seeking to fulfill these wishes.[15]

Normally, the possessing spirit states its wishes in *kuari*, the possession trance entered by a patient while he is being treated by the *bhagat*. In case a patient cannot enter the *kuari* state, the *bhagat* falls back on his own experience to select the proper ritual that will tempt the *shaitan* to leave. The most common ritual in such cases is called "setting up a bird." The spirit is asked to enter a chicken or a pigeon and is assured that it will get a regular supply of food. The bird is kept in the patient's house and great care taken of its welfare. After about six months, assuming the patient has completely recovered and not suffered a relapse, the bird is killed and fed to invited guests—the *bhagat* remaining silent about the fate of the *shaitan* or, for that matter, of the guests. The pacification of a possessing spirit by the offer of food, then, is a common element in most treatment rituals; the appeasement of the *shaitan*'s hunger being one of the *bhagat*'s primary concerns. "Sometimes the *shaitan* gets to eat and sometimes he goes hungry. When he [the *shaitan*] doesn't get to eat, he punishes the person he is possessing. Our duty is to pacify him and get him his share of food," says one *bhagat*. "If the *shaitan* is given the sacrifice of a chicken or a goat then he'll usually go away. The *shaitan* is very greedy. After all, everyone has a stomach—you, me, the *shaitan*," says Ayata, emphasizing the point that a people who have known hunger will breed hungry spirits and must constantly struggle with the persecuting demon of greed.

The *bhagat*s are unanimous in their opinion that spirit possession occurs mainly because of the envy of a person's neighbors at seeing him eat and drink well. The evil eye of envy directed at someone who is faring better than others renders him defenseless against the *shaitan*'s incursion. When asked to explain the relationship between envy and *shaitani* illness, Ayata went into a semitrance, rocking his body and speaking in the rhythmic singsong he normally employs for divination. "I shall make you understand. Soon you'll understand.

He-Who-Is-Above tells us, always talk small. I say the truth, not lies.
I speak with the voice of the sun. Do not be afraid, fear gives birth
to *bhuta*. Fear comes from envy. He who eats well is afraid. The
others ask, 'Where does he get all this from?' The gaze is envious,
the look is fearful. Then the *bhuta* comes."

Envy settles down like a "chill on the ego"[16] when we compare
and find another possessing and enjoying something we desire. In an
affluent society, wealth, power and the good things they are thought
to bring (including prestige and status) are the objects of envy. In
a society as poor as the Oraon, the ego chill emanates primarily from
food. The feeling of resentful privation at seeing others eat more or
better may be traced back to Oraon childhood, where rivalries with
siblings and the struggle for parental love were inextricably bound
up with the issue of sharing and distribution of scarce food resources
—a distribution that was often experienced as unfair. Interestingly
enough, the *bhagats* too locate the origins of envy in early childhood,
though they do not quite plumb Kleinian depths, where the first stir
of envy is attributed to the infant's awareness of the breast as a
source of life and all good experience, together with his resentment
at not being himself the source of such perfection. In the Oraon
metaphor, envy is "the shit every child eats," a base emotion lodged
in the child to reappear in adulthood. As Ayata states it, "We all
have the evil eye in our heads. The child eats, defecates, dips his
hand into the excreta and puts the hand back into his mouth. The
dirt travels up and settles inside his head. When the child grows up
and looks at anyone who is eating, the dirt of his evil eye will affect
the other person."

In large societies, as George Foster reminds us in a stimulating
essay, envy can be more easily concealed than in the smaller, simpler
societies.[17] In a large society, subsocieties separated by social, psychological, cultural and often physical boundaries are built up. The
enviable in each subsociety stands out much less distinctly and
comparisons across boundaries are discouraged. Such envy barriers
are absent among the Oraon, as indeed they are in other "primitive"
societies where people spend much of their time contriving to avoid
being envied.[18] Envy, which as Helmut Schoeck points out appears
in its worst form in conditions of social proximity or among near
relatives,[19] is constantly stimulated among the Oraon, where noth-

ing can be hidden from the prying eye that may easily become evil, and where members of the tribe live in a close, almost familial proximity. Because of its feared virulence, the overarching ideal of tribal solidarity demands that envy in the individual be stamped out as early as possible, the differences within the village minimized and egalitarianism encouraged. The institution of the youth dormitory —the *dhumkuria*—in which boys and girls spend a major part of their childhood and youth participating in common activities and undergoing an identical regimen, can then be seen as a major cultural effort to contain envy by standardizing Oraon childhood and youth. Such an attempt at standardization, however, seems to have met with as little success in reducing envy among the Oraon as it has elsewhere. As A. F. Davies remarks, "the lesson of the Kibbutz is that the standardization of childhood augments envy in adults; and communes, as social experiments designed precisely to deal with this problem, set up conditions which notoriously exacerbate it."[20]

The *bhagats*, we saw earlier, have more or less successfully erected psychological defenses against their own envious impulses by a voluntary and periodic renunciation—and thus a devaluation—of food, the focal object of envy among the Oraon; a disparaged object does not arouse envy. Others, however, whose defenses against the corrosive power of envy are not of a similarly high order, remain markedly sensitive to the slightest manifestation of envy in their environment. For an Oraon villager, I suggest, to be looked upon with envy stirs up a whole complex that contains his own split-off envious impulses together with guilt feelings at the possession of these forbidden impulses, which are so contrary to his tribal ethos. To be punished by a *shaitan*, then, provides relief from a far more painful inner conflict and the feelings of "badness" it has generated in turn. The *shaitan*'s departure signals the restoration of defenses against greed and envy—a repression and denial of base, "demonic" desires. Once again the individual can feel "good," lovable and thus loved by his superego.

In discussing the nature of the *shaitan*, Ayata hints at a similar conflict between badness and goodness—and their underlying unity in the individual psyche in a theological rather than psychological language: "It is God who is also the *shaitan*. Just as from one womb two different babies are born; just as there are two different kinds

of rice paddy—the green kind when the sweet wind blows from the
north and the red paddy when the bitter wind blows from the south
—so too has God given himself two forms: one good and the other
bad. He comes in the form of a *shaitan* when the bitter wind blows.
Why does he become the *shaitan*? Who else will punish us for our
bad deeds? Who else will remind us that there exists a power higher
than us?"

By seven in the morning, when Ayata emerges from his prayer
room to begin the day's work, there are well over a dozen people
waiting. Squatting silently in the courtyard or milling around in
small groups, it is not easy to distinguish the patients from those who
have come for some other purpose. Among those waiting, there may
be one or more former patients who have dropped in to greet the
bhagat, who tries to maintain a close contact with his ex-patients;
in fact, each year Ayata takes a group of eight to ten of his former
patients on a week's pilgrimage to the nearby temple complexes. In
addition, there are always a few spectators present: some have come
to witness the excitement of a healing drama while others presumably attend to fulfill their own deeper needs to be near the sacred. To
get an amulet *(tabiz)* from the *bhagat* as a protection against unknown future threats may be one man's purpose, while yet another
may consult the *bhagat* about a recent theft or loss. *Bhagats* not only
take care of mental illness among the Oraon but are also general
practitioners of reassurance and specialists in faith. Ayata normally
begins by asking the would-be patients and supplicants to step forward with the sal leaf they have brought with them held in the open
palm of the right hand. The *bhagat* loudly hails each of his six deities
in turn and begins to take quick, deep breaths. His neck swells up
in the shape of a gourd and the veins stand out prominently. He
expels the air in explosive bursts through the nose, each exhalation
accompanied by an eerie sound somewhere between a bark and a
yowl. The head and the upper part of his body slowly shake as the
god "mounts" him and Ayata begins to divine a patient's problem
by "reading" the leaf.

"Ancestors, no," he says in a singsong voice to a woman in her
early thirties. "In the earth, no. Gold and silver, no. Four legs, no.
Sometimes she is well, sometimes she is sick. The family sent a
dayan. She is afraid." The man next to her is told: "He is afraid of

enemies. Are there enemies? Only God knows. Three, four kinds of sickness. No peace. One sickness comes, goes; the second comes, goes. The sickness on the leaf, is it there? The child's destruction. It's not his fault. Catch hold of someone else. What can I do? Nothing. Only God can help. God, you are not blind, I am. Bathe in milk, God, and grind the *shaitan* into dust."

During divination, it is invariably Ayata who is possessed by the deity. But when it comes to the treatment, either the patient or both the healer and the patient will be similarly possessed. Ayata's possession trance, voluntary and controlled, is predictably within a certain range of intensity. The patient's possession trance, however, varies greatly—from a mild state (indicated by a gentle trembling) to a violent rolling of the head or a frenzied thrashing about of the body. An example of a treatment in which only the patient is possessed is a sixteen-year-old girl to whom *jhar-phook* had been recommended. The girl was badly frightened one day when, walking alone near a garden, she saw an old man coming toward her. Nothing seemed to have happened but the girl could not eat or sleep well after this "encounter." "What was the old man's caste? A Munda*?" the *bhagat* asks after telling the girl to sit down on the floor. The girl nods her head but does not speak. Ayata tells her to stretch out her legs and the girl complies. The *bhagat* squats down in front of her and begins to chant a mantra. In contrast to the local Oraon language he uses when talking to a patient, the *bhagat*'s communications with the divine, either through the mantra or prayer, are invariably in Hindi, stressing both the formality and the privilege of the *bhagat*'s position vis-à-vis the divine. The *bhagat* now holds his left hand above the girl's head, the index finger pointing upward, while his right hand sways a couple of inches above the girl's knees. He continues to chant the mantra and moves his right hand down till he comes to the girl's feet, where he pauses and then makes a quick movement as if pulling something out through the toes. He repeats this jerky movement several times. There is a pronounced tremor in the girl's body and her toes wriggle whenever she senses the *bhagat*'s hand above them. After a while, Ayata smites the floor with his left hand every time he makes the pulling movement with

*The Munda are another tribe that lives in the same area as the Oraon.

the right. "You must leave, you must go," he shouts. He repeats this several times and then tells the girl in a quiet voice, "He has left through the toes. He won't be back." Again the girl nods her head. She looks tired and there is a sheen of perspiration on her dark skin.

Jhar-phook, I have mentioned earlier, is required in cases involving lower-order spirits who can be driven away by the power of the *bhagat*'s mantra. In psychological terms, the *bhagat*'s suggestion, backed by his immense personal and cultural authority, has sufficient curative power in milder cases. In *puja*, designed to take care of more stubborn, higher-order *shaitans*, mantra power is not sufficient. Here both the patient and the *bhagat* are possessed for the duration of the healing ritual. The patient is helped to get into this state by many different means, including the rhythmic beating of a brass tray kept in the room specifically for this purpose. The following excerpt from a conversation between the healer and the patient when both are possessed—the woman rather violently—gives a flavor of the healing encounter and hints at the deeper psychological levels that may be touched on these occasions.

WOMAN The *shaitan* has come. The enemy has come. Face the guru, child.

BHAGAT What enemy? Give it a voice. Speak your name.

WOMAN Yes, oh, yes. It is Budhan *shaitan*. Belongs to another caste. Speak! Will you speak, boy? Dare you be higher than the guru? How far will you walk, *shaitan?*

BHAGAT From earth, from dust. Ah, there is a *shaitan* in my house. Will you walk as far as to the cradle? I shall feed you a black goat.

The woman's eyes are shut tight; the expression on her face is one of exaltation. She is holding up the pot she has brought with her. It contains bangles, leaves, flowers and dust, and is the *shaitan*'s intended prison cell. She holds the pot near the flame of an earthen lamp that was lit at the beginning of the ritual. "The *shaitan*'s liver burns," she says, her voice exultant. "Oh, *shaitan,* your jaw will break, your teeth will break, your limbs will break."

BHAGAT [In a tone of urgency] Catch him now. Don't let him go.

WOMAN What will you do now? Answer. No mistake was made, none at all. She walked properly. She gave water properly and she gave milk properly. He came like a cat. You want to spring higher than everyone else?

The *bhagat* places his hand on the patient's head and threatens: "If you stay you will be given piss to drink. From all directions the gods will come to grind you into dust." The woman is making a choking sound and then, as if by a prearranged signal, both the healer and the patient are suddenly still. Their eyes begin to lose their unfocused look and they seem exhausted.

Obviously more than suggestion is involved in the ritual and the conversation reported above. The exchange between Ayata and the woman reminds one of Pfister's remarks on Navaho healing ceremonies, that the unconscious of the medicine man speaks to the unconscious of his patient, reaching the core of the patient's inner conflict and avoiding resistances that would be stirred up if only consciousness were involved.[21] The woman's remarks on her demon going too far and her denial of any misconduct on the part of "the woman who did everything properly" are certainly suggestive in this direction. However, without an intimate knowledge of Ayata's patients, the notion of the *bhagat* practicing a kind of "instinctive psychoanalysis" will be highly speculative, and it may be more useful to look elsewhere for the psychotherapeutic mechanisms involved in this kind of shamanic healing. Raymond Prince, reviewing a number of studies from different parts of the world, has suggested that the altered state of consciousness during the possession trance—technically known as dissociation—when another ego seems to take control, may itself be a major therapeutic agent.[22] For though in the West dissociation is traditionally linked with the existence of psychopathology, in many other cultures—ranging from cults in Ghana to rural villages in Japan, from shamanic healing in Dahomey and Nigeria to the Paulau islanders in Micronesia, from the *zar* cult that is found all over the Middle East to the snake-handling cult in the American Southwest—dissociation is widely employed in psychotherapy.[23] It may indeed be the single most widespread psychotherapeutic technique in the world today. The methods of inducing a dissociated state—rhythmic music, dance, overbreathing and stimulation of the semicircular canals by rotation of the head—may vary.

Yet, as Prince points out, there are a number of characteristics of
this state which suggest a common neurophysiological substratum:
a fine tremor of head and limbs and sometimes the occurrence of
grosser, convulsive jerks, the return to normal consciousness, often
followed by a sleep of exhaustion from which the person awakes in
a euphoric state but with a more or less complete amnesia for the
period of dissociation, and so on.[24]

How dissociation actually works in helping a mentally ill patient
is still a mystery, though there are a few speculations. Sargant, for
instance, feels that the excessive sensory stimulation during this state
results in a neurophysiological change, with the breaking down of
the patient's former patterns of conditioning and increasing his
susceptibility to the new pattern suggested by the healer or the priest
—the therapeutic effects being due to mechanisms similar to those
which operate in electroconvulsive therapy, brainwashing practices
and Wesleyan type of evangelical preaching and conversions.[25]
Prince, on the other hand, following Freud's remarks (in the Scher-
ber case) on psychosis as an endogenous attempt at healing by the
shattering of an overly rigid ego, sees in the dissociation of a possession trance a kind of micropsychosis in which the ego is dissolved
and a more adaptive ego sought to be rebuilt.[26] Let me note that
dissociation techniques are not solely the province of shamans but
are also employed by at least one contemporary guru—Bhagwan
Rajneesh. Of the many psychological experiences offered in his
Poona ashram, there are certainly two that depend largely upon
producing dissociation in the seeker-disciple: "rebirthing," generated with the help of quick, deep breathing; and the "energy darshan" in the ritual initiation into the cult, where dance, rhythmic
music and variation in lighting masterfully combine dissociation
techniques from different shamanic traditions.

The Lama of Macleodganj

In the foothills of the Himalayas, fifteen hundred miles northwest
of the country of the Oraon, there lives another community at the

margin of Indian society. These are the Tibetans who have come to India after the Dalai Lama's flight from Lhasa following the Chinese invasion, and who are settled in and around the town of Dharamshala. Macleodganj, the abode of the Dalai Lama and therefore the spiritual center of the community, is a small town high up in the hills above Dharamshala. Buddhist monks, known as lamas, with closely cropped hair and characteristically dressed in their flowing maroon robes, are conspicuous in the streets of Macleodganj, as are the more casually attired Westerners in search of esoteric wisdom. The local population calls these young Europeans and Americans "hippies," although these earnest young men and women have little of the innocence and ebullience of their predecessors from the heady days of the late sixties and early seventies. Among the lamas, there are mystics, doctors practicing the ancient art of Tibetan medicine and "shamans," although the Tibetans would not make sharp distinctions between the three—seeing in the vocation of each more a matter of emphasis than of exclusive specialization. Our chief informant, Nagpalla, a monk in his mid-thirties, who is in the last phase of his apprenticeship in demonology with one of the most respected lamas of the community, is then a shaman only in this special sense.

To enter the world of a Tibetan shaman involves a sustained hermeneutical effort which is difficult for a psychoanalyst—even an Indian one whose own cultural background is presumably closer to the Tibetan world view. Strongly influenced by the substrata of the native religion Bon (a form of Northeast Asian shamanism) and the later imports of Mahayana Buddhism and tantric ideas from India and Nepal, the Tibetan world view is uncompromising in its insistence on the "softness" of all phenomenal reality. The question of "apparent" versus the "real" in relation to phenomenal existence, which has long been a preoccupation of Western philosophy, was in Tibet long ago firmly decided in favor of the former; *stong pa nyid* ("emptiness," "voidness") is part of everyday speech of a Tibetan and the explanation he offers for the many riddles of life. In the Tibetan view, all that exists is a mirage of the mind, imperfect images on a screen covering "absolute" reality, which can only be realized in liberation. Everything in the universe, then, has a meaning other than the apparent one, and the world is full of oracles and signs that need to be interpreted. Imagination reigns supreme and all that can be imagined is as real as all that exists. There is no place for the supernatural in this world since one may arbitrarily choose to regard everything either as miraculous or as commonplace. As David-Neel describes it, "None in Tibet deny that such events may take place, but no one regards them as miracles. . . . Indeed, Tibetans do not recognize any supernatural agent. The so-called wonders, they think, are as natural as common daily events and depend on the clever handling of *little known laws and forces.* "[27] Since phenomenal existence is believed to be created by the mind, then phenomenal reality can also be controlled, the relationship between its elements varied, and new phenomena created, by special types of mental effort involving concentrated meditation, elaborate rituals and the transforming power of mantra.

In the sphere of illness and healing, the Tibetan world view leads to a blurring of the distinction between physical and mental sickness as far as their causation is concerned; both kinds of illness ultimately originate in what may be called a "fault" of the mind. Ignorance of the "really real" gives rise to anger, desire and mental darkness— what the medical texts call the "three poisons of the mind." In turn, the mental poisons disturb the balance between the three bodily humors—wind, bile and phlegm.[28] An increase in one of the humors produces the characteristic symptoms of a disease connected with that particular humor. A thorough cleansing of the entire mental and emotional world is then necessary for the cure of every sickness.

Obviously, to hardworking physicians and shamanic healers concerned with concrete symptoms of physical and mental disorders and confronted with the patient's wish to be rid of these symptoms expeditiously, the Buddhist philosophical equation of cure with realization of absolute reality has only a limited practical value. Tibetan doctors therefore tend to relegate ignorance to the background as the long-term cause for illness and turn their attention more to the immediate causes. These immediate causes are four in number: the period or season of the year; food; habit and behavior; and, finally, an attack by one of the three hundred and sixty spirits. If wind, bile or phlegm gets disturbed by any one of the above causes, diseases arise, and the medical education of a Tibetan doctor is built around the symptoms, methods of diagnosis, remedies and prognoses of these diseases.

Nagpalla, like other shamans, is a specialist in spirits—one of the four acknowledged causes in *all* types of illness. These spirit beings, whether the gods *(iha)* of the upper regions or the serpent spirits *(klu)* of the netherworld, share the cosmos with humans—the *sab-dag,* or "earth lords." Cutting across this basic tripartite system, spirit beings are divided into categories of three, five, eight, nine, ten, twelve, thirteen, sixteen, eighteen and so on up to three hundred and sixty.[29] According to the iron law of karma that governs all beings—gods, serpent spirits and the "earth lords"—the individual spirit beings are moved within congeries, promoted to higher ones as they evolve or demoted if they falter, in the constant flux and change that is part of the Buddhist theory of existence.[30] Swarming above, in midspace and in depths, some spirit beings are beneficent, others perhaps more wrathful than intrinsically evil, and in fact Nagpalla claims that of the three hundred and sixty spirits mentioned in the texts, there are only eighteen who afflict human beings with illness or insanity. It is important to note that in the Tibetan system, madness and possession by an evil spirit are not coterminous; spirit possession can cause *both* mental disorders and physical illness. Concomitantly, though a mental disorder may be caused by an evil spirit, it may also be due to other causes such as a sudden loss of possessions or a loved one, the effects of a prolongation of a wind disease, and, finally, the power of a mantra which an enemy has directed against the victim. "Sudden losses usually produce grief so that the person loses his will to live," Nagpalla says. "What we usually do in such cases is to focus his thoughts on those deprived ones who never had any possessions to begin with. We remind the person how lucky he is to be given an opportunity by God to enjoy the possession for so long. We also refresh his ambition that the ultimate goal of human life is knowledge of reality and freedom from earthly attachments. Even Buddha was shocked, as you are now, we say, but reflect how the shock helped him to move forward on the path of enlightenment.

"Mild insanity can also be caused by recitation of certain mantras that have a bad effect on a person's mind. We find this practice—of affecting someone's mind through the power of mantras recited during black magic rites—particularly widespread among Indians."

There are various ways of establishing whether the mental disorder is due to spirit attack or whether it has some other cause. An impending spirit attack usually announces itself through certain omens in dreams. Symptoms of dizziness and nightmares are also widespread among victims of spirit attack. "Often," Nagpalla says, "the man becomes a child of his dreams. Whatever he had wished for during childhood, he tries to realize that wish. For instance, if he had imagined becoming a carpenter, he starts asking for woodworking tools. In short, the child is reborn in the insane man." The most important tool in diagnosis, not only of spirit attack but in determining the particular spirit involved, is called the Mo, the Tibetan counterpart of the I-Ching. The eye movements of the patient are also important to identify the possessing spirit. For instance, if the patient is possessed by a *bhuta*, his eyes move downward toward the left; in case of possession by a *dakini*—a female spirit often addressed as "Mother," who is said to bestow esoteric knowledge and power on its devotees—the eyes move upward toward the right.

Nagpalla denies that there are any particular reasons for an attack by a spirit. "It all depends upon the state of one's karma. There are times in every man's life when there are dangers to his life, his body, his personal dignity and his luck. If all four factors are unfavorable, then a spirit is sure to possess him. We have the remedies too. For danger to one's life, we ask the person to have the 'initiation' ritual performed; for danger to the body, we change the name of the person as well as his clothes; for dignity and luck we hang certain prayers on flags outside his house. You must have seen flags with the pictures of a flying horse. This is the *lung-da* [lit. 'wind horse'] or luck, and these flags are put up to enhance it. In all cases we insist that a *puja* be performed. *Puja* is very important to instill spiritual strength in the potential victim or actual sufferer. Besides *puja*, we have the 'entreaty' [*yachna*] mantra chanted to prevent the evil spirit from entering the person." From the accounts of Nagpalla and other lamas, the main therapeutic agent in the various *puja* rituals is the mantra. We have discussed the nature of and beliefs about mantras earlier and need only to emphasize that for Tibetans, as for Indians, mantra is power and not merely speech which the mind can contradict or evade. When a lama chants a mantra, then he is calling forth its healing content into a state of immediate reality, so profoundly is the magic of the mantra experienced by a Tibetan.[31]

One of Nagpalla's patients was a monk in his early twenties who had recently suffered an attack by a spirit. On the day of the attack, the monks of this particular monastery had gone for a celebration to the Tibetan children's village a couple of miles away in the hills. In the evening, while the senior, older monks used a jeep for their return journey, the younger monks, the lama's patient among them, went ahead on foot, taking a shortcut through the hills. Running up and down the steep curving path in an effort to beat the jeep to the monastery, the young monks playfully turned the journey into a competition. The patient was faster than others and had opened up a wide gap when he thought of slowing down his pace and found that he was unable to do so. "I don't know what happened then," he says. "Suddenly I was lying unconscious on the path." He recovered consciousness after a while and found his companions crowding around him, asking him what had transpired. The young monk was unable to give a satisfactory answer. He was badly bruised, his palms and elbows bleeding, but he did not feel any pain though he did feel dizzy when he stood up. Supported by two of his friends, the patient slowly walked toward the monastery till he came to a waterfall. As it was getting late, he asked his friends to go ahead while he washed his face and cleansed his wounds. Two "hippies" were washing their soiled clothes and dirty dishes in the same stream under the waterfall, and they bandaged his wounds. When the monk returned to his room in the monastery, he asked a friend to fetch some medicine for his cuts and bruises. The medicine did not help. His face swelled up so much that he could barely see through his eyes, which were mere slits, and he had to be helped by others in the performance of his daily activities. By the third day, he was so embarrassed by his swollen looks that he confined himself to the room. Finally, he asked one of his friends to go to the lama and urge him to perform a *puja*. The lama played the Mo and gave his verdict that it was definitely a case of spirit attack. He also asked the friend whether the patient had recently washed himself in a stream. The friend had not known about the washing incident at the waterfall and expressed his ignorance. But the lama was certain that such an event had taken place and sent the friend back for further details. "After listening to what

the lama had said, I remembered washing my wounds at the waterfall," said the patient. "I also remembered that people believe that
a spirit, either a *naga* ['serpent'] or a *lu* ['wind'] lives in the stream
under the waterfall. I must have angered the spirit by pouring all that
filth in its house. *Lu* and *naga* spirits are very sensitive about cleanli-
ness."

Both *lu* and *naga* are spirits of an order lower than human beings
and normally cannot attack a person unless they are angered—as the
lu was by our patient "pouring filth" in his home. When aroused,
these spirits become powerful enough to attack and to possess.
Another aspect of these spirits is that they are considered rather
dim-witted since they cannot distinguish whether an affront to their
home or dignity was intentional or unintentional. Whenever the
Tibetans are about to start a new construction, they go to the
construction site two to three days before the work of digging is to
begin and urge the spirit who may be living there to look for a new
home. The prayer to the spirit goes something like this: "O *naga* or
lu or whoever you are living here, we find this place best suited for
our building, and so you will have to move to a different place. We
are sorry to trouble you and cause discomfort but we cannot help it
since the book forecasts this site to be the best for our purpose. So
in accordance with the wish of His Holiness [the Dalai Lama], please
move away within two days."

To continue with our account: the patient told the lama through
his friend that he had indeed washed his wounds at the waterfall.
The lama again played the Mo and discovered that the possessing
spirit was a *lu.* He performed the required *puja* and the patient took
the *puja* offerings to the waterfall to offer them to the *lu.* "I had
to be alone with the *lu* when I gave it the *puja* offerings. I spoke
to the *lu* in three languages—Tibetan, Hindi and English—since I
did not know to which community this *lu* belonged. It is written in
our scriptures that the spirit should be addressed in all the languages
one knows. 'O *lu,*' I said, 'forget whatever happened the other day.
You know I had fallen and hurt myself. In that moment of pain I
completely forgot that the stream could be your residence. So whatever my offense, I have come to make amends. I offer you these gifts
as a gesture of compensation for the annoyance I caused. So let us
forget the whole matter. I hope the *puja* and this request will be

accepted.' " The reparation made, and evidently accepted, the swelling on the monk's face receded and he was soon well enough to participate in the normal life of the monastery.

Our young monk has plausible explanations for why the *lu* did not attack the hippies. "There is a difference," he says. "Blood is a kind of filth which arises from within your body, whereas they were washing away the external dirt. The dirt from inside is considered more offensive by our scriptures. Besides, their *lung-da* might have been higher than mine. Another reason could be that those who believe in the spirit's existence are more prone to be attacked. The *lu* thinks, this man is afraid of me, so he attacks. In case of the hippies, the *lu* knows that they don't believe in him, and he cannot change them in any way, so he does not attack."

Like other Tibetans, the monk does not attribute any particular reason to the *lu*'s attack. "Who knows? Perhaps my *lung-da* was weak. It is quite simple. There are moments when one's *lung-da* is not as good as at other times. And this happens with everyone. It could happen to you. My *lung-da* is probably low these days and I may be attacked again. Even while running I had the feeling I was being pursued by an evil spirit. I still think a spirit possessed me at that time, otherwise why couldn't I slow down? They say one of the signs of a low *lung-da* is when an intelligent man continues to act like an idiot or a monk starts playing and goes on playing."

I suspect that the young monk, in expressing his feeling of a continued vulnerability to spirit attack and of being pursued and possessed even *before* he transgressed against the *lu*, has some reservations about the lama's diagnosis and treatment of his condition. In other words, despite his apparent cure, the monk's unconscious knowledge of his own illness does not match the available cultural blueprint used by the lama. Shamanic cures, I suggest, either do not take place at all or are jeopardized if the shaman's use of the cultural myth received from the collective tradition (as Lévi-Strauss describes shamanic healing) does not also offer the sick person some kind of resolution for his individual conflict.

A skeletal psychological reconstruction of the individual, unconscious factors behind the young man's anxiety attack (for that is how the *lu*'s predatoriness appears to the psychologically minded) will very likely pick on his last statement, about the monk who starts playing and cannot stop, as a vital clue to what probably happened on the evening of the attack. The hypothesis is that once he started running, the young monk's initial playfulness soon turned into a deadly serious affair that his ego could not quite control. The competition with the older monks must have stirred up forbidden feelings of unconscious hostility against the "fathers" of the monastery, while racing ahead of his "brother" monks reactivated the (also forbidden) feelings of rivalry and the threatening, retaliation-provoking idea of his being "better" than others. Unable to cope with the conflict between his competitive hostile wishes and the fear and guilt aroused by these unconscious wishes, the young man "chose" fainting (and later the somatic symptoms) as a way out of a painful inner conflict. The lama's therapeutic efforts, then, consist of providing a cultural container for a psychic state that threatened to become chaotic. He further strengthened the ego defenses through the *puja* ritual that is "known" to instill spiritual strength, and lessened the guilt by requiring the young man to make reparations for his "transgression." Needless to say, this simplified version of what could have triggered off the illness, even without an attempt to trace its origins in the monk's personal history, was met with utter incomprehension on the part of the lama. It was not the language of determinism which was the problem, since the lama is quite comfortable with notions of cause and effect in other spheres of life. What appeared to baffle him was the notion of an *individual, personal* causation of illness.

In drawing some intriguing parallels between shamanism and psychoanalysis, Lévi-Strauss has suggested that whereas a psychoanalytic cure is based upon the patient's recovery of his individual myth, constructed with elements from his past, the cure in shamanism is predicated on the patient's receiving the social myth from his collective tradition.[32] The collective myth used by the shaman does not correspond to the patient's personal state but reintegrates his alienating experience of sickness within a meaningful whole. Both of these myths, whether re-created by the individual or borrowed from tradition, have to be lived or relived by the patient for the healing experience of "abreaction" to take place. Lévi-Strauss further speculated that the contents of the two kinds of myth may be different but their structure, through which the healing symbolic function operated, remained the same.[33] From our studies of Indian shamanic healing, however, it seems premature to assign precedence to form over content. The separation between the use of collective and individual myths in healing is not fundamental but appears to be a matter of relative emphasis and elaboration of the collective versus individual aspects of sickness. The diagnostic and treatment rituals of shamanism—and thus the collective myth which they elaborate—must also offer the patient an opportunity for "airing" his individual conflict and some kind of resolution on the personal plane. We saw this "airing" of the patient's personal conflict in the dream communications made to the *pir*, in the possessing spirit's exchanges with members of the patient's family in the exorcism rituals and in the nightly group sessions at Balaji, in the patient's exchanges with the possessing spirit and the possessing spirit's exchanges with the healer in the case of Ayata and other *bhagats*. A successful shamanic ritual is not merely the healing operation of a collective myth subscribed to by the community, but also attends to the individual elements of the patient's sickness. In some cases, the collective myth used by the shaman clearly addresses the dominant individual conflict in the community—for instance, the sexual anxiety of young Muslim women in the case of the *pir* and the conflicts around envy among the Oraon in the case of the *bhagats*. In other words, the stock of representations in a collective myth is not a matter of indifference but embodies a potent distillate of the modal conflict experienced by individuals within that community. Conversely, an effective individual resolution of psychic conflict in psychoanalysis and psychoanalytically oriented therapy will, in some measure, also incorporate the collective myth shared by the patient, the therapist and the community of which they both form a part. Normally, this collective myth, based on the Western tradition of which individual autonomy and individual worth, knowableness of reality and the possibility of real choice are some aspects, remains relatively unarticulated. Nevertheless, as the elaboration of the individual myth proceeds (and this is especially noticeable in psychoanalytic practice across cultures), the collective myth often becomes audible, as a theme here and just a faint echo there, providing the patient with an opportunity to relate and reintegrate his illness with a larger meaningful whole. In contrast to the explanation of two different healing mechanisms (and their ultimate identity) employed by the shaman and the psychoanalyst, I would suggest that both shamanism and psychoanalysis operate with collective and individual myths, though each chooses to focus on one part of the dual healing mechanism and underplay the other.

II

MYSTICAL
TRADITIONS

5

THE PATH
OF THE SAINTS

To study the theory and practice of a sect that lies in the mainstream of Indian religious and cultural tradition is a task fraught with difficulty. The difficulty does not arise from the fact that I propose to look at Santmat ("the Path of the Saints") advocated by the Radha Soami Satsang from the perspective of healing. As we shall see later, though the Santmat may be explicitly catering to what Aldous Huxley called "a principal appetite of the Soul," namely the urge to transcend a self-conscious selfhood, the sect's implied promise to remove suffering, mental and otherwise, is a key factor in its attraction for the thousands who stream to the Satsang in the hope of receiving peace and direction to the flow of their lives.

The difficulty I allude to pertains more to the existence of a deep gulf that divides Freudian psychoanalysis from the practical psycho-philosophical schools of self-development and self-integration in India, which are generally grouped together under the common label "mysticism," and to the fact that I am an *Indian* psychoanalyst. Unlike his Western counterpart, the Indian analyst has at one time or another consciously faced and reflected on the conflict between an absorbing intellectual orientation—psychoanalysis—which is the mainstay of his professional identity, and the workings of a historical fate which has made the "mystical" the distinctive leitmotif of a dominant Indian cultural tradition and thus a part of his communal identity. This conflict has certain consequences that need to be spelled out in greater detail.

As one of the premier sciences of man, psychoanalysis has an implicit paradigm of human nature, a model of man with an unspoken consensus on the boundaries of acceptable inquiry. The psychoanalytic paradigm, however, clashes strongly with the implicit model of man—*and* the concept of reality—that anchors the Indian mystical approaches and propels their practices. Inevitably this clash has often led to a passionate condemnation of the mystical approach under the guise of detached observation and the expression of an ill-disguised antagonism behind the mask of reasonable argument. Whereas Freud's basic evaluation of the mystical "oceanic feeling" as a memory of a relatively undifferentiated infantile state was an original (and plausible) speculation at a time when European knowledge of the mystical approaches, techniques and results was rather limited, I am afraid that many subsequent psychoanalytic comments in a similar vein (for example, Franz Alexander's opinion that Buddhist meditation training was designed to achieve "the pure narcissism of the sperm"[1]) show the operation of a paradigm's blinding factor more than any genuine attempt at the increase of understanding.

The tendency to fight the mystical paradigm with the weapon of psychopathogical labeling has indeed been persistent in psychoanalytic thought. There is, however, more than a clash of paradigms involved when psychoanalysts venture out of the clinical domain to condemn the mystical model of man on social and historical grounds. Consider, for instance, the following remarks by an eminent analyst: "I am afraid that Hindu striving toward Nirvana may well be related to the terrible failures and cruelties of this culture (as the appalling prevalence of abysmal poverty, the infantile death rate, the infamous caste system, with its ugly notion of the 'untouchable,' the dismal failure to control overpopulation) and the dangers of escapism implicit in a too unworldly approach to life. The unhappy results are of a magnitude which cannot be overlooked; I am afraid that reality testing may well have fallen by the wayside in the striving toward 'moksa.' "[2] Such sweeping remarks can only lend credence to the position of an increasing number of third-world intellectuals, who maintain that the Western sciences of man, including psychoanalysis, are in fact culture-bound ethnosciences whose claim to universality is an aspect of the global political and economic domination by the West.[3] The "refusal" of psychoanalysts to engage themselves with the mystical model of man and their predilection to dismiss it perfunctorily are thus seen as other examples of Western parochialism in the human sciences, especially since the contemporary mystical paradigm, in spite of a rich European past, is generally perceived as a non-Western product that has its origin in the Hindu, Buddhist and Sufi traditions.

On the other hand, it would be a grievous mistake if the ethnocentricity of a few psychoanalysts and their profligacy with psychopathological labels for non-Western cultural phenomena led non-Western intellectuals to dismiss psychoanalysis summarily. In their effort toward cultural emancipation and discovery (or rediscovery) of models of man congruent with their own history and society, non-Westerners need to be on guard against the danger of losing the liberations that Freud initiated—the freedom from unnecessary hypocrisies and enslaving ideologies.

In the clash of two paradigms, the mystics, secure in the hoariness of their tradition, have generally gone their own way. Serenely unaware of the psychoanalytic challenge to their particular model of man, they have ignored the psychoanalytic claim to have discovered the "true," unconscious meaning of mystical aims and practices. "There are at least four levels of the knowledge of man," a mystic would say, "arranged in an ascending order. There is the shrewd level of common sense, the rational one of the scientist, the imaginative level of the artist and the spiritual one of the mystic. It is meaningless, if not foolish, to make statements about one level from the viewpoint of the other." The psychoanalyst would, of course, doubt whether "spiritual knowledge" exists at all except as a transformation of emotions.

Not unlike their counterparts in psychoanalysis, a few eminent mystics have been unable to resist the temptation to take contemptuous swipes at the opposing paradigm. For instance, although he is a yogi who is supposed to have reached the "highest state" and thus to have transcended human passions, especially *krodha* (anger), Sri Aurobindo displays a certain peevishness when he states that he finds it "difficult to take psychoanalysis seriously," that "one cannot discover the meaning of the lotus by analyzing the secrets of the mud in which it grows," and that as a science it is "still in its infancy—inconsiderate, awkward and rudimentary at one and the same time."[4] Other comments have been gentler though equally condescending and, I am afraid, equally uninformed as to what constitutes the aims and practice of psychoanalysis. In a letter to an American disciple, Maharaj Charan Singh, the "Living Master" and head of the Radha Soami Satsang of Beas, writes: "As regards the course of psycho-analysis, we have no prejudices, but the same result can be achieved, as you rightly guess, by a continued and faithful course of proper meditation. Hundreds of people seek interviews with the Master for their internal problems and this, combined with the exposition during the Satsang, solves their difficulties and secures for them even greater results than psychoanalysis. You may continue this course [of psychoanalysis] as long as you find it helpful but do not depend too much on it."[5] But perhaps it is our soft spot of yearning for omniscience and perfection in parental figures that makes us surprised to find that mystics too can be narrow specialists of spiritual knowledge, and that sages may be men of wisdom but not necessarily of (profane) knowledge. Agehananda Bharati, himself a "professional" mystic and anthropologist with an impressive personal experience of Indian mystics and mystical orders, states this much more strongly when he maintains that mysticism is a skill that can be learned. Its practice leads to an achievement (the mystical experience) which neither confers supernatural powers or superhuman status on the practitioner nor imbues him with any moral excellence beyond what he can acquire through accompanying efforts of a nonmystical kind: moral, artistic, intellectual.[6] The widespread Indian belief to the contrary, there is little evidence that the mystic is somehow a "better" human being because of his mystical efforts and experience. Indeed, some of the best-known mystics have been and continue to be pompous and self-righteous, woman-haters and politically fascist. As Bharati puts it: "In other words, by knowing *brahman* one does not know anything but *brahman*: not physics, not mathematics, nor the stock-market—else the monastic profession in India would be much more affluent than it is. The naive assumption is that yogic vision, the zero-experience, also brings about knowledge of all things to be known. This is nonsense. The implication is quite clear; that the knowledge of the Absolute, the mystical knowledge, the zero-experience, is of a precious sort all of its own and does not generate other types of knowledge."[7]

The Sect

The historical beginning of the Radha Soami sect can be dated to 1861, when the mystic Shiv Dayal Singh, or Soamiji as he is known among the Satsangis, established an organization with that name in the city of Agra.[8] Coming from a deeply spiritual family and influenced by the saint Tulsi Saheb of Hathras, Soamiji's new sect was very much in the mainstream of Indian devotional mysticism as it has been expounded in the discourses, songs and poems of such venerated medieval saints as Kabir and Nanak, the founder of the Sikh faith. The two main pillars of the cult, described in *Sarbachan*, the collection of Soamiji's discourses, are guru *bhakti*—the devotion to the guru—and a particular kind of mystical discipline known as the *surat shabd yoga.*

The guru *bhakti* demanded in the Radha Soami sect (and described in medieval mysticism) is not a matter of mere intellectual acceptance and respect for the guru as a teacher or guide. For one, the guru referred to is the *Satguru* ("True Master"), who is the "embodiment of the divine and is in fact the Supreme Being himself." Sharing the Indian penchant for a hierarchical classification of all things—from plants to human beings—the Radha Soami sect has an elaborate ranking order of saints and gurus. The ranking of a guru depends upon the mystical realm he himself has access to—whether it is one of the lower or higher realms of consciousness—since the guru's own level of "attainment" will set the limits to the inner transformation of his disciples. A *Satguru* can take his devotee to the highest realm, where the disciple is united with the Supreme Being and redeemed from the cycles of birth, life and death. The *Satguru*, however, must be a living one. *Satgurus* of the past such as (perhaps) Buddha and Christ (for did he too not say "I and my Father are one"?) have performed this work of . . . well one can choose one's term from "salvation," "transcendence," "liberation," *"moksha"* and so on—only for the devotees of their own times and not for any future ones. According to the Radhasoamis a seeker must then necessarily seek out the *Satguru* of his own time and surrender himself totally to his worship before he receives the guru's grace that helps him to progress on the mystical path.

The idea of the *Satguru* and the need to achieve a complete surrender and develop an intense love for him are the patrimony of many medieval saints, especially Kabir and Guru Nanak, as also of the Muslim mystics, who have highlighted the emotional and ecstatic aspects of the devotee's surrender. Other notions connected with the Radha Soami institution of the *Satguru*, for instance, the importance placed on Satsang ("True Association"), where devotees congregate for the holy service conducted by or under the authority of the *Satguru* and where they can partake of the guru's presence (*darshan*), and the possibility of a *Satguru* naming his successor, which can make this kind of guruhood hereditary, show the deep influence of the religious tradition of the Sikhs on the sect's practices.

The second main feature of the Radha Soami faith is the exercise of a mystical discipline known as *surat shabd yoga*—literally, the joining (*yoga*) of the spirit or soul entity (*surat*) with the Divine Sound or Word (*shabd*). According to the metaphors of this yoga, a spiritual current of sound, emanating from the highest region of creation, the abode of the Supreme Being, is resonating permanently within every human being. With proper guru *bhakti* and the practice of *surat shabd yoga*, the individual soul can become attached to the sound current which pulls it up through the various "mansions of the soul" till it reaches the highest realm of consciousness. The key to the door behind which the *shabd* can be heard lies with the *Satguru*, who is the disciple's guide on the journey through the mystical regions. The actual practices of the *surat shabd yoga* will be discussed later; here it only needs to be said that the Radha Soami cult considers it to be the easiest yet the most potent form of all the yogas. Since it involves neither arduous mental regimen nor ascetic excesses, it can be practiced by everyone, young or old, householder or recluse, man or woman. The Satsangis believe their yoga to be far superior to the breathing and other physical exercises of hatha yoga and claim that it constitutes a decisive improvement on the *shagal-i-awaz* of the Sufis or even the *sahaja yoga* of the medieval saints.

Like many other mystical-religious movements, the Radha Soami Satsang did not survive long as an organizational unity after the death of its founder. Schisms leading to open splits appeared soon and by the early part of the twentieth century the Satsang had been split into three larger groups and almost a dozen smaller ones. Ostensibly, the splits were due to differences in interpretation of the founder's theology or to a group's accentuating one part of Soamiji's teaching at the expense of others. Yet the evidence is strong that most of the splits were dictated by personal rivalries and struggles for power within the organization and for status outside it.[9] At present, since each of many of these groups is headed by its own guru, the claimants to being the *Satguru* of the time are many and a seeker is apt to be confused by a profusion of "True Living Masters." In any event, as a psychoanalyst with a historical legacy and a continuing experience of similar schisms within my own discipline, I can ill afford to be condescending and can easily appreciate and accept the fact that what is common to various groups far outweighs their differences. The existence of rivalry between the gurus and the claim of each group to be in the direct line of descent from the founder need not diminish the basic "truth" of the Radha Soami theory or the efficacy of its practices.

It is important to note here that for the Satsangis (of whichever persuasion), as indeed for members of all mystical cults, a historical account of the cult's origin that does not read like the unfolding of a divine plan and biographical sketches of their gurus that are not exercises in hagiography are *essentially* false. They feel that historical accounts are misleading since they reduce the eternal to the temporal and limit what is universal to the confines of a particular geographical region. The spiritual base and mystical regimen of the Radha Soami cult, they claim, are not the products of individuals or of historical movements, nor can they be explained by recourse to any psychological or sociological constructs. To its adherents, the Radha Soami faith is the *real* teaching of *every* saint at *all* times of history. Christ and Buddha, Krishna and Kabir, the Sufi saints and the Sikh gurus, have all talked of and taught exactly the same journey on the road to self-transformation. When the original core of major religious writings is uncovered, the misunderstandings introduced due to later interpolations are removed and the missing links restored, then the mystical kernel of all religions, the Satsangis say, stands revealed as being identical with the teachings of Santmat.[10]

In its concern with the permanent, unchanging part of man which it regards as the *central* expression of his being, the mystical tradition is close to the traditional psychoanalytic position of an unchanging core of human nature; though, of course, they differ implacably on whether this essential core is spiritual or instinctual. Mysticism, however, is even more radical than psychoanalysis in its uncompromising exclusion of the other pole of man which involves his temporality and historical-cultural conditions—the "outer crust" of his being—and which is the subject of the sciences of man.

The attempt at *universalization* and *eternalization* (and hence at achieving permanence) of the sect's theory and practice is also extended to the personage of its gurus. Instead of being individuals with distinctive names and personal histories, the gurus become the "embodiment of the same Supreme Spirit" and in a sense flow into each other. They receive respectful appellations that seem so totally familiar—Swamiji, Maharajji, Perfect Master and so on—which differ from each other only marginally. In fact, these appellations seem to be interchangeable not only within the same sect but even between different mystical cults. Indeed, as we shall discuss later, the negation of human finitude, the denial of human limits and the claim to transcend history and time are perhaps the distinctive therapeutic levers of all mystical cults and comprise the essential building blocks of their theory and practice.

The Radha Soami sect studied here is the Beas group, the first one that splintered off from the main movement in 1903. Its founder was Jaimal Singh (Babaji), an intimate disciple of Soamiji, who settled down to lead an ascetic life in the Punjab. Babaji seems to have been a genuinely otherworldly man who could neither abide by nor take seriously the newfangled rules and regulations promulgated by the Central Administrative Council set up after the death of the first gurus to look after the affairs of the Satsang. As a result, Babaji's license to initiate was canceled.[11] Unperturbed, Babaji built a small hut on the west bank of the river Beas, between Jullundur and Amritsar, eight miles away from his native village. In an understandable wish to lend distinction to an otherwise undistinguished place, the legend among the faithful has it that it was at this precise spot that the army of Alexander the Great rebelled against his plans to march farther east and complete Alexander's self-chosen mission of conquering India. In any event, peasants from neighboring villages, following an immemorial Indian tradition, were drawn to the holy man outside the gate of their settlements and the settledness of their humdrum lives. Many came to hear him discourse upon matters of soul and ultimate meanings, while a few remained to be initiated into the mystical practices of the sect. Babaji did not formally disassociate himself from the main group at Agra till 1903, the year of his death. It was his chosen successor Sawan Singh ("Huzoor Maharajji") who established the Beas group as a separate organization. Guru *bhakti* and *surat shabd yoga*, however, remained the main pillars of the Beas Satsang as it did of other Radha Soami groups— the theological differentiation of the Beas Satsang from others being influenced more by its geographical surroundings than by any matters of faith. Located in the heartland of the Punjab and drawing the bulk of its following from the Sikh peasantry, the Beas Satsang naturally sought to emphasize its links with the Sikh spiritual tradition and to strengthen its kinship with the Sikh gurus. For instance, it propounded the theory that Radha Soami is not the true spiritual resonance *(dhunyatamak nam)* but an addition to the already existing fifteen hundred names of God in the Sikh scriptures and that Tulsi Sahab of Hathras, the spiritual father of Soamiji, had been himself initiated into the mysteries of Santmat by the last Sikh guru.

In the forty-five years of his stewardship, Huzoor Maharaj set the Beas Satsang upon a path of expansion which built a flourishing township out of a single hut and transformed a sect with a handful of members into a mass mystical movement.[12] By the time of his death in 1948, Huzoor Maharaj had initiated over a hundred thousand people into the sect's mysteries; the Radha Soami Satsang of Beas had begun to claim an increasing number of devotees in most major Indian towns and in many foreign cities. Today, with Huzoor Maharaj's grandson, Charan Singh ("Maharajji") at the helm of its affairs, the Beas Satsang is a flourishing enterprise by all standards. In the last twenty-eight years during which Maharajji has been the "Living Master," he has initiated over half a million people into the Santmat. There are now more than three hundred Satsang centers spread all over India and two hundred centers in the rest of the world. The resident spiritual community at Beas lives in a well-organized township that might well be the envy of most Indians,

supplied as it is with all the civic amenities such as plumbing,
electricity, a safe water supply, hospitals, libraries and a community
kitchen which, on special feast days (*bhandaras*) commemorating
the past gurus, feeds as many as eighty thousand people at a single
sitting. Maharajji's Satsangs at Beas and in other Indian towns attract congregations that often number over a hundred thousand,
while every year thousands seek initiation into the cult. With its
demonstrated popularity and strong appeal for seekers, the Radha
Soami Satsang of Beas is certainly one of the major mystical-spiritual
movements in the world today.

The Healing Offer

I attended my first Satsang immediately after my arrival in Beas on
a cold December morning. The Satsang was to be held in the large
open space behind the Satsang Ghar, the imposing congregation
hall, built during the early part of this century, that dominates the
township and the plains around it. With its hundred-foot-high ceiling, marble floors inlaid with mosaic designs and a profusion of
arches, columns and towers, the Satsang Ghar is a medley of ar-
chitectural styles. In fact, at first glance, before the aesthetic eye can
become clouded over by the film of faith, the Satsang Ghar looks
like a Punjabi petty official's fantasy of a building that combines both
Victorian imperial grandeur and Mughal oriental splendor. On this
particular day, the *bhandara* of Babaji, the congregation was especially large, numbering well over fifty thousand. Swaddled in rough
woolen blankets and huddling close together for warmth against the
chilly wind blowing down from the distant Shivalik hills, barely
visible through their shroud of steel-gray haze, the crowd was impressive in its silent orderliness. The noise, the bustle and the confusion
that are an inherent quality of a large Punjabi or, for that matter,
any Indian gathering, were remarkable by their absence.

As I made my way through the patiently squatting men—the
women were sitting on the other side—my strongest impression was
of a pervasive friendliness, bubbling over into welcoming smiles and

the low-murmured cultic greeting of "Radha Soami!" Most of the men and women in the congregation belonged to the Sikh peasantry —the men tall and bearded, with fierce faces yet gentle eyes, and the women stately in their traditional knee-length shirts and floppy trousers that narrowed down sharply at the ankles. There were others too: hill people from Kangra and Jammu, petty traders and small housekeepers from dusty towns of the Punjab and from as far away as (I discovered later) Mehsana in Gujarat and Bhopal in Madhya Pradesh. Right up at the front, in a separate enclosure just below the fifteen-foot-high dais from where Maharajji would address the congregation, sat the "elite" Satsangis. Among these fifty-odd European and American Satsangis—many of them reclining comfortably on cunningly designed chairs without legs that give a person an appearance of squatting cross-legged without his actually doing so—there was a sprinkling of industrialists, former diplomats, retired high government officials and an ex-prince of an obscure Indian state with a retinue of daughters, daughters-in-law and a brood of solemn-eyed children.

While we waited for Maharajji, we sang. The mellifluous voice of a *panthi*—the chanter of Sikh scriptures—drifted out of the loud-speakers strung out on the grounds as he sang of man's spiritual longing for the *Satguru*. The crowd joined in the refrain at the end of each familiar and well-loved verse, fifty thousand voices merging into one deep-throated chant that was scarcely a song any longer but more an emotion, a yearning broken into patterns of sound. To anyone sitting within the vast belly of the crowd, a choir of fifty thousand feels like an elemental sound of nature—the rumbling of a volcano full of melody and meaning or, perhaps, like the sound of high wind and torrential rain which has been shaped into a musical pattern. Here I am deliberately emphasizing my subjective experience of the Satsang, on this day as on the following days, and the fantasies that bubble up to the fore of consciousness as one sits esconced in the warmth and closeness of thousands of bodies. At first there is a sense of unease as the body, the container of our individuality and the demarcator of our spatial boundaries, is sharply wrenched away from its habitual mode of experiencing others. For as we grow up, the touch of others, once so deliberately courted and responded to with delight, increasingly becomes ambivalent. Coming from a loved one, touch is deliciously welcomed; with strangers, on the other hand, there is an involuntary shrinking of the body, their touch taking on the menacing air of invasion by the Other. But once the fear of touch disappears in the fierce press of other bodies and the individual lets himself become a part of the crowd's density, the original apprehension is gradually transformed into an expansiveness that stretches to include the others. Distances and differences—of status, age and sex—disappear in an exhilarating feeling (temporary to be sure) that individual boundaries can indeed be transcended and were perhaps illusory in the first place. Of course, touch is only one of the sensual stimuli that hammers at the gate of individual identity. Other excitations, channeled through vision, hearing and smell, are also very much involved. In addition, as Phyllis Greenacre has suggested, there are other, more subliminal exchanges of body heat, muscle tension and body rhythms taking place in a crowd.[13] In short, the crowd's assault on the sense of individual identity appears to be well nigh irresistible; its invitation to a psychological regression —in which the image of one's body becomes fluid and increasingly blurred, controls over emotions and impulses are weakened, critical faculties and rational thought processes are abandoned—is extended in a way that is both forceful and seductive.

It was in such a mild state of "altered consciousness," pervaded with a feeling of oneness and affection for every member of the crowd, that I waited for Maharajji to appear. There is little doubt that I (along with the rest of the crowd) was in a heightened state of receptivity for whatever might come next.

The chanting stopped and there were minutes of hushed silence as Maharajji's chauffeured Fiat car came into view, driven slowly down the empty road and stopping behind the high podium from where he would hold the Satsang. All eyes were now raised up to the dais. The canopy above it fluttered lightly in the breeze that rippled through its bright-blue canvas. And then Maharajji appeared at the top of the steps behind the dais. A majestic figure with a long white beard and a neatly tied white turban covering his head, he was dressed in a cream-colored *kurta,* well-cut *churidars,* a sleeveless tan woolen jacket and a beige *pashmina* shawl wrapped round his shoulders. Tall and well built, Maharaj Charan Singh is a stately figure and I remember the fleeting thought that this is what God's younger brother must look like. With a brisk tread belying his sixty-three years, Maharajji stepped up to the low divan at the front, bowed and touched his forehead to the seat in a gesture of reverence to his predecessors. He then mounted the divan and sat down cross-legged, adjusting the shawl around his broad shoulders as he pulled the microphone in front of the divan closer. The silence continued, broken occasionally by a cough, while Maharajji sat there impassively, slowly turning his head from one side to the other in a wide sweep, surveying his flock from under bushy white eyebrows and through slightly hooded eyes while his right hand moved up and down rhythmically, stroking and smoothing down errant hair that had escaped from the luxuriant growth of his beard.

The people around me were transfixed, overwhelmed by the presence of the Satguru who to a Satsangi is God made flesh, divine made human. This was *darshan;* "viewing," in its most intense form. There were tears of emotion running down the cheek of the middle-aged man sitting next to me, merging with drops of saliva dribbling out of the corner of his mouth, and I had the distinct feeling that my neighbors were visually feasting on Maharajji's face. Meanwhile, there was movement on the stage as a frail old Sikh appeared and sat on one side, where a second microphone had been strategically placed. Untying the knots of a bundle wrapped in a red muslin, he took out a thick tome—the Adi Granth—and peered nearsightedly at the pages, which he riffled through rapidly till he came to the page he was looking for. Replacing the open book on the book rack in front and crossing his arms across his chest, the old *panthi* settled back, slowly rocking on his haunches as he too waited for the *darshan* to end.

Maharajji cleared his throat, a rasping sound instantaneously amplified into a thunderous rumble by the loudspeakers, and as if he were only awaiting this signal, the *panthi* started singing a poem by Guru Amar Das from the Adi Granth. His voice was indescribably appealing, full of wise tranquility and spirited longing at the same time, both old and childlike at once, melodious and yet somehow also conveying that it was unmindful of such criteria as timbre and melody. He sang a short verse before Maharajji began to elaborate on the verse in clear and idiomatic Punjabi. His voice was soft and low, the tone intimate, the diction full of assurance and easy authority.

"Look where we will," he began, "we find nothing but pain and suffering in this world. The more we try to find peace and happiness in the shapes and forms of this world, the deeper is our misery. By their very nature, the things we seek are transient. Consequently, the pleasure derived from them is invariably short-lived."[14]

The devaluation of the objective world contained in Maharajji's opening sentences, his emphasis on the misery of the world and his perfunctory dismissal of its splendors, are of course in the mainstream of Indian spiritual tradition, the prism through which Indians have traditionally viewed the outer world. It is however deeply reassuring for a sufferer to be told that his suffering does not connote any individual failure or deficiency on his part, something of which almost every patient is unconsciously convinced. On the contrary, Maharajji ennobles individual suffering by characterizing it as a part of the eternal "nature of things"—part of a scrutable divine plan. For someone in pain, it is even more comforting to be told that everyone else too is a sufferer, actual or potential. This *democratization* of suffering was made more concrete as Maharajji proceeded to give homely illustrations that were obviously resonant with the situation of the members of his audience and addressed the concerns of their daily life. "Marriage is a happy and festive event in our life, but if our partner turns out to be quarrelsome, overbearing and unaccommodating, the resulting tension and strife turn the whole household into a veritable hell. Some are dogged by illness, others by the curse of unemployment. Some are denied the privilege of parenthood and they yearn for a child day and night. Others have children who cause them endless misery and worry. Some are worried because they cannot secure a loan, others because they cannot repay one. We daily witness the sorry spectacle of beggars and destitutes clamoring for alms by the roadside. We have only to visit a hospital to hear the doleful cries of patients writhing in agony, or a jail to listen to the tales of woe and distress of the unfortunate inmates. If this is the fate of man in this world, the position of the lower species can better be imagined than described. One shudders to think of their lot. Man is considered the 'top of the creation' and made in the image of his Maker. Yet no one, even in this coveted form, can claim to be happy and contented. By far the largest number of people look for happiness and peace in amassing wealth.

They toil day and night and sacrifice many a principle in this ignoble pursuit. But soon they are disillusioned to find that riches and happiness are not synonymous. Stark misery stares them in the face when the pile starts shrinking, for money soon begins to slide into the doctor's pocket for treatment of all kinds of ailments, or into the lawyer's purse when they get involved in prolonged and expensive litigation.

"Then, again, some seek pleasure in wine and whiskey and in eating the flesh of animals, fish and fowl. These things may give them pleasure of the palate; they may appear to be rich and savory, but quite often they also land them in hospitals and nursing homes, sometimes even in prison cells, entailing hard labor."

Maharajji then went on to the riddle of why peace and happiness are so elusive and why pain and pleasure are so intermingled in every life. Taking the question of personal misery onto the existential plane, he proceeded to give the traditional Indian answer to the cause of suffering, namely, the workings of karma.

"Sages and seers have called this world the 'field of karma,' for here we have to reap what we have sown. Crops of pleasure and pain, joy and sorrow, grow strictly according to the seeds of good and bad karma. If we sow seeds of pepper, we shall harvest pepper. If we plant mangoes, we are entitled to enjoy the taste of mangoes. It's the load of karma that is keeping us in this prison house of 'eighty-four.'* Look at our present state. After every death, the messengers of Death lead us before Dharma Rai, the Divine Accountant, who takes into account our unfulfilled desires and wishes and accordingly decides where and when we have to be born again. We are not yet rid of the shackles of one body when the sheath of the next one is already there to confine us. Like branded habitual criminals, we are fettered and shifted, as it were, from one cell of the prison house to another. Neither through good deeds nor through bad ones can one obtain release from this prison of lives. If bad deeds are iron fetters then good deeds are fetters made of gold. After exhausting their fruits, we are back to misery, sorrow and pain. Our situation is indeed like that of man clinging to the branch of a tree whose roots are

---

*Here he is referring to the traditional Indian notion of there being 8,400,000 species in creation—"wombs" through which one must be successively reborn to attain *moksha*.

being gnawed by rats while a deadly cobra waits for the man to fall on the ground. In this predicament two drops of honey [of sensual pleasure] fall on his tongue and he becomes oblivious to everything as he savors their sweetness."

The *panthi* sang:

> All treasure is within thy home
> There is naught without
> Thou shalt attain it through Guru's grace
> When thy inner door is opened.

Maharajji continued, "If we long for permanent peace and happiness and freedom from the laws of karma, we must seek the Lord within. Our soul is of the essence of the Lord. 'Just as oil is in sesame seeds,' says Kabir, 'and fire is in flint, so does he reside in your body, the Lord whom you seek day and night.' Jesus Christ also pronounces in the Bible, 'The kingdom of God is within you.' As Christ says, our body is the 'temple of the living God,' for it is within our body alone where he can be realized and experienced.

"One can see for himself how ignorant we are when we look for the Lord in man-made shrines instead of the temple made by God himself to reside in. The saints advise us, therefore, that if we want to realize God, we must look for him within ourselves and nowhere else. Naturally the question now arises that if God is within our own body, which is the true temple of God, why do we not see him? What is the obstacle and how can it be removed? The obvious reply is that it is our desires and wishes, our love and attachment for the world and its objects, that generate the love and attachment in us. Naturally, it is our own mind. Whatever karma the mind impels us to do, the consequences have to be suffered by the soul also, for the mind and soul are knotted together. We know that water in the clouds is pure, but when it falls on the ground as rain, it gathers all kinds of impurities. The condition of our soul is no way different from that of rainwater. It is of the same essence as God himself, but having become subservient to the mind it has gathered dirt and dross and lost its purity. As long as the soul does not free itself from the clutches of the mind, it cannot know its source.

"All genuine seekers realize the importance of controlling and subduing the mind. To that end they try diverse methods and techniques. Some resort to austerities and repetition of holy names, some indulge in charitable acts, others leave their hearths and homes and seek the seclusion of mountains and forests. There are still others who make endless rounds of temples, mosques, churches, *gurudwaras*, and devote themselves to the study of scriptures and sacred books and listen to learned discourses. All these functions are solely directed to one end, namely to control the mind. The truth, however, is that the cravings and desires of the mind have only been suppressed for a while; they have not disappeared, nor have they been conquered. The more we suppress a thing, the more it re-bounds and reacts."

Maharajji then went on to say that the only way of detaching the mind was to attach it to something higher—to the God within. This could be done by seeking the company of like-minded believers in the experience of Satsang such as the one we were all engaged in; by devotion to the guru who is a conduit to the divine and especially by the spiritual practices of *surat shabd yoga*, through which the "divine nectar within can be tasted, the divine melody resounding within can be heard and the divine light shining within can be seen."

The direct quotations of passages from Maharajji's long discourse —a discourse which he has delivered hundred of times before with minor variations—are intended to convey its flavor as much as its content, if not more. I certainly realize that without giving due attention to the nonverbal signals contained in the movement of his hands, the play of his body, the changes in the pitch of his voice, flavor can only be imperfectly conveyed, even by a verbatim repro-duction of his imagery and metaphors. I have also omitted here some of the parables Maharajji is so fond of using—parables obviously suggesting to members of his audience that each one of them is like a child in an amusement park who is happy only as long as he is holding on to his father's hand; or that he is like a child absorbed in play but only as long as he does not remember his parents.

The intellectual contents of Maharajji's discourse are familiar since they are common to many mystical traditions, Indian as well as of other societies. To list some of these repetitive elements: there is the derogation of the perceived real world and an emphasis on its painful, withholding nature; there is the suggestion of mystical withdrawal as a solution to the individual's psychic needs and life problems; there is the offer of a system of psychological and physiological practices by which a person can deliberately and voluntarily seek detachment from the everyday, external world and replace it with a heightened awareness of inner reality; and, finally, there is a shared conviction that this inner world possesses a much greater reality than the outer one.

Emotionally, to an Indian, the familiarity of the message, repeated often enough since the beginning of childhood, constitutes its greatest strength and attraction. Once again the men and women were transported to the time when, their small hands clutched in those of older family members, they had sat up late into the night, in the midst of a group of neighbors and kinsmen, sleepily listening to wandering *religiosi* expound the mysteries of life. It was familiar from the many after-death ceremonies where they had listened to the priest and the family elders talk of the laws of karma, the cycles of birth, life and death and the *mukti* that was every being's goal. Maharajji's talk was then a murmur from the past—both individual and collective—that had suddenly become audible. I too must confess to a curious mixture of elation and unease that gripped me as I listened to him. The source of the elation was difficult to pinpoint then, though now I would describe it, somewhat fancifully to be sure, as a stirring of the blood to the call of the Indian Passion, the overflow of a feeling of oneness with one's (idealized) community and its traditions. He had touched an atavistic chord in me of which I would have perhaps preferred to remain unaware.

The unease is much easier to define. It sprang from what I can only call an outrage to "liberal, humanist sentiments" that too are a part of my inheritance as they are of all those, in every country around the globe, who are the heirs to a still-emerging modern world. I was neither bothered by nor am I referring here to what appears as an element of medieval feudalism in the relationship of the *Satguru* with the members of his cult. Maharajji, of course, means "great king" and the translation of the *gaddi* he sits on—and has succeeded to—is "throne." The lithograph of Soamiji, the founder of the cult, that hangs in many public places and in the homes of devout initiates shows him clad in expensive-looking silks and brocades, richly bejeweled and benecklaced, and quite indistinguishable from the coppery daguerrotypes of Indian princes and "nabobs" that occasionally used to adorn the pages of turn-of-the-century British periodicals. Nor am I too much troubled by the fact that in the Satsang (as in most Indian mystical cults) favored treatment is given to the wealthy and powerful and that these marks of favor are rationalized by the gurus as being deserved by the disciples on account of their past good karma. I have also little quarrel with the very comfortable, if not opulent, life-style of Maharajji and other mystics. The proverbial problems of the rich man trying to negotiate the eye of the needle are more a part of the Christian than the Hindu heritage; the link between asceticism and poverty on the one hand and spirituality and transcendence on the other has been denied by Indian saints more often than it has been affirmed.

My unease had more to do with the repeated assertion of Maharajji (and of his predecessors) that a "seeker" should not only endure but cheerfully and actively *accept* the iron law of karma. Saints, he says, perhaps rightly, are not social reformers who have come to change the world—although even here too one may doubt the validity of such a clear-cut demarcation between inner and outer changes, individual and social transformations, saints and revolutionaries. To recommend, however, a joyous acceptance of the existing social order—with its economic, social and sexual inequities—as the *prerequisite* for a state of mind that leads to highest mystical truths, to advise women to cheerfully conform to the meek subservient roles laid out for them by a repressive patriarchy, does go against the grain of modern identity, even if Maharajji considers them to be absolutely essential for progress on the mystical path. (A cynic, pointing to the fact that Maharajji himself is a rich landowner who is allied by kinship and marriage ties to some of the wealthiest families in northern India, might observe the curious coincidence that the will of God and the "eternal law of nature" seem to be identical to the economic and political interest of a feudal elite and the convenience of a patriarchal order. This, however, would be doing Maharajji an injustice, since his position on the law of karma and its individual and social consequences is not idiosyncratic but is shared by a vast majority of his countrymen and lies unexceptionably within the mainstream of Indian religiosity.)

After the Satsang, I took a leisurely walk through the Dera town-

ship. People streamed past me in groups—small contingents of Satsangis from different villages, large families with women and children placed protectively in the middle while the men walked at the
periphery, guarding them like sheepdogs. Many of them were on
their way to the huge tents erected near the Satsang Ghar, each of
which could accommodate up to a thousand people in its cavernous
insides. Others strolled through the freshly swept streets, the claw-
like marks made by the twig brooms still visible in the earth, their
festive mood proving to be more than a match for the whipping cold
wind. The afterglow of the Satsang was still reflected on their
friendly faces and in their smiles that seemed to affirm joyously each
other's existence and value. I remember that my own greetings of
"Radha Soami!" in response to those directed at me by total strangers were without a trace of the earlier self-consciousness and embar-
rassment I had felt at being (in a sense) an imposter among true
believers. For a short while, I was prepared to believe that social
relations need not necessarily be organized according to either of the
two fundamental categories that sociologists since Toennies have
prescribed for them. The Satsangis were neither a *community*, with
the community's uncritical acceptance of roles and relationships,
where the individual tends to merge into others, nor did they constitute a *society* with its rational-contractual bonds and its calculating
coolness, where the individual is at a distance from others with
whom he is also in competition. The sect members seemed to be
living, however temporarily, in a third kind of association which
Eugen Schmalenbach has called "communion" and which only a
few social scientists have explored as being either desirable or possible.[15] Here a more or less freely chosen, nonbinding brotherhood
dominates; the individual is enhanced (unlike community) and yet
the emotional bonds go deep (unlike society).[16] I could therefore
understand how the Radha Soami Satsang (and perhaps most mystical sects) can become a haven for so many Indians who are in flight
from the oppressiveness of an all-embracing community, as well as
for those Westerners who are moving in the other direction, namely,
away from the cold isolation and competitiveness of an individualis-
tic society.

In the meantime, Maharajji had returned to his house, its approaches guarded by volunteers who politely but firmly turned back

the more curious and intrepid of his disciples. Behind the high walls surrounding his mansion, Maharajji reclined on a wicker chair in his rose garden, attending to his correspondence and affairs of the trust that manages the Satsang's far-flung activities with exemplary efficiency. A dozen of his intimate disciples—the specially special ones —sat around him at a respectful distance. They watched Maharajji work, savoring the great privilege of his nearness, grateful for being allowed to participate, however vicariously, in his activities. Maharajji's every movement—whether the opening of a letter, the adjustment of his reading glasses or a gentle burp as he meditatively stroked his beard—seemed to be greeted by silent hosannas. They followed him, again at a respectful distance, to the guesthouse where Maharajji was to give a special *darshan* to seventy-odd mostly foreign members of the cult. The *darshan* itself did not take too much time. Maharajji approached them with folded hands raised in greeting and sat down on a sofa placed in the middle of the guesthouse lawn, with rows of chairs arranged in a semicircle around it. Without any preliminaries, he looked steadily for a couple of minutes at one section of his small audience, regally turned his face and stared unblinkingly at another section—a virtuoso use of look and silence. The transformation of the disciples' faces as their eyes looked into his was remarkable. The eyes glazed over as they drank in his visage. Visibly, their brows smoothened out, their jaw muscles slackened and a beatific expression slowly spread on the faces. The whole transformation was startingly similar to the nursing infant when he takes the breast into his mouth and the milk begins to spread its soothing warmth, generating those good feelings that gradually obliterate all the earlier unease, the tension and the plain anxiousness.

The *darshan* ended around noon. Keeping a few paces behind him, all of us followed Maharajji to the venue of his next engagement, the blessing of the food at the *langar*—the community kitchen. "Kitchen," of course, is a euphemism for a sprawling complex of large rooms and open spaces where eighty thousand meals were being prepared for lunch and where hundreds of volunteer cooks and helpers—men and women—were carrying out their assigned tasks with a military precision. Thick *masur dal* steamed and gurgled in a row of burnished-copper vats, each one the height of a man; the cloying sweet smell of jaggery-flavored rice wafted out of oval cauldrons; flat, pancake-shaped breads—the *rotis*—were being taken out of clay ovens dug deep into the earth and then stacked up in mounds. As we approached the *langar*, we could already hear the women, busy in kneading and rolling the dough for the *rotis*, singing:

> *Charan kamal tere dho dho peeyan*
> *Deen Dayal Satguru mere*
>
> (I wash your lotus feet and drink the water
> O my compassionate and merciful Satguru)

The scene as Maharajji briskly walked around the "kitchen" with his hands raised in benediction is one of my most striking memories of Beas. Squatting on their heels, their hands clasped together in supplication, the glittering black eyes shining with the light of purest pleasure and the broad smiles expressing a child's unreserved delight, the women sang louder as Maharajji passed close to them, while their heads and the upper halves of their bodies seemed to strain toward him in unbearable longing. In contrast, the men quietly raised their faces toward Maharajji in a look of dumb devotion that was also full of awe—if not fear. In fact, whenever the Satguru came upon a man working alone, the man would immediately squat down on his heels and visibly cringe, as if prepared to receive a capricious blow. The Punjabi daughter's early experience of her father, I reminded myself from clinical experience, is indeed very different from that of the Punjabi son; the mutual adoration and idealization characteristic of the former relationship is missing in the latter.

The Tie to the Master

In the afternoon I had watched the selection of those who desired to be initiated into the cult and receive the *nam* ("Word") from Maharajji. There were about four hundred men squatting patiently in one corner of the open ground next to the Satsang Ghar while an almost equal number of women waited in another corner. One by one, the men and women went up to two large tables, each manned by four hawk-eyed and officious-looking men whose sharpened pencils hovered menacingly above the open registers lying in front of them. The first official asked each applicant a few questions. If the answers were satisfactory, the aspirant was passed on to the next official, who noted down his or her personal details. In case of an unsatisfactory response, the person was summarily directed toward the exit. I had asked the man next to me, a tall and gaunt Sikh who was interestedly watching the proceedings, what was going on. "Oh, everyone is asked how long it has been since he has given up eating meat and drinking liquor, how old he is, and from which district he comes," the man replied. "To be accepted for registration one must have given up eating meat and drinking liquor for more than three months and should be at least thirty years old. The older you are the better are your chances for receiving *nam*. Naturally some lie about their age or about having given up drinking, but I always say that lying in the good cause of getting salvation cannot be a sin. I myself received *nam* last year and lied about the drinking bit. The *nam* will be given by Maharajji the day after tomorrow and he, of course, knows whether one has been lying or not. But then he is God and will often forgive the lie and accept the person."

We had drifted into a conversation and I had asked Harnam Singh (that was his name) as to how he had become a Satsangi. Harnam Singh was the youngest of four sons in a Sikh peasant family from a Patiala village who had tilled their own land for many generations. As the "baby" of the family, Harnam Singh had been much indulged during childhood, especially by his mother. She had died when he was eighteen and ever since her death, he said, a peculiar *udasinta* (sadness) had taken possession of his soul. Though he had all the comforts at home, enough to eat and drink and an abundant measure of affection from his father and elder brothers, the *udasinta* had persisted. For fifteen long years, he said, his soul remained restless, yearning for an unattainable peace. His thoughts often dwelt upon death, of which he developed an exaggerated fear, and he was subject to crippling headaches that confined him to the darkness of his room for long periods. Then, suddenly last year, he had a vision in a dream of Maharajji (he had seen his photograph in a Satsangi home in his village), who told him to come to Beas and take the *nam*. He had done so; the *udasinta* disappeared, as did his fear and headaches, and he felt the loving omnipresence of the Master as a protection against their return.

In my interviews with the Satsangis, I found that many of them shared a common pattern in their lives that had led them to a search for the guru and to initiation in the Radha Soami cult. Almost invariably the individual had gone through one or more experiences that had severely mauled his sense of self-worth, if not shattered it completely. In contrast to the rest of us, who must also deal with the painful feelings aroused by temporary depletions in self-esteem, it seems that those who came to the Radha Soami cult grappled with these feelings for a much longer time, sometimes for many years, without being able to change them appreciably. Unable to rid themselves of the feelings of "I have lost everything and the world is empty," or "I have lost everything because I do not deserve anything," they had been on the lookout for someone, somewhere, to restore the lost sense of self-worth and to counteract their hidden image of a failing, depleted self—a search none the less desperate for its being mostly unconscious. This "someone" eventually turned out to be Maharajji and the "somewhere" the Satsang at Beas, to which the seekers were led by events—such as the vision of Maharajji—which in retrospect seemed miraculous. The conviction and sense of a miracle having taken place, though projected to the circumstances that led to the individual's initiation into the cult, actually derived from the "miraculous" ending of a persistent and painful internal state, the disappearance of the black clouds of *udasinta* that had seemed to be a permanent feature of the individual's life. Perhaps a few vignettes from life histories will illustrate this pattern more concretely.

K. was a fifty-year-old woman from a rich business family in Ahmadabad who had been deserted by her husband when she was thirty-five. She did not remarry and, unable to "plant another garden of love" around her, she had busied herself with the running of the household (which in any case was efficiently managed by the servants) and with her grown-up children, who needed her less and less. Gradually, she lost whatever interest she had been able to summon up in life after the shock of her husband's desertion. She attended a couple of Satsangs in Ahmadabad, heard Maharajji speak and was deeply impressed though she did not take the *nam*. One day, sitting alone in a hotel room in a strange city, she was overwhelmed by the hopelessness of her situation and felt that she had come to the end of her tether. She had closed her eyes in utter weariness, she says, when she felt Maharajji's presence in the room and had the distinct sensation of a hand squeezing her shoulder like that of a kind father. She says she knew at that moment that if she went to Maharajji for protection all her problems would be resolved.

Sixty-year-old B. was a small shopkeeper in Jammu who did a modest business in buying and selling gunnysacks, a business he had inherited from his father. Some years before, when he had entered the fourth stage of his life (the last stage of the Hindu life cycle), he said, he had felt gripped by a strong sense of dissatisfaction. His only son had turned out to be a delinquent who could not hold a job and was in constant trouble with the police. B. felt terribly ashamed of his son and "realizing the futility of all attachments" he had turned to spiritual life, listening to the discourses of various saints and attending the Satsang in his city. Four years ago he came to Beas, took the initiation from Maharajji and, though he could not sit as long in the *bhajan* (the required daily meditation) as he would have liked to, he had known peace since then. Maharajji, all-loving and all-compassionate, was now constantly with him.

R. was a forty-four-year-old businessman whose parents had emigrated to South America from an eastern European country and whose father died when he was young. Thirteen years before, R.'s business had failed and he became bankrupt. His wife left him since he had little time for her, and he was left with the responsibility of bringing up three small children. As if this were not enough, his mother had a stroke that left her paralyzed. R. became depressed and often thought of suicide. On the suggestion of a friend he began attending evening classes at a theosophy school. Here he came into contact with the mystical thought of Gourdjieff and Ouspensky. During one of the relaxation exercises at the school, while R. was sitting with his eyes closed, he saw the face of an old man with a long white beard. This happened twice again and the third time, R. says, the following dialogue took place:

R.: Where are you?

Old man: Look for me.

R.: How can I when I have no money?

Old man: When you get some, then come.

After a few years when the children were grown and R.'s finances improved, he remembered his promise and set out on his search for the old man of the vision, who was "somewhere in the East." He traveled through Japan and Hong Kong and when he came to Bangkok he saw Maharajji's picture hanging in a shop where he had gone to buy a silk shirt. "I recognized him at once!" R. exclaimed. "He was the old man of my vision! I took the address from the shopkeeper and made straight for India and Beas. And there he was, waiting for me! I had come home."

The above accounts of events that led people into the Radha Soami fold are obviously also capable of straightforward psychological interpretations. R.'s vision of the old man, for instance, which occurred at a time of deep personal crisis, can be viewed as the symbolic expression of R.'s yearning for the guiding presence of the father of his childhood who would rescue him from his state of helplessness and take over the responsibility for his shattered life. In another, more complicated explanation, a Jungian might interpret R.'s vision more in terms of a collective rather than a personal unconscious by suggesting that what R. experienced that day in the theosophy school was the healing archetype of the Old Wise Man, who symbolizes the preexistent hidden meaning in the chaos of life and represents the understanding of life processes which are never fully comprehended consciously. To the Satsangis, however, R.'s vision and similar experiences of many other "seekers" are a proof of Maharajji's omnipresence and omnipotence, a testimonial to his miraculous power to leave his physical body at will and journey through the astral regions into the dreams and visions of his present and future disciples.

Initiation into the Radha Soami cult undoubtedly restored a sense of well-being to many whose emotional lives had been marked by starkly depressive features. It seems that in most cases the sense of at last being at peace with oneself followed the abandonment of a long and futile struggle to obtain the required supplies of love and esteem from "significant others" in both the outer and inner worlds. The route now taken to restore the self to its pristine glory and powerfulness was very different. The first steps on the new road involved a conscious deprecation and a further *willed* depletion of the self, accompanied by a corresponding idealization of Maharajji. The Satsangi renounced all claims to self-aggrandizement, underlined his or her unworthiness ("I am not even fit to be the dust on his feet") and forcefully projected all the positive aspects of the self —its strength, power, knowledge, goodness, gifts, etc.—onto Maharajji, who became the fount of omniscience and omnipotence. The next step was a sharing of this projected goodness and greatness through "identification," a psychological process in which Maharajji's supposed power was assimilated into the self, which was thereby transformed. The whole transformation process has its roots in, and is a replication of, psychic events in that early period of childhood when the child, in the face of the many narcissistic hurts and disappointments that the ending of infancy brought in its wake, sought to recapture his early feelings of "greatness" through a new route, where he projected this greatness onto the idealized image of a parent and then partook of it himself by setting up a configuration in the psyche: "You are great but I am a part of you."[17] At the level of manifest behavior, the almost exaggerated humility I encountered in every Satsangi (coupled with his paeans of praise for the Master) did not mask the underlying bedrock of a very high self-esteem. Nowhere, it seems, is Nietzsche's observation that "he who despises himself nevertheless esteems himself thereby as the despiser" more true than in case of the followers of a mystical cult. Perhaps I should note that the healing transformation of the self I have described here is not unique to the Radha Soami Satsang but is a characteristic feature of many mystical sects, independent of the uniqueness that the followers may ascribe to their own particular sect and the "true divinity" which they may credit to their particular guru.

It is evident that the two psychological mechanisms of idealization and identification, which give a newfound centrality to the self, need to be kept intact if the individual follower is not again to be exposed to the crushing and crushed feelings aroused by a reactivation of the image of a failed and empty self. Perceptions, information and knowledge that have the potential to lead to the slightest disillusionment with the Master and to a more realistic image of the Satguru, as well as mental events that threaten to disturb the feeling of unity with him, need to be denied access to consciousness. Beneath the tortuous effort to perfect the particular *Sadhna* (mystical practice) of the mystical school to which he belongs, the follower is also engaged in an unconscious struggle to deepen the processes of idealization and identification.

Idealization and identification are certainly not exclusive to the mystical sects but, avowed or unavowed, are also present in most psychotherapies. During certain periods of psychoanalysis, for instance, a patient *needs* a temporary idealization and identification with the analyst in order to take the initial steps toward self-exploration, which are otherwise prohibited by the archaic and punitive elements of his superego. The difference between the two "healing traditions" lies in the fact that whereas idealization and identification are tactical and temporary in psychoanalysis, they are strategic and intended to be permanent in the Radha Soami Satsang and other mystical cults. The cult's group activities such as the Satsang, its philosophy as expounded in the cultic literature, by senior disciples, and by the guru himself, all propel idealization to its culminating point, where the guru can be experienced as God, and take the identification to *its* logical conclusion, where the disciple has the feeling of complete unity with the guru. Besides its specific therapeutic and adaptive aspects,[18] the required daily meditation of four hours for the novitiate, with the Master's face as the object of meditation, further cements the idealization and internalization of the guru since he is daily experienced as the benevolent protector against the anxieties that arise during the meditative process.

The apparently quiescent figure of the Indian guru, self-absorbed in his meditative stillness, is then quite misleading. In actual fact, he is a veritable psychological powerhouse who actively drives forward the processes I have described above. Take, for instance, Maharajji. As a counterpoint to the disciple's dependence he emphasizes his dependability and his assumption of total responsibility for the disciple's welfare throughout eternity.[19] To the disciple's feeling of insignificance, the guru offers his omnipotence, his ability to perform miracles (not only spiritual but physical ones) and generally function above the laws of nature.[20] To the disciple's feeling of crippling inertness, Maharajji offers his energy: "We are in a deep, deep sleep. We are all dead. We need somebody to put life into us. We need somebody to give us that eye with which we can see inside, we need somebody to give us that ear through which we have to hear, somebody to give us that living water by which we have to come back to life again, from death."[21] To the disciple's feeling of limitation and circumscription, he offers his all-pervasive presence.[22] All of these bounties can be shared by the disciple if he chooses to fuse his identity with that of the Master. He must strive for a psychological symbiosis which, the Master assures him, is vital for his rebirth and reemergence. As a poem by Kabir (which I heard often at Beas) puts it:

> When I was there, then the Master was absent,
> When the Master was there, then I was not,
> The lane of love is narrow,
> There is room only for one.

The striving for symbiosis with the Master is, of course, consistent with the Hindu view that solutions to problems are relational, with dyads and not monads being the basic units of problem resolution.[23]

A Satsangi's acceptance of the Master's offer and the transforming processes of idealization and identification that follow in its wake have been so far presented as a more or less abstract portrayal of what I believe is happening "inside" him. Turning to some aspects of concrete behavior, my most striking impression of the Satsangis I met was their relatively greater childlikeness that made for easier access to the emotional treasures of childhood. The spontaneity and trusting friendliness, cheerful acceptance and sunny optimism I encountered were charged with a compelling appeal. From the clinical viewpoint, however, I also felt that at least some of my interviewees seemed to be striving toward some kind of surrender of adulthood. By "surrender of adulthood" I do not mean the presence of childlike qualities enumerated above. These are precious attributes of human beings, of all ages. I am alluding here more to a hankering after absolute mental states free of ambiguity and contradiction in which the onerousness of responsibility is renounced together with the burdens of self-criticism and doubt. Concomitantly, the followers seemed to show an intolerance for what clinicians would consider the "more adult," integrated mental states that invariably contain a modicum of conflict and pain. The childlike state a Satsangi seeks to re-create is very much an ideal one, where questions of morality are simple: the father (Maharajji) is only loving and kind and does not have any of the attributes of the "bad father," who is liable to be absent, frustrating, punishing or rivalrous. Perhaps both the inner dynamics and the outer behavior can best be illustrated by reproducing, without distracting psychological asides or psychoanalytic exegeses, parts of a disciple's account of her days with Maharajji at Beas. Of the first meeting with Maharajji she writes:

"And then . . . then I saw the Master for the first time. He met me at the door and took both my hands in His. I looked upon His face, a kind, beautiful face, unlike any other. My throat constricted and I couldn't speak, but He looked into my eyes and said, 'I'm so glad you've come.' At that moment the world was mine! The love and the warmth and the power emanating from Him filled me with joy. . . . [Afterward] a short entry in my diary which reads: 'I have just met the Master. Ah, but the dream has finally come true. How wonderful and beautiful He is. Words cannot describe His glory. I wish now only to be alone and not think or work but just be happy. Is it really me?' "[24]

After a dinner for the "elite" Indian and foreign disciples at which the Master had been present, her account reads:

"It passed far too quickly for us all, and soon the Master was leaving. We followed him in a little band; it was just too difficult to say good-bye. When He heard us behind Him, He turned and started to smilingly protest. 'But it is on our way,' we chorused. The Master laughed: 'Just like little sheep you are,' He said. This entirely destroyed our attempts at seriousness about the matter. We broke into laughter, and it continued all the way to the Guest house entrance. I think we were laughing more from happiness and gratitude than anything else. I had the strong feeling that everyone in the group was very glad to be one of His little sheep."[25] Then comes the long-awaited personal encounter:

" 'Maharajji, do you know everything?' I asked him bluntly. It was my first private interview with the Master, and I had been sitting in His living room for about ten minutes. There was so much I wanted to say to Him. In fact, as is the experience common to many disciples, I wanted to burst into tears, to fall at His feet, to let out every problem inside all at once. . . . And again, as in that first interview, He gave me one of those very special looks, the kind of look that makes one feel that one is the Master's sole concern and that the Master knows each and every hidden nook and corner of one's being."[26]

These extracts happen to be from a book by a young American woman and thus by a "special" disciple. But the psychological state of discipleship they portray bears an unmistakable stamp of many mystical cults and seems to be independent of the follower's cultural background, language or socioeconomic status. Another young woman, a *dudhwali* (milk seller) from the small northern Indian town of Firozpur, confided in me: "Maharajji slapped me [in her meditation] some days ago because I put water into the milk I sold. He watched me for two days and on the third day he slapped me during *bhajan* [meditation]. It didn't hurt, though, for afterwards he lovingly stroked my cheek." Her brother, who was standing next to her, exclaimed, "How lucky you are that the Master touched you!" And then turning toward her he remarked, "This is why we Satsangis keep on becoming better. Because the Master can see everything we are doing or thinking! He can see through us. Our head is like glass and he knows everything that is going on there, even when we are far away from him."

I have attributed the uncritical eulogizing of the guru, the dependent worship of the Master's contrasting strength, wisdom and all the other components of hagiolatry, to the disciple's desperate need for idealization and identification with the Master. These processes, in turn, are the basis for the disciple's own healing transformation. Essentially, such is the raw material from which legends and tales that ascribe superhuman powers and miracles to mystics get manufactured. We have, however, still to explore the other side of the relationship: namely, what happens to the guru who is the recipient of such flattering projections? Normally, for most of us, malignant projections are easier to handle since they cause severe discomfort, compelling us to reject them by discriminating inside between what belongs to us and the alien attributes that have been projected onto us. This painful motivation for repelling the invasion of the self by others does not exist when the projections are narcissistically gratifying, as they invariably are in case of the adoring followers. To be consistently thought greater, more wonderful and more intelligent than we are is a burden only in the sense that we may feel impelled to be greater, more wonderful and more intelligent. And indeed there is many a guru, including the fictional one in R. K. Narayan's *The Guide*, who has become a guru because of the followers' ascription of gurulike qualities to him. Most often, however, the guru simply accepts these projections as belonging to his self and enters into an unconscious collusion with the followers—"I am uncannily sensitive, infinitely wise, miraculously powerful; *you* are not"—thus making the followers more stupid, more infantile and more powerless than they actually are. Such unconscious transactions in the relationship between the Master and the followers are a common occurrence in most mystical cults and were also conspicuous in the Radha Soami Satsang.

The Satsangi of course, if he is polite, will consider such psychological reflections on the transactions between the Master and the disciple and on the seeker's motivations, irrelevant to the purpose of the mystical enterprise. What psychoanalysts see as the "infantilization" of the seeker and his search for the ideal parent, the Satsangi will consider as part of the vital surrender to the Master that Maharajji and other gurus demand for a very good reason. It is a surrender to the divine in the Master, he would say, and the way of the infant is the only way to approach the divine; it is just too bad if this also happens to be the way parents are approached. Ontogeny is not necessarily a one-way street and spiritual growth may take a direction opposite to psychological development. Your critical tone, the Satsangi may continue, springs from the Hindu mystic's affront to your psychoanalytic preference for the model of an individual striving for autonomy and for an increase in the range of his choices in the face of all the inner and outer forces that impinge upon him. For the Hindu, however, boundaries are obstacles, the body a prison, autonomy a curse.[27] Gaining irreversible insights into the events of one's mental life is not the only way to "maturity," the Satsangi may further argue, for one *can* detach oneself from one's biography by following the mystical path. Such a detachment is not defensive but a "virtue"—particularly of middle age—which the mystical way and the guru can help you to cultivate. With this imaginary defense, we return to the original gulf between psychoanalysis and mysticism, though, I hope, with an improved understanding of what separates them.

6

TANTRA AND
TANTRIC HEALING

In the emerging global civilization that draws increasingly and eclectically from many different cultural sources as it begins to span the urban centers of the world, the rumor about tantra has reached most educated persons. The rumor is still vague; it is about the mysteries of Tibetan lamas and Indian yogis, about mandalas and goddesses of light and darkness, about meditations and esoteric rites that supposedly yield the practitioner uncanny, occult powers but can as easily drive him into the terrifying world and visions of schizophrenia. Many, who have a slightly greater knowledge of tantra and especially of its central sexual ritual, are tempted to dismiss it as a metaphysical justification for a protracted saturnalia. Yet tantra's attraction has never lain solely in its orgiastic aspects. As Edward Dimock has aptly remarked in his study of the Sahajiya cult, an offshoot of tantra, "One's lusts would have had to be very strong indeed, and one's frustrations very great, to carry him through the stringent and arduous, though interesting, training necessary before the sexual ritual was undertaken."[1] Tantra is indeed more than a series of yogic exercises applied to the sexual act, more than a *coitus reservatus par excellence,* and more than just a sad attempt to mechanize the mysteries of sexual love.[2]

Tantra's adherents, of course, claim that it is *the* modern path toward "enlightenment"; the word *modern* used in its Hindu sense for Kaliyuga, an era that started some three hundred thousand years ago. Setting aside the mystical-religious context within which tantra has so far received scholarly attention, my aim here is to focus on tantra more as a system of mental health and healing. As a healing system, tantra has two aspects. First, tantra, like psychoanalysis, proceeds from a philosophy of human nature which was (and is) as radical in the Indian context as were Freud's contributions in changing the concept of the person in the West. Tantra has defined specific mental and behavioral traits of the "healthy" (in its original sense of "whole") person; it has described the impediments in the way of this personal integration; and it has developed a series of mental exercises designed to lead to body-mind states which tantra considers as coming close to its vision of human potential. Tantra, however, also possesses a circumscribed healing system, a modest theory of the causes and relief of certain forms of mental distress.[3]

Tantra is said to have appeared in India at the beginning of this era. Assimilated, though uneasily, in all the great Indian religions, tantra had become a pan-Indian phenomenon by the sixth century and remains one to this day.[4] There are Hindu, Buddhist and Jain tantras, with many common features and some identical ritual practices. Though tantra has greatly influenced many spheres of Indian life, especially art, through its resurrection of the ancient, pre-Aryan "religions of the Mother," it has tended to exist as a set of more or less secret cults at the fringe of Indian society. This marginality even extends to the geographic concentration of practicing tantriks. Bengal, Assam, Kerala and Kashmir, where tantric practices and cults have historically flourished, are at the edges (today, even politically) of the Indian subcontinent. Reviled, disapproved or barely tolerated, tantra's relationship to the dominant religious orthodoxy has never been easy. It could hardly be otherwise, given the fact that tantriks have always flouted orthodox tradition and rejected conventional morality. Today, when Bhagwan Rajneesh offers his own particular brand of tantra to the thousands who flock to his Poona ashram, he is, in the best tantric tradition, also making fun of a scandalized Hindu establishment. As Agehananda Bharati has pointed out, the contemporary official Hindu culture, essentially formulated by Vivekananda, Gandhi and other "reformists," is decidedly antitantric and keeps tantra well outside the ken of permissible interest.[5]

Tantra has always provided a cultic home for many types of deviants from Hindu orthodoxy, as well as for those who, because of their lower caste or their sex, could not fully participate in the Brahminical system. Befitting its status as the cult of the Great Goddess and the Divine Female, tantra has welcomed women members; Yogeshwari, the tantric guru of one of India's greatest modern sages, Sri Ramakrishna, was a woman, and female teachers are not uncommon. I must, however, add that though tantra admits equality between men and women—the rituals and practices for female tantriks are the mirror image of those for males in the sense that (wherever it is required) Shiva is substituted for Shakti, a god is replaced by a goddess, a vulva is exchanged for a phallus—the texts invariably proceed from and reflect the viewpoint of male practitioners. As we shall see later, this is not solely a matter of stylistic conventions in a patriarchal society but may also reflect tantra's greater resonance for the male psyche and physiology in Indian culture.

Of the many Indian mystical-spiritual cults, tantra is perhaps the most congenial to a psychoanalyst. Partly, this may have to do with the low tastes of this particular analyst who, in his interpretations of Indian culture, prefers as his data the lusty folktale, the lewd wedding song, the legends surrounding a fearful goddess rather than the minutiae of a Vedic ritual—and who finds Puranic stories infinitely more exciting than Upanishadic metaphysics. But tantra's affinity to psychoanalysis extends beyond individual matters of taste to its antispeculative thrust and to its emphasis on increasing the individual's awareness of his mental life—with all its fantastic gods, ghosts, demons and the clamor of a hundred voices of human desire. This is not to say that tantriks do not believe in "liberation" *(mukti)* as the overall goal of their path or that they do not subscribe to the mystical axioms of transcendence of duality and the unity of "I" and the phenomenal world. The tantric goal of "liberation," however, is like the psychoanalytic ideal of "genitality," a speculative construct that does not unduly interfere with its vastly more important practice. Both in tantra and in psychoanalysis, this practice remains the discovery of psychic contents and structures and the possibilities of their transformation. I would agree with Bharati that in its unremitting preoccupation with psychic experimentation, to be carried out over many years under the guidance and with the help of a senior colleague, the most appropriate analogue to tantric training in the modern world is the training analysis that every intending psychoanalyst must go through before he is recognized as an "adept."[6]

Tantra's analogy to psychoanalysis goes beyond the common concern of both these disciplines and the similarities in their training methods. Both are commonly misunderstood in their respective cultural milieus. Just as opinions about psychoanalysis are often based on a more or less perfunctory knowledge of psychoanalytic literature, especially Freud's writings on metapsychology and theories of culture, neglecting the far more important question of what a psychoanalyst does, *i.e.*, the whole question of psychoanalytic technique and what actually happens in the analytic encounter, so too does the understanding of tantra commonly derive from an interpretation of its ambiguous texts without due reference to the details of its practice. It is only through a consideration of the practice of both disciplines that one becomes aware of their emancipative core; in the case of psychoanalysis, an "enlightenment" which is not only individual but also societal in nature[7] and, in the case of tantra, a "liberation" not only in the mystical sense but one which is also relevant to the individual's concrete, historical condition. Finally, like psychoanalysis, tantra is based upon a recognition, even a celebration, of man's sensuous nature.

In cautiously hinting at the parallels between psychoanalysis and tantra, I have no intention of reducing one to the other or glossing over their considerable differences. Psychoanalysis, whatever its later developments and the status accorded it in Western culture as a philosophy of human nature, did begin as an empirical psychotherapy promising freedom from particular pathological conditions; and tantra, whatever its empirical therapeutic content, does aim at a "mystical" freedom from *all* human conditions and predicaments. Critics, following the late Ananda Coomaraswamy, may then object that my treatment of tantra as an empirical psychotherapy is like expounding Taoism without Tao or Brahmavada without Brahma, and thus cannot be taken seriously as a scientific account of a traditional psychology.[8] Yet tantra, avowedly a system of psychic experimentation which has over the centuries successfully attracted so many people searching for salvation, must be based upon and deal with what evolution has created: human growth and development and the inevitable mental and physical pain encountered in this process. Tantra's analysis of human disease cannot (and, we shall see below, *does not*) substantially differ from similar analyses by psychoanalysis and other modern "depth" psychologies. Of course, the solutions tantra propounds to malformations of the human psyche and the resolutions it offers to human dilemmas are radically different from those offered by Western psychotherapies.

Leaving aside the experience of birth, of which we know next to nothing, most of the psychic pain we experience on the path toward becoming a person is occasioned by the two great (and inevitable) experiences of life—*separation* and *differentiation*.[9] Separation refers to the process extending through the first three years of life, a period which Freud called the "prehistoric" part of man's psychic story, when the infant Narcissus painfully separates his image out of a flux of primordial unity and sorts out a "me" from a "not-me" environment. Melanie Klein and her followers have illuminated (insofar as this dark space before language is born *can* be illuminated) the psychic turmoil of this period.[10] They have talked of the loss of the magical breast mother and the necessity of creating mental objects to compensate for this loss. They have described the anxieties associated with the primal separation, anxieties that hover darkly in a threat of annihilation and disintegration. As adults we sense these primal menaces dimly, if at all, though they are deeply embedded in the substratum of our psyche and lie at the core of our personal identity.

The second major traumatic experience is the acquisition of a gender identity which follows the dawning awareness that human beings are differentiated into two sexes. The process begins with children of each sex feeling a sense of mystery—and developing an anxiety—about genital differences. Perhaps the mystery is greater in relation to the hidden female genitals; a phallus is dangerous but not mysterious. Masculine anxiety about sexual difference may be accentuated in cultures where there are restrictions, as there are both in India and in the West, on a boy's free exploration of female bodies which, in turn, are based upon and magnify the ancient fears of female genitalia and generativity.

Freud, of course, was the first one to uncover the traumas caused by the difference between the sexes. His descriptions of the mortification of little Oedipus, the symbolic structures around the Oedipus complex and castration anxiety, the child's relinquishment of aggressive and erotic incestuous wishes, are the stuff of classical psychoanalysis which have given it its popular reputation as a primarily sexual psychology.

Tantra's image as a sexual pneumatology also stems from its recognition of sexual difference as a major problem of human life. Tantra claims that a person can become "whole" (and, in the extended, mystical sense, "liberated") only when he annuls sexual differentiation and dissolves his gender identity into a certain kind of bisexuality. The realization of both masculinity and femininity within the tantrik's own body, the experience of a constant, doubled joy of "two-in-one," the re-creation of a primordial androgyny, looms large as the goal of a bulk of tantrik practices. This is indeed a radical and, many psychoanalysts would say, regressive solution to the traumas of sexual difference. Nevertheless, the implications of this desired androgyny as the core of the "whole" person, which forms the cornerstone of the tantric system, need to be discussed in some detail.

I am aware that the notion of *divine* bisexuality is not a tantric peculiarity but is also met with in other cultural traditions. It is present in the Chinese concept of Yin and Yang, in the gnostic syzygies but also, as Coomaraswamy has pointed out, in the Christian form of transmitted revelation.[11] Yet the tantriks I interviewed did not speak of biunity in the symbolic, religious sense characteristic of other traditions, but as a concrete phenomenon and a personally attainable goal. When tantric texts represent this experience as a sexual embrace, and when Ramakrishna, in his tantric phase, describes it as if each pore of the skin were a vulva and intercourse were taking place over the whole body, they are not merely using a sexual metaphor. The tantric language of sexuality which also pervades its mythology and cosmology is both concrete and symbolic at the same time; God and penis, coitus and enlightenment, are interchangeable, making tantric texts difficult to decipher and virtually untranslatable.[12] In my own conversations with tantriks, I sometimes had the impression that they deliberately (and mischievously) used the multivalence of tantric terminology to befuddle the perhaps too-earnest outsider. Whenever the term *ananda* came up in a text —and *ananda* comes up often, since it is the name of the state in which every tantrik must aspire to live perpetually—and I translated it as "supreme bliss," I was told to forget all the mystical balderdash since *ananda* was the pure and simple pleasure of intercourse. If I took the concrete meaning—which, incidentally, can also change to signify other pleasures such as that of drinking wine and, on occasion, is the name for wine itself—then I was invariably chided for my literal-mindedness since the word in that particular context just happened to stand for "enlightenment."

For the male tantrik, apprehending and experiencing the nature of femininity (it is the opposite with female tantriks) form a major part of the tantric practice. The process may begin with simpler forms of understanding the mystery of sexual difference. Here is how a tantrik recollects the first conversation with his guru on the subject.

"I was sixteen at the time and acquiring the secrets of the svadhisthan *chakra** when my guru once asked me:

" 'Can you tell me under what circumstances you get an erection?'

" 'Guru, I don't know. But I often have an erection.'

" 'When you get an erection, what do you feel about it?'

" 'Well, I feel pleasure but I am also uncomfortable.'

" 'What do you do when you get the erection?'

" 'Sometimes I go to the bathroom, run a hand over it till sperm is released and then I feel good.'

" 'Yes, that's fine. This is one way of doing it. But this shouldn't last. Would you like to use your hand for ever?'

" 'No, what I'd like to do is find a woman, put my erection in her and drive as hard as possible.'

" 'What do you think the woman thinks about that?'

" 'I don't understand what you mean.'

" 'Well, she is not dead, is she? Would you have intercourse with a corpse?'

" 'No.'

" 'Then she must somehow participate in it. She must have something for it, mustn't she? Why should she do it? What is it that you are giving her?'

" 'Guru, what do you mean by this giving? I just want to find a hole and jab.'

" 'Why should the woman enjoy your jab? What does she get and what happens to her? The moment you give me a good answer I'll get you a woman.'

"He then gave me a mantra to help me meditate over the ques-

---

*The second of the six (or seven) "centers of consciousness" which are located along the central axis (the cerebrospinal cord) of the tantric "subtle" body; in other words, the *chakra* is an element of the tantric model of the psyche.

tion. I came to him after a few days, after having thought over our previous conversation and meditated with the mantra he had given me.

" 'Guru, I think what a woman wants is to fill a vacant spot.'

" 'Correct. That is one of the right answers. Most women suffer because they have an empty space which a man fills with the penis. You fulfill a lack in her. Similarly, your penis is incomplete without the vagina. In the act of union, both of you become complete. Do you want a woman?'

" 'Not immediately.' "

From simpler forms of understanding, the young neophyte progresses through a series of graded *sadhanas* (lit. "methods"), which can be best described as a combinations of guided imaginative activity, meditative routines and ritual performances. Although a *sadhana* may incorporate meditation procedures and bodily "exercises" from other yogas, the chief tantric techniques involved in a *sadhana*, which we shall discuss later in some detail, are: (a) a sequence of *sound* units (mantra); (b) patterned *gestures (mudra)* and; (c) visual *imagery*, which includes the full range of tantric iconography *(pratima)* as well as the use of "mystical" diagrams *(yantra*, mandala and *prastara)*.

Looking at tantric practice, it seems to me that knowledge through devotional worship, rational understanding and a "direct" knowledge through identification are the chief modes of understanding which are aspired for in a tantric *sadhana*, with identification holding the pride of place. The attempted identification with Woman in tantra refers to a psychological process where the adept attempts to assimilate a particular feminine aspect, in order to be transformed, wholly or partially, after the feminine model. Most often, the feminine model is provided by the tantrik's personal goddess *(ishtadevi)*, assigned to him by the guru as his particular divine consort—a femininity of his own.

Identification with female sexual experience seems to be the primary aim of one set of *sadhana*. For instance, one of my informants belonging to the Kali-kula tradition described a *sadhana* where the adept, after a period of preliminary training, strives to experience the sensations *inside* his penis during ritual coitus since it is postulated that the inside of the penis corresponds to the vagina and the sensations experienced here will be those of a woman.

The attempted understanding and identification with the Feminine extend beyond female sexual experience to other aspects of femininity. As Herbert Guenther in his study of Buddhist tantrism states it, "The man may experience his femininity through all female members of his family, leading to a multiplicity of projective images."[13] In the typical fashion of tantric texts, this "knowing" of the female experience of motherhood, sisterhood and daughterhood is expressed in frank sexual imagery. Thus the *Guhyasamaja-tantra*, an early (fourth-century) Buddhist text, says: "The adept who has sexual intercourse with his mother, his sister, and his daughter, goes toward highest perfection, which is the essence of Mahayana."[14]

In practice, in most tantric schools with which I am familiar, the "conquest" of the incest taboo involved in "knowing" the mother, sister and daughter takes place with the help of one's wife. It is the wife (referred to as the *shakti* [power or energy] by most tantriks) who, with the help of certain *sadhanas*, is sought to be transformed into the mother, sister or daughter during ritual intercourse. When tantriks attribute the attainment of singular powers to a successful practice of the particular *sadhanas* that "break" the incest taboo, we are once again reminded of the fact that the problem of sexual difference lies squarely in the middle of tantric theory and practice. As post-Freudians, we know that the child's unconscious incestuous fantasies, consequent to the momentous discovery of gender identity, provoke major anxieties which the child's immature ego copes with by building defensive structures in the psyche. Tantric practice, not unlike psychoanalysis, seeks to resurrect the elemental fantasies around incest, together with their associated anxiety, in order to find a new resolution for an old yet nagging dilemma of human development. Of course, the tantric resolution, unlike that of psychoanalysis, where one strives for a final renunciation of the incestuous fantasy, aims at its anxiety-free reenactment and symbolic fulfillment. The "power" acquired by the tantrik is then another name for the feeling of expansiveness which follows the reduction of anxiety and which has its source in the release of psychic energy that was bound in maintaining inappropriate defensive structures.

In his effort to penetrate to the core of femininity and comprehend its manifoldness, a tantrik is expected to ignore all the externals of a woman's age, appearance or social class. "He must not," a text says, "despise a woman even if all her limbs are attacked by leprosy.

Regardless of what standing she is, he may adore any woman when she is in possession of the Vajra."[15] Different schools (*kulas*) may emphasize different aspects of femaleness which the adept belonging to that tradition learns to experience and to identify with. In the Kali-kula tradition mentioned above, the feminine aspects that are accentuated above all others are (in the words of an informant): "Woman as something who gave you birth and nourished you, woman as something who loved you and woman as something who will devour you at the end."[16] Ramakrishna was very much within this tradition when he "created" the following vision through tantric *sadhana*: " . . . he saw a female figure of great beauty arise from the Ganga [Ganges] and approach the Panchavati with dignified gait. She was far advanced in pregnancy, and soon gave birth to a beautiful baby, which she nursed with great affection. But the next moment he saw that the woman had assumed a very cruel and terrible appearance, and was actually devouring the baby; she then re-entered the waters of the river."[17]

Before considering the question of a modern psychologist's attitude to the tantric quest for androgyny one must first specify the psychologist's theoretical leaning. The Jungian, of course, will find himself at home in the world of tantric discourse. Tantric practices, he might argue, clearly aim at making conscious the inherited, collective image of Woman which exists in every man's unconscious and through which he "knows" Woman. This preformed image—the anima—has both a pure and noble side and a dark side. The former is represented in the "ten great knowledges" (*mahavidya*) of tantra by such goddesses of light and liberation as Tara and Kamala. Anima also has a dark face which is unveiled by other goddesses, for example, Dhumavati, Matangi and Bagla. The tantric *sadhana* tries to attract the relevant psychic experience to each of these goddess images till it forms a strong enough complex to emerge into consciousness as a created (and creative) "vision." Many may be uneasy, as I am, with notions such as "inherited, collective image of Woman" existing "preformed" in the unconscious. One may suspect, as I do, the operation of life-historical factors rather than of archetypes, when one reads that Ramakrishna, in the course of his tantric practice, had an unexpected, "hideous vision of a middle-aged prostitute, seated with her back to him, from whose large hips issued a mound of filth."[18]

In any event, if we attach importance to human infancy and life history in the formation of personal strivings and goals, then we must turn to a Freudian for a psychoanalytic perspective. By Freudian, I do not mean the crusty clinician who will summarily dismiss the whole realm of tantra as a collective perversion, but rather someone who will be sensitive to the developmental aspects of bisexuality and to its cultural variations. For even with our present, insufficient knowledge of the beginnings of gender identity and the development of masculinity in men and femininity in women, I am convinced that the tantric striving for androgyny can be discussed without either falling into the trap of psychopathological labeling and reductionism on the one hand, or of cultural apologetics and a thoroughgoing relativism on the other.

Psychoanalysts who have explored their patients' fantasies of being both sexes and possessing both male and female genitals agree on the universal occurrence of this fantasy in young children.[19] We also know that the infant boy does not start off life as a psychological male, with his mother as his first heterosexual love object, as postulated by Freud, but goes through an even earlier phase in which he is "merged" with his mother.[20] In this early, "symbiotic" period of human development, the boy has yet to distinguish his body and psyche from the female body and the feminine psyche of his mother; he still has to separate himself from her before he can begin the process of becoming masculine. Masculinity in men, as Robert Stoller has remarked, is not a naturally occurring state; it is not a given; some rudiment of femininity is there from the start.[21] In every man, therefore, there remain traces of the early merger with the mother, a "primary identification" with her femaleness and femininity and thus a minimum, irreducible tendency toward bisexuality.

If our self-image is composed of many facets, both conscious and unconscious, then we also have an early female aspect which is not only feminine in tone but which includes the presence of breasts and vagina. The early self-image disappears—not in the sense of vanishing but in the sense of lying quiescent and buried in psychic depths —once the core masculine identity is formed. The process of acquiring masculinity which follows an identification with the father and other males also involves giving up the fantasy of being both sexes and accepting the fact that one can only be one sex. The acceptance of this limitation, like all the other limitations experienced by the child in his mental development from a state of undifferentiation to a state of greater differentiation, evokes a sense of loss at the giving up of the fantasy of omnipotence—at the imposing of limits and the drawing of boundaries.

How blissful the early experience of oneness with the mother has been for a boy and how magnetic the pull of his feminine aspect remains in the psyche, forever drawing him back in a longing to repeat the experience, depends upon the vicissitudes of an individual mother-son dyad and also varies across cultures. I have discussed elsewhere that in India, because of a host of social and cultural factors, the mother-and-son connection is both longer and more intense than in many other societies.[22] For many years and many hours a day, the infant is surrounded by the pleasures of the mother's all-giving body while she attempts to maintain a close physical and psychic contact. Fueled by the long blissful closeness with the mother, the female aspect of the son's self-image gains great strength. It must be remembered that we are speaking here of unconflicted and nondefensive aspects of the mother-son bond. Normally, since the mother does not restrain the child from exploring the outside world and encourages the growth of his ego functions, the Indian boy's greater propensity to merge with his mother has little to do with psychotic fusion, a state where there is a lack of differentiation between the self and the nonself. The infant son is indeed helped to define all borders between the self and the outside world save one—the border between the self and the mother.

In men in whom the original experience with the mother was pervaded by an underlying maternal hostility, the inner femininity takes on a malevolent visage. Masculinity acquires an exaggerated importance. Constituting the only bulwark against the threat of being overwhelmed by a dangerous femininity, the penis seems both infinitely precious and fragile. As an adult, defensive, neurotic maneuvers are instituted to shore up the male self-image and to keep the female aspect of the self from gaining control of the personality and of vital ego functions. Many such men cannot live lovingly with a woman over long periods of time; often, they cannot trust her with the endangered penis and must get up and move away quickly after intercourse. The intensity and duration of the mother-son bond in

India ensure that just as there will be many men in search of the early bliss, and thus open to their femininity, there will also be others for whom the experience contained more distress than pleasure and who need to cling fiercely to their sense of masculinity. In other words, the issue of inner femaleness, desired or desperately defended against, is much more emotionally charged in the Indian context, where it remains one of the chief issues of human development. Tantra then provides both a focus and a "laboratory" for dealing with these preoccupations. Indeed, as in many other spheres of human fantasy, what in the West is repressed and relegated to the unconscious finds a cultic home in India, where it can be consciously engaged with and ritually acted out. Here we may add that since the same tendency for merging with the mother in a woman need not be a threat to her gender identity (in fact, it augments and sustains her femininity), we are in a better position to understand why tantric texts seem to be addressed exclusively to men.

I am suggesting here that the tantric desire for androgyny, the promise to the adept that he can retain his masculinity and yet recapture the *ananda* of his early femininity, has a special meaning in the Indian cultural context. Tantric practices aiming at an identification with the *mother* goddess, of course, try to ensure that the practitioner is not passively swept away by waves of inner femininity, with all the attendant threats to his gender identity. The *sadhana* attempts a gradual, step-by-step, controlled and, above all, an *active* integration of the feminine in the psyche.

We should note that tantriks do not deny their maleness (indeed, they esteem it highly) but simply insist on "realizing" the unconscious female aspect of their self-image. Nevertheless, for the Freudian psychoanalyst, the tantric wish to be both male and female and the belief that this wish is in fact realizable points to early fantasies of omnipotence and of complete gratification as well as the childish denial of limits to human possibilities. Tantriks, on the other hand, would claim that a psychic bisexuality—the resurrection of the early feminine aspect of the self, as psychoanalysts would put it—is indeed possible and even desirable for the experience of "wholeness." Such a bisexuality, they would continue, fits well with the Indian context, where there are also many nontantriks who subscribe to the doctrine of "wholeness" through psychic androgyny. These sympathizers, while recognizing the radical nature of tantric practice, maintain that this particular tantric goal for a person is not very different from the aims of other Indian religious traditions.[23] Buddhism, Vedanta and devotional theism, for instance, also seek to overcome a sexual consciousness and to establish a nonsexual identity at the individual's deepest core. From this particular viewpoint, the tantric striving for androgyny is a concrete form of an abstract religious ideal. Because of its "normality" in the Indian setting, it does not require any particular psychological elaboration or causal explanation. The tracing of a phenomenon to its roots is necessary only for manifest absurdities and self-evident falsehoods; a psychological exegesis is then required for illness but not health.[24]

Cultures, it seems, differ with regard to which of the major universal human concerns they pick and choose to highlight. Androgyny, and thus the son's encounter with the mother's femaleness and his own femininity, is highlighted in India, just as, perhaps, "Oedipality," where sons and fathers encounter each other in conflict, has been the chosen theme of modern Western cultures. The classical Oedipal complex, which has received a great deal of Western literary attention as well as exquisite psychological analysis by Freud, is not the major "nuclear" complex in the Indian setting. The father-son encounter in India tends to be overshadowed by the earlier confluence of mother and son and the pressing needs it has generated in the latter. Let me illustrate this through two clinical vignettes:

M. was a twenty-six-year-old engineer who had come for analysis because of a general loss of interest in work, inability to relate to people and suicidal thoughts. He was the eldest son of his parents and had spent the first three years of his life with his mother at the home of his maternal grandparents who were farmers in a village in Uttar Pradesh. When he was four years old M., together with his mother, moved to a different village, where his father was a policeman. M.'s first memories of his father were of a harsh and authoritarian man who had broken the blissful intimacy between mother and son but who, luckily, was rarely at home. As the analysis progressed, M.'s memories and feelings about his early childhood years began to change. He discovered that under the overt hostility against the father, there were considerable feelings of affection and admiration.

At the same time, the mother's image began changing from a loving mother absorbed in her son's welfare to an overpowering mother who clung to her son and belittled his efforts at becoming an individual separate from her. M.'s resentment against the father, he discovered, had less to do with the so-called Oedipal rage and more with the fact that the father was so often away and did not provide the son any emotional access to him. Once, after his marriage, when M.'s earlier feelings of helplessness in the face of an overpowering femininity had been activated again, he had the following dream:

"I am in our village home when a gang of dacoits led by a girl attacks our house. The female leader of the band chases me through the rooms of the house. I pass my father in the hall. He is lying on the bed with a gun but it is not effective and he cannot help me though he wants to. I am very frightened as the girl bandit runs after me, laughing and mocking me for not being able to defend myself."

Another, borderline patient with severe identity problems, who was struggling with his very ambivalent feelings toward his mother, with whom he had a "symbiotic" relationship till late into childhood, dreamed:

"I am lying on my bed when I see my mother approaching. She is almost naked and has a laughing, gloating expression on her face. I am very scared. Then I see you [the analyst] sitting in a corner of the room with an enormous penis next to your chair which is rising from the floor and going up to the ceiling. I hold the penis and feel safe."

Clinical fragments of course do not "prove" anything, but they can be illustrative—in this case of the thesis that the son's struggle with the overwhelming mother and her femininity is a major theme in Indian psyche and culture. The son's need for the father to help him get out of this primary danger, *i.e.*, the necessity of Oedipal alliance, outweighs the hostilities of the Oedipal complex.

Turning from individual case histories to the wider culture, we find that androgyny, the attempt to deal with a pervasive desire and an equally ubiquitous (male) human anxiety, is not restricted to tantra—though tantrism takes it as its central concern—but has been an important theme in Indian cultural tradition. Wendy O'Flaherty has insightfully commented on a number of Hindu myths and on many examples of Indian art in which androgyny is the central theme.[25] In the Vedic period, Indra, the king of gods, is an alternating androgyne, a man among men and a woman among women, as well as a simultaneous androgyne when, as a result of a curse, he is marked by a thousand vulvas. In the early Puranic texts Prajapati, the Lord of Creation, is depicted as a primeval androgyne who broke apart because of its desire to create. And, of course, Shiva is the supreme Indian androgyne. Both as *ardha-narishwara* ("half-man, half-woman") and in his iconic representation as the phallic *linga* that is always accompanied by the *yoni*, the symbol of the sexual organ of the goddess, the origins of Shiva's androgyny are detailed in a number of myths in the later Puranas. His androgyny is praised and satirized in Sanskrit court poetry, and visually represented in many artistic traditions ranging from Chola bronzes to the folk paintings of the women artists of Madhubani. As O'Flaherty remarks, "The Hindu myths assume that a man can be a woman; there is no problem about it at all."[26]

Sexual difference is one major hindrance to living in *ananda*. In the tantric scheme, the second major hurdle lies in the way we are accustomed to approach and interact with the outside world. The normal (and according to tantriks wrong) body-mind state in which the "average expectable person" (to vary Heinz Hartman's well-known phrase) lives is fueled by desire and constantly acts upon the environment with the intention of changing it and bringing the world in line with the desire. The tantrik view of the "healthy person" is radically different, yet not a simple reversal of man as desiring actor. The healthy personality in tantra is neither passive nor desireless; it has only redefined the terms of the struggle between desire and a world which is often unable or unwilling to gratify it.

Here, let me reproduce extracts from a series of interview with A., a Bengali economist in his early forties, who belongs to a family who have been tantriks for three generations and who has been a practicing tantrik himself for over twenty years.

"The true tantrik is always in a state of nonsuppression and enjoyment. The purpose of every moment of life is to experience *ananda*. *Ananda* is active enjoyment of everything that comes your way. If there is a heat wave, I will not try to make it less by using a fan or an air conditioner. Nor will I try to put up with the heat by turning my mind away and bearing it in the manner of the Stoics.

The true tantrik puts himself, or rather *is*, in a body-mind state where he *enjoys* the heat . . . as he will enjoy the cold. Ideally, a tantrik is in such a state of attunement with his environment, with what is possible, that his desire awakens just at the moment when the environment is willing to grant it. If a woman desires him, his desire for her is there; if food awaits him, his appetite is keen. A tantrik has only those desires which the environment is ready, willing and in a position to satisfy. This is not because he denies any of his wishes or rationalizes them later, but because he has developed his capacity for attention and is intensely aware of where he is and what he is doing at every single moment of time. For example, in my own case (and I am not yet a very advanced student), I can tell you that I have the appropriate desire for whatever food is put before me. If it is fish, I discover with pleasure that fish was exactly what I wanted; if it is meat, I cannot imagine it could have been anything else. So every day I eat exactly the meal I want to."

How does this square with the widespread Indian belief that a tantrik has "occult powers," that he can command the elements, bend any man to his will and possess every woman he desires? I ask.

"These are ridiculous statements. The truth is exactly the opposite. Partly, such statements arise from a misunderstanding of tantrik texts. For instance, let us look at this passage"—here A. read out from the *Panchastavi*, a ninth-century tantric text from Kashmir, which I have been trying to understand with his help—" 'Lovely women, tormented by the fires of *kama*, with eyes like those of frightened young deer, in every way succumb to the fascination of those men of concentrated minds, O Goddess, who even for a moment meditate on Thy lustre (of crimson hue) covering the sky with clouds of vermilion dust and submerging the earth in folds of molten lac.'[27]

"There are many similar passages scattered throughout tantric literature; they depict women running after a tantrik be he ever so hideous. If we understand this specific passage as a description of objective reality, of what happens when a tantrik concentrates on a particular goddess, then those sentences seem ridiculous, a child's fantasy of omnipotence. But remember, we must read tantric texts as accounts of certain subjective states and not of objective situations. The text simply describes what happens when a tantrik concentrates on, or rather *attends* to, the realm of sexuality. Let me explain this passage.

"In tantric iconography a crimson or vermilion goddess represents woman as a sexual partner. A goddess of crimson hue and 'molten lac' will, for instance, never have the big, heavy breasts characteristic of a blue-colored goddess who is woman-as-mother; the crimson goddess is desirable in the classical Indian, *padmini* form. By learning to pay attention to sexuality, the adept will become very finely attuned to sexual desire in the environment. His own desire will be ready the moment a woman desires him. Subjectively, it would appear that every time he desires, his desire is fulfilled. In fact, in his state of nonsuppression and attunement, a real tantrik becomes aware a little earlier than others when a storm is due or a heat wave is coming so as to be prepared to enjoy them. Similarly, if he pays attention, he can become aware of a woman's desire for him even before she has recognized it in herself.

"What the passage then expresses in a crude way is not a wish for omnipotence. It is describing a state of attunement in which one is exquisitely aware of the desire potentials existing in the environment. There is no question of forcing your desire on the world through magical means: that is both childish and impossible."

The explanation is ingenuous, but the tantrik belief in occult "powers" is widespread and cannot be dismissed as mere descriptions of subjective states.

"Tantra recognizes three chief causes for not being in a state of nonsuppression and attunement: impossible desires, trying to get *ananda* wrongly (primarily because of incorrect perception or false use of language) and, finally, undigested karma. Much of tantric training is designed to surmount these causes. There is a traditional list of one hundred and eight impossible desires, which is not exhaustive but only indicative. "My son will always obey me"; "my wife will remain faithful but I will not," are a couple of examples of impossible desires. Impossible desires may be implanted in you by your environment, by your parents for instance. That is why the guru says, 'Put your parents in the funeral pyre and burn them.'

"As for trying to get *ananda* wrongly, tantra claims that sensory inputs do not betray you; you go astray by wrongly interpreting them; for instance, if a woman blushes and you interpret the blush to mean that she is in love with you. Tantriks are also taught to be very precise in their language, especially before children. When I say 'we must do something,' my son will always ask which 'we' do I mean. My own *guru* even discouraged the use of metaphors, claiming that they mislead by making a part of reality seem like the whole.

"Undigested karma is, of course, the tantrik's greatest enemy; undigested karma is bad karma, or rather it is the other way around and this is important to remember. Actions, thoughts, feelings, that constitute karma cannot be good or bad; they can only be digested or undigested. I am not speaking of the undigested karma of previous life; that has already determined which parents you choose, their temperaments, social class, as well as your own constitutional endowment and so on. It may happen that the undigested karma of a previous life has given you such a deficient body-mind scheme— afflicted you with a grave constitutional lack or a congenital disease, for instance—that nothing can be done; you can only live out your life and die. When I talk of undigested karma, I am talking of those people who start life with a reasonable body-mind state and a tolerable environment and who have to digest the karma they produce in this life. To give an example: when I was ten, I had a good-looking teacher and I imagined myself being married to her. I thought this was very bad and promptly "forgot" about it. This was a piece of undigested karma. In the state of full selfhood, we may avoid karma that disturbs us but we do not pretend that it never happened. Can you imagine the great task of digesting all the karma we have 'forgotten'?"

Before I come to the major tantric techniques that are employed to usher in the mental state for which A. has used such words as "concentration," "paying attention" and "attunement," I should mention that tantric texts prescribe different ways or rather sets of practices (*acharas*) for different classes of aspirants. The assignment of an individual into one or another class is based on his "disposition" or "character" (*bhava*). The three major dispositions described in the texts are the godlike (*divya*), the heroic (*vira*) and the animal-like (*pashu*). Roughly speaking, this threefold classification corresponds to the gnostic distinction between the spiritual, psychic and material man or the *sattvik, rajasik* and *tamasik* temperaments of traditional Hindu psychology, which have become well known through the Bhagavad-Gita.

Tantric texts do not agree upon the precise meaning of these dispositions. Most of them use the classification in an evaluative, judgmental fashion: the godlike type is then superior, the heroic type is mediocre and the animallike is positively objectionable.[28] Consequently, of the seven types of tantric practice identified in the texts —*vedachara, vaishnavachara, shaivachara, dakshinachara, vamachara, siddhanthachara* and *kulachara*—the first four are meant for the animallike, and are inferior to the next two, which are the paths for the heroic man, while the highest form of tantric practice— *kulachara*—can only be undertaken by the godlike man.[29] Other texts, such as the *Kalivilas-tantra,* see the personality dispositions in relatively value-free terms: "Listen to the three dispositions, O Devi! They are classified as the divine *(divyabhava),* the heroic *(virbhava),* and the animal-like *(pashubhava).* The first is god-like, the second is intensely exciting, the third is always pure and shining white."[30] A.'s interpretation of the dispositions is more in line with the above distinction. "The animallike man," he says, "is the kind of man who primarily reacts and reacts instinctively. Abused, he abuses back; when hit, he hits back. A man whose balls have been crushed by the environment cannot act like a *pashu.* For him it is important to learn to be a *pashu.* To know what is instinctive in oneself and to react instinctively are the hallmarks of a *pashu.* He who learns this perfectly becomes *pashupati* [Lord of the *pashu*], which is another name for Shiva himself.

"The hero has gone beyond the *pashu* stage in the sense that he does not have such maladaptive instinctive reactions as running around in circles in a panic. To be heroic is to feel, 'I do not have to meet my environment merely reactively but can also act on it and change it.'

"The godlike [*divya*], of course, is nearer the tantric ideal since he goes beyond the *pashu*'s reactivity and the *vira*'s activity, toward an attunement with his environment."

The whole discussion of the various types of dispositions, and the sets of practices suitable for each, seems academic if we look at modern tantric practice and/or if we heed the warning of some tantric texts (such as the *Kubjika-tantra*), which claim that in the modern age of Kaliyuga the animallike and godlike dispositions are rarely to be found and that tantric practice must be solely tailored to the needs of the heroic type.[31] Indeed, modern-day tantrism chiefly distinguishes between two sets of practices: the "right-handed" way *(dakshinachara)* and the "left-handed" way *(vama-chara)*. On the basis of the texts, Bharati differentiates between these two ways mainly in the manner in which each approaches the well-known sexual ritual.[32] In the left-handed way, where the female partner sits to the left of the adept, the ingredients employed in this particular ritual—meat, fish, wine, etc.—are physically used and actual intercourse with the female partner takes place. In the right-handed way, where the female partner sits on the right, either the ingredients are meditated upon or innocuous substitutes are used. The actual sexual intercourse is also replaced by a mental act. Bharati also mentions a third way, *kulachara* (the practice of a tantric in-group) which seems "to unite and transcend both the right- and left-handed traditions in a sort of dialectical synthesis."[33]

One of my informants, who belongs to a *kula*, elaborates further on these divisions. All *kulas*, he says, belong to the right-handed way. In the sexual ritual, as performed by his particular group, meat, fish and wine and other intoxicants are physically used but the female partner is invariably one's wife, who is also a tantrik. He character-izes left-handed tantriks as radical. They (the *vamacharis*) believe that tantric goals can be reached in as short a time span as three years —in contrast to the twenty to twenty-five years of practice which his own tradition regards as a reasonable period for reaching the highest degree of adeptness. The left-handed practice also breaks most of the rules that govern his own right-handed tradition, espe-cially the rule permitting ritual sexual intercourse only with one's wife.

Tantric Techniques

Irrespective of the path a tantrik chooses or—in case of a *kula*—is born into, the use of mantra in tantric *sadhana* is common to all traditions. Mantra is so central to tantrism that tantriks are often called mantriks and tantra itself is seen as synonymous with mantra-*shastra*—the science of mantra. Since my aim here is a psychological account of tantrism and particularly of its psychotherapeutic aspect, I will not go into the formal, ritual and metaphysical aspects of mantra which have been comprehensively discussed by other scholars.[34]

In popular Hindu culture, a mantra is considered a sacred yet magical formula, whose rhythmical repetition *(japa)* can fulfill many desired purposes. Mantras, it is held, aid a person to ward off evil spirits, propitiate wrathful gods and goddesses and help in the acquisition of religious merit. They are also believed to encourage friendly supernatural powers to intercede on the mantra user's behalf in the more mundane matters: for instance, in ensuring the favorable outcome of a court case, the birth of a son rather than a daughter, the spiting of an enemy, the acquisition of wealth that does not have to be worked for and other such desirable matters. In tantric practice, the use of mantra is more sophisticated. Mantra *japa* (silent or otherwise) holds a preeminent position in realization of the tantric goals of establishing the adept's identity with a goddess and in helping the tantrik to "concentrate" and enter a desired psychic state.

Essentially, a mantra is a sequence of sound units or *sphotas* (Bharati calls them morphemes)[35] with a characteristic pronunciation and intonation which the disciple normally learns from the guru. The major constituent of a mantra is a combination of *bijas* (seeds). A *bija* is a syllable without apparent meaning yet possesses the greatest significance for the initiate. To me, *bijas* appear to be aural symbols for certain forms of inner psychological experience ranging from simple sensations to more complex emotional states. Thus the *bija* "Am" is connected to the sensation of starting, being ready to begin, genesis; "Ram" is connected to burning; "Ham" is connected with the blowing of wind and the sensation of being carried up, whirled away and so on. Other, complex *bijas* symbolize particular emotional states: for instance "Klim" is regarded as the *bija* of erotic desire, "Aim" of wonder, and "Sauh" of fulfillment or "of what the infant vocalizes when he is replete with milk."

My tantrik informants (as well as the texts) insisted that the connection between a *bija* and its corresponding psychic state was not merely symbolic. A *bija* intonated properly and repeated according to instructions, they maintained, produced certain vibrations *(spanda)* which, acting through an unknown physiological process, created characteristic emotional states. In other words, each psychic state has a corresponding sound pattern and the activation of this sound pattern can evoke the particular psychic state. My own suggestion that the association between a *bija* and a psychic state was established by the awesome authority of the guru, supported by the belief and fervor of fellow disciples, reinforced by the cultural network of tantric tradition and lore and enhanced by the hypnotic effect exercised by repetitive chanting, did not find much favor with my discussion partners.

Besides the crucial *bija*, a mantra may have other elements. First, there may be an opening syllable which will be either Aum (signifying that the mantra is aimed at a peaceful state), Kraum (signifying that the psychic state aimed at is one of "active struggle") or Vam (signifying that the psychic state aimed at is of "expanded awareness"). Second, there may be names of particular gods or goddesses who symbolically correspond to the state or experience aimed at. Third, there may be ordinary words interpolated to amplify, interpret or direct the mantra. Finally, there may be a concluding syllable showing the intention of the mantra. If it is Hum, it means that the psychic state/experience is to become a part of the adept's consciousness. If it is Phat (spoken out with a kind of staccato disdain), it means the psychological experience is to be split up into its components, analyzed and deprived of its emotional power. If it is Svaha, then the psychic state, after being experienced, is to be returned to the unconscious realm. If a *bija* is a sound symbol, then a mantra can be called an autohypnotic shorthand for a psychological experience. The probability that an adept can enter into a desired psychic state by the repetition of a mantra is increased by the fact that mantra *japa* is not performed in isolation but often together with a contemplation of the corresponding visual symbols. Each mantra has its accompanying image, which is simultaneously visualized. Both the inner ear and the inner eye are directed toward the same psychic state and, in many *sadhanas*, the suggestive power of the aural and visual symbolism is further reinforced by the use of corresponding gestures or postures *(mudra)*.

In the preliminary phases of tantric training, the neophyte uses mantra to prepare himself for ordinary actions of day-to-day life such as studying, listening to music or making love. The beginner's aim is to learn to concentrate with the aid of the mantra and to make himself fully receptive for the experience that awaits him. To listen to music, for instance, he will follow a sequence where he recites "Vam" x number of times, followed by "Aim" y number of times, and then repeats "Aim-Vam" together. The tantriks say that this clears the listener's inner ear and prepares his mind to enjoy the music and therefore such mantras are purificatory. As the student progresses, purificatory mantras are no longer needed since their operation has been internalized and does not require conscious effort. Used in this way, the mantra acts as a ritual which raises the emotional level of the user to a point where the actual signals are received with the utmost clarity and acted on in the most appropriate way.

Though mantra-*japa* is the chief technique in learning to concentrate and pay attention to experience, A. tells of other supplementary methods which were employed in the first years of his own training:

"One way of increasing concentration is to learn to make two speeches at the same time, one sentence spoken on one subject and the second sentence on a completely different subject. The trainee is regarded as having arrived when he can make seven simultaneous speeches.

"My own guru also placed emphasis on memory training as an aid to concentration. After one of our talks, when I went back the next Saturday, he asked me to repeat verbatim what had transpired between us in our previous conversation. He ponted out my memory lapses and corrected my errors, and the next time I had to reproduce the first conversation together with the additions and corrections made by the guru in the second. This went on for some time. Every time we met, I was expected to repeat the first conversation together with all the additions of the subsequent meetings. These are not difficult things to learn; they are merely matters of practice, as in a circus. Of course, people believe that we tantriks have extraordinary powers merely because some of us have such good powers of recall or have a kind of concentration that shuts out all sensory inputs except the one to which attention is being paid to at a particular moment."

Mantras are used not only as a preparation for receiving future experience but also to look back at the past and make some of the undigested karma more palatable. I find it an intriguing (and innovative) therapeutic notion that one can enter a particular feeling state with the help of a mantra and then look back at one's past so as to highlight the situations in which that particular feeling state—say, anger—played a vital role. It is as if one were illuminating the topography of one's life with a certain kind of emotional light—it could be sadness, fear, sexual desire or shame—in an attempt to rediscover some of the experiences connected with that particular emotion which were "undigested" at the time they happened and still remain to be integrated into consciousness.

Mantras can be classified in many different ways. One class of mantras represents the particular goddess with whom the tantrik is seeking to identify. These so-called *ishta*-mantras are communicated by the guru to the disciple after a long period of preliminary training. The goddess *(ishta-devi)* represents the incomplete part of the student's self, which needs to be accepted and integrated in the psyche before he can become "whole." Since the *ishta-devi* (*devata,* for women) is an intensely personal concept, her (or his) name is never to be revealed and the mantra must also be kept a secret. The *ishta-sadhana* has been described by A. as follows:

"This *sadhana* has three stages. In the first stage, the goddess is the mother and we try to penetrate through her outer [*avarna*], terrible and destroying form to reach her inner and basic [*mula*] nurturing core. The form of the *ishta*-mantra at this stage will contain a set of syllables protecting against the outer, terrible form of the goddess and another set of syllables opening the psyche to the experience of the nurturant goddess. The mantra is inevitably rather long and divided into two sets of syllables, Kraum . . . Phat, and Aum . . . Svaha, the first directed against the destructive aspect and the second toward her sympathetic aspect.

"At the second stage, the *ishta*-mantra, as directed by the guru, changes into a different pattern. Here the psychic operation is visualized as becoming one with the goddess-as-consort through sexual union. According to the *kula* in which I was instructed, that is best done with a female partner who has a complementary pattern. Indeed, the arrangement of tantric marriages is dictated by this requirement; the wife selected by the guru is your complementary *shakti*. The *ishta*-mantra at this stage has two parts: Kraum . . . hum, and Aum . . . hum, the first part relating to self-visualization and the second part to the visualization of the desired partner.

"At the third stage, the goddess becomes the daughter and the *ishta*-mantra changes accordingly. The first part of the mantra now signifies a nurturing intention toward the goddess and the second part a handing over of the goddess to her natural consort.

"Another class of mantras are called the basic or *mula*-mantra, which are common to all tantric traditions and initiate a programmed sequence of psychic experiences. These basic mantras can be divided into many collections. For example, there is the sixty-four-yogini collection, which is said to be appropriate for tantriks whose main orientation toward life is of 'balance' and 'harmony,' *i.e.*, ordinary human life but at a higher level of consciousness. Then there is the "ten great knowledges" *(dasha mahavidya)* collection, for those who approach life primarily through knowledge and reflection. We also have the eight-*nayika* collection, suitable for those who have a fundamentally artistic-creative approach of life."

I have already mentioned that mantras are used not in isolation but as part of a complex routine which blends together many other techniques. Mantras also have visual counterparts, the tantric iconography being as complex as the mantric *aurologie* to which it exactly corresponds. In the visual sphere, besides the images *(pratima)* of the goddesses that the adept "creates" there are: (1) diagrammatic forms *(yantra)* symbolizing divine manifestations, or, in secular language, human potentials to which the practitioner aspires; (2) symbols of protection and invulnerability (mandala) which the tantric uses to contain the anxiety that may be released during the *sadhana;* and (3) there are symbolic elaborations of central themes *(prastara)* which are contemplated in order to create certain emotional states.[36]

In connection with visual techniques, I should also mention *nyasa*. This is a technique in which the tantrik visualizes the goddess and then introjects her into the various parts of his body by touching them. Indeed, to a psychoanalyst, many psychic processes such as identification and introjection, which operate automatically and unconsciously, appear to be actively dramatized in tantra—as if some of the tantric techniques were conceived in a script written by Freud in collaboration with Céline.

My intention here is not to describe these ancient techniques in any detail but to convey the flavor of the emotional states and psychological experiences they seek to create. The precise nature of the psychic experience produced by a tantric *sadhana* remains elusive since its hallucinationlike intensity is beyond the ken of our everyday psychic life and commonsense reality. One may speculate that the kind of imaginative reality tantric exercises seek to create is akin to artistic creativity and may well have its source in that particular human capacity and propensity which create metaphors in the waking state and dream images in sleep.[37] The tantric imaginative reality is not the personal, imaginary reality of the psychotic, though it may sometimes slip in that direction. The imaginative reality created by tantric exercises is both shared and public in the sense that it is based upon, guided and formed by the symbolic, iconic network of the tantric culture which the adept inhabits. In other words, if tantric visualizations are conscious dream creations, then they are dreams which have been dreamed by others. A tantric vision does not seem to be imposed by unconscious forces, nor is it idiosyncratic (as in the case of the psychotic), but it is consciously chosen and controlled, its form and content preselected to the last detail.[38]

As an outsider to the tantric tradition, I hesitate to speculate further on the meaning of these psychic states and experiences; nor do I wish to venture an opinion on the therapeutic efficacy claimed for them by tantriks. My major interest in these training techniques lies in what they reveal about issues that tantra considers vital to man's quest for psychic integration and "wholeness."

In helping a person to learn (in A.'s words) "to concentrate," "pay attention," "be attuned," the tantric *sadhanas* intend to usher in a permanent psychic transformation whose outcome is a state of *focused receptivity*. By focused receptivity I mean the circumscribing of a particular psychological state ("state of consciousness" in the currently fashionable jargon) which differs from our normal, intellectually active and problem-solving mode of thought that is the legacy of our development from infancy to adulthood. Similar in some respects to what Keats called the "negative capability" of the artist, a condition where there is "no irritable reaching after fact and reason,"[39] the attention of a person in a state of focused receptivity is concentrated yet not seeking. The kind of receptivity I mean here cannot be simply equated with a passive, fuguelike state. Focused receptivity pulsates with an intense concentration which, however, is not used for a categorizing mode of thought or for an active grasping of percepts, but for an alert, nondiscursive "contemplation." Psychoanalysts will recognize in focused receptivity elements of the "free-floating attention" required of the analyst, the nonselective, nondirective, evenly suspended and evenly hovering attention with which he (ideally) listens to the patient. Focused receptivity comes even closer to those moments in the process of analysis when the normal analytical empathy with the patient imperceptibly changes into a kind of unconscious alignment with his psyche and material, and insights, surprising by the force of conviction they carry, begin to emerge without being sought or anticipated. I would therefore suggest that when tantric texts talk of an immobilization of semen, thought and breath, their urgent desire for stillness is not masking early fears of sexual excitement, emotions or death,[40] but something simpler. The tantric formula of threefold immobility, it seems to me, expresses the underlying idea of a desired cessation of (masculine) physical and mental activity and its transformation into the kind of receptivity I have discussed above. The tantric striving is to conceive oneself not as an ego opposed to an alien environment which must be mastered by "irritably reaching after fact and reason," but an ego with a permanent "absorbing" and "receiving" stance toward the outside world. Charles Rycroft's impression of individuals possessing a high degree of "negative capability" will, I suspect, also apply to tantric adepts: ". . . in other and in psychoanalytic words, their relationship to external reality is identificatory without impermeable 'ego boundaries' drawn between themselves and others or between their 'I' and their 'It.' They also seem to be refreshingly free from the conventional notion that activity is masculine and passivity is feminine and can therefore oscillate between active and passive states of being, between objectivity and subjectivity, without feeling that their identity is threatened by doing so."[41]

Let me add that I am not contrasting the tantric goals for the "healthy" person with their counterparts in Western systems of psychotherapy in any evaluative fashion. The tantric ideal of an androgynous identity—as contrasted with the goal of "true" masculinity or femininity in most Western systems, and the tantric preparation for an ego *receiving* the world in "concentration"—as against the Western, Faustian notion of the ego advancing against the world on a broad front in order to change it, are not simple, right-or-wrong alternatives. An acquaintanceship with the tantric system only makes us more aware of the existence of a wider range of human potential than we are normally prepared to acknowledge. At the same time tantra points out an ancient and arduous route to the pursuit of *ananda* and the restoration of well-being which lies to one side of the well-traveled highways of Western psychiatry and psychotherapy.

Tantric Psychotherapy

Before we come to tantric healing in the narrow sense of a removal of specific pathological conditions, we must discuss briefly the whole issue of tantric "powers" (*siddhis*), which are closely connected with tantric healing and healers. Apart from tantra's public notoriety as an orgiastic cult, there are a vast number of Indians, including members of the business and political elite, who believe that tantriks possess, and tantra promises, occult powers.

Many tantrik texts resemble manuals of black magic insofar as they teach the casting of spells (*jadu-tona*) and the creation of illusions (*indra-jala*) while they describe the *sadhana*s necessary to obtain various kinds of miraculous powers.[42] The major powers are the ability to exercise, through occult means, complete control (*vashikarana*) over "women, husbands and kings," attraction (*mohana*), immobilization (*stambhana*), pacification (*shantikarna*), causing death (*marana*) and sowing enmity (*videshana*). Naturally, each power is the province of a particular goddess whom the adept has to first woo and make his own. For instance, the *sadhana* for gaining the power of immobilization—not only of human beings (the immobilizing of an enemy army would have been a particularly desirable power from the viewpoint of a king), but also of natural phenomena such as flowing water or burning fire—is addressed to the goddess Rama.

The phenomenon of occult tantric powers and miracles can be viewed in different ways. The dominant view perhaps will be that of people whose consciousness has been formed in the crucible of that psychological revolution which has narrowed the older, metaphysical scope of the mind to mind as an isolated island of individual consciousness, profoundly aware of its almost limitless subjectivity and its infantile tendency to heedless projection and illusion. In this view, the widespread Indian belief in tantric "powers" and miracles is an expression of an ancient (in history) and infantile (in life history) magical world view. Tantric claims and assertions are then mental phenomena based on the unconscious dispositions of both those who make and those who believe them; and it would be better for the society and people who affirm the reality of these phenomena to bid farewell to that miraculous world in which mind-created things live and move. This view would also see the tantric preoccupation with the control of the environment through "powers" as the darker side of its receptivity ideal. The concern with "powers" is then an expression of defenses against relinquishing conscious control and against the unexpected and the unknown—defenses which are activated by the "unnatural" tantric striving for what I have earlier called focused receptivity.

Essentially this is the modern "commonsense" attitude (ancient common sense was different), which is justifiably wary of the realm of unchecked subjectivity and tends to equate the products of imagination—the imaginary—with the false. As the source of subjectivity and of private images, the psyche too is apt to be regarded here with a degree of suspiciousness. As Jung wrote some forty years ago:

" 'Psychic reality' is a controversial concept, like 'psyche' or 'mind.' By the latter terms some understand consciousness and its contents, others allow the existence of 'dark' or 'subconscious' representations. Some include instincts in the psychic realm, others exclude them. The vast majority consider the psyche to be a result of bio-chemical processes in the brain cells. A few conjecture that it is the psyche that makes the cortical cells function. Some identify 'life' with psyche. But only an insignificant minority regards the psychic phenomenon as a category of existence *per se* and draws the necessary conclusions."[43]

Jung's observations are as true today as when they were first made; indeed, as an Indian and an Asian, I am constantly struck by how few Western psychologists believe in the psyche as a condition of human existence. Moreover, the number of psychiatrists who are really comfortable with the notion of psychic reality seems to be steadily decreasing, with very few left who pay more than lip service to the idea of the unconscious—either their patients' or their own.

Another view, which for the sake of convenience may be prefixed as traditionally Indian, South Asian or perhaps simply Eastern, will look at the phenomenon of the occult somewhat differently. In this view, which takes the existence of the psyche and psychic reality for granted, there is greater acceptance of psychic products, including the mind-created gods and goddesses.

Generally speaking, this view does not adopt the extreme position of Indian Buddhist philosophers who, in the words of Stephan Beyer, "had long made an axiom of the 'softness' of reality and given an ontological status to the omnipotence of imagination: it developed upon them to explain not why imagery is private but rather why reality is public."[44] As O'Flaherty has pointed out, lying somewhere between the Buddhist "soft" reality and the "hard" line of modern Western psychology, the traditional Indian view occupies "a middle path, in which reality has a status somewhat like that of equality in *Animal Farm*: Some things are realer than others."[45] For most Hindus, the stories of tantric miracles are like that; not as real as the dentist pulling out a tooth perhaps but nevertheless real enough. Tantriks themselves attach different degrees of reality to their "powers." "Many of our powers are a product of practice like that of a stage magician," said one. "Others are a little more complicated since they involve the control of others' perceptions of the world. For example, if I wish to become beautiful to a woman, I can. The whole idea of objectivity is something a tantrik is not worried about." If I can create a private "reality" for myself, he seemed to be saying, and if I can get others to verify it by influencing their perception, then what I have created is certainly real. The creation of such real illusions which invite and involve the participation of the patients and others—healing illusions, if one will—is a major part of the tantrik healer's repertoire.

Healing in its narrow sense is then a part of the underworld of tantra that is full of miracles and peopled by practitioners of the occult. There are many well-known tantriks in this world who are spoken of with dread and awe. There is the reputedly six-hundred-year-old Bhubhru Baba who, in turn, is a mere stripling compared with the inmates of the legendary Siddha ashram, reportedly tucked away somewhere deep in the vastness of the Himalayas. In this world, where normal laws of time, space and causation are suspended, one hears of Trijata Aghori, who has the power of reviving a corpse; Devahura Baba possesses the *samharini-kritya* power which instantly kills anyone—an individual or a multitude—against whom it is directed. Pagla Baba and Baba Bhairavnath can fly through air or enter other bodies at will; Dhurjata Aghori has Brahma's power of beginning a new Creation; and the female tantrik Debul Bhairavi controls a legion of female spirits eager to do her slightest bidding.

Tantrik healers belong to this occult world and are widely believed to be men with "powers." These powers, which can be used either to harm or to heal, are acquired by undergoing difficult and even dangerous *sadhanas*. As an illustration of the popular notion of the occult world inhibited by healers and other tantriks and the kind of *sadhana* that a healer must undergo, let me reproduce excerpts from a "letter," purportedly written by a disciple to his teacher. The disciple is a small-time astrologer who wishes to possess the secret of time—certainly a useful asset for a man who needs to look into the past of his clients and accurately predict their future. The *sadhana* is directed toward the demoness *(pishachini)* Karna ("one who tells in the ear") and the disciple has insisted, in spite of the guru's reluctance, to carry out the *sadhana* in the "left-handed" way since this way promises quick results.

"You had told me that this *sadhana* needs three days. It can be begun in any month three days before new moon but it needs ten days of prior preparation, and a further ten days of rituals to be performed after the *sadhana* is over.

"According to your instructions, I stopped bathing on the third day of Posh.* For ten days, I cleaned neither my teeth nor scraped

*The Indian lunar month starting from middle of January.

my tongue nor changed my clothes. I continued with my astrological work, though people were surprised at my dishevelled appearance. I stopped saying my daily prayers. I did not go to a temple, nor did I recite the Gayatri and the Vedas since you had said that I should abstain from all the sacred acts prescribed for a Brahmin since these rituals hinder the realization of the Karna Pishachini. For ten days I did not make my bed. After eating, I did not wash my plate and used the same dirty plate for every meal.

"According to instructions, on the thirteenth day after full moon, I took some of my own feces from the chamber-pot and ate it. Although I felt thoroughly disgusted, I wanted to complete the *sadhana* in the left-handed way. In the three days of the *sadhana,* whenever I felt hungry I ate my feces and whenever I felt thirsty I drank my own urine.

"On the same night, I locked the doors of my house from inside and lit eleven big lamps in my room. Each lamp contained more than half a litre of oil. Spreading a woollen blanket on the floor, I sat down facing south. I had eaten some of my feces from the morning. I smeared the rest all over my naked body and rubbed a little into my hair.

"I had prepared two strings of bones, each containing fifty-four bones. The bones had been dug up from the cremation ground at night. I wore one string of bones around my neck and held the other in my hand.

"I then started reciting the mantra of Karna Pishachini. The mantra goes like this:

> 'Aum hring Karna Pishachini
> Amodha Satya Vadini mum Karne
> Avatar-avatar satya Kathya-kathya atita anagata
> Vartamana darshya-darshya ain hring hring
> Karna Pishachini svaha'

"I went on reciting [*japa*] this mantra. You had told me to do the *japa* for one hundred and fifteen strings. If there is a need to urinate during the *japa,* you had said, then I should urinate while seated; if there is a need to defecate, this too should be done wherever I am sitting. Without breaking the rhythm of the *japa,* the urine should be sprinkled and the feces rubbed all over the body. That night I urinated and defecated many times. I was amazed, as this had never happened earlier. The room was stinking. It was difficult even to breathe but I managed to complete a hundred and fifteen strings of the *japa*. It was five in the morning when the *japa* ended.

"As instructed, I lay down on the floor to sleep. Around nine in the morning, I felt ravenous, as if I had not eaten for a whole month. Tears came to my eyes. I wished that I had listened to you and not undertaken this *sadhana.* If only I had heeded your advice I would not have landed myself in this mess. My Brahminhood was lost and I lay in that room a degraded being—a *pishacha.*

"In the afternoon, while I was lying down I felt the door open. Although the room was locked I felt that someone had come in. I even pinched myself to make sure that I was awake. I saw an attractive woman, twenty-five to thirty years old, completely naked, standing next to me. She lay down without saying a word. I was frightened and tried to get up but she forced me to lie down besides her and started to stroke my penis. I was frightened and did not know what to do. I could not even bear to look at her while she shamelessly continued to stroke my penis and incite me to the 'act.' There was no intercourse though, and around five in the evening she disappeared. I felt utterly drained and almost decided to discontinue the *sadhana.* But you had told me that anyone who leaves the *sadhana* unfinished is certain to be slain by the Pishachini and that having once started one obtained either the desired power . . . or death.

"I woke up in the evening, my head splitting from the stink inside the room. At eleven in the night I once again lighted the lamps and started the *japa.* After about an hour, the woman of the afternoon appeared and sat down next to me. Her teeth were protruding. She had short, closely cropped hair and wore a necklace of bones. Otherwise, she was naked. She seemed to be in good spirits and constantly fondled my penis. Sometimes she stroked it, sometimes she kissed me and put her arm around my waist. I was sweating with fear but did not interrupt my *japa.* I urinated and defecated five to six times. Each time the woman smeared both our bodies with the urine and feces. She sat with me till five in the morning and went away as soon as the *japa* was over. Once again I thought of stopping the *sadhana,* but the fear of death drove me to persist.

"On the third, new moon day, the woman again came and lay next to me. I tried to get up but she kicked me hard on the waist and forced me to lie with her. She again played with my body and incited me to intercourse. Around three in the afternoon she finally succeeded and left as soon as the act was over. I went on lying there, miserable and full of fear, shame and remorse.

"When I started the *japa* at night, the woman appeared instantly and sat down on my lap. I went on chanting the mantra while she urinated and defecated all over me and smeared my body with her urine and feces. At five in the morning she got up from my lap and said, 'I am your lover now and I'll stay with you all your life. I'll do all your work but if you ever think of leaving me, I shall kill you.' Then, like a newly wed bride, she exchanged her necklace of bones for mine. I was silent but she said: 'Don't be shy, you have obtained me and I shall stay with you. Whenever I want intercourse I'll come to you and you will have to satisfy my desire. Whenever you ask a question I'll whisper the answer in your ear. But do not tell anyone about me or I'll strangle you.' After saying this, she kissed my penis and disappeared."

The disciple completed the other prescribed rituals. For the next ten days, he was in a state of great mental agony since he could neither worship any of the Hindu gods nor carry out the daily rituals prescribed for a Brahmin. His economic situation, however, greatly improved. "The Pishachini collects hordes of people and drives them toward my house. Everyday, more than a hundred people come to consult me. Scenes from their past come unbidden before my eyes. Whenever someone asks me a question the Pishachini whispers the answer in my ear. The questioner is generally astounded by my knowledge of his past and falls down at my feet in reverence."[46]

This letter is interesting on many counts. First, it gives us an accurate representation of the popular beliefs regarding tantra— especially its left-handed practice and of how tantriks acquire their "powers," be they astrological or curative. Second, it reveals the social function of tantra as a receptacle of unconscious fantasies, not only of tantriks but of large sections of Hindu society as well. Here, for instance, the description of the Pishachini *sadhana* dramatizes some of the hidden aspects of the Brahminical ideals of ritual purity.

The pollution fantasy underlying the stringent Hindu social regulations that govern what is to be touched or eaten—when, where and
with whom—is no longer buried in the depths of private psyches but
becomes publicly shared in tantric practice—actual or imagined. As
I have mentioned earlier, there are very few unconscious fantasies
which do not have a public home in India—either in a "living" myth
or in a cultic practice; a striking characteristic of Indian society is
that everything is allowed in fantasy but very little in practice.

Coming back to tantric healing, since the healer is believed to be
endowed with suprahuman powers, there is a general belief that all
he needs to know is the right mantra for a particular psychic affliction and success is inevitable. Such a belief in the healer's powers,
as we know, is of immeasurable value since it harnesses the patient's
state of expectant trust which is vital for the healing of emotional
disorders. For someone given to fits of rage, the healer gives the
mantra "Hring thing thing krodhaprahmana hring hring ham kling
sa sa svaha" and requires that the mantra be repeated one hundred
and eight times a day for twenty-one days. For someone possessed
by a spirit, a sacrificial fire is lit and the healer touches various parts
of the patient's body with the smoke from the fire while he chants
the mantra "Aum hum ksham, sa svaha." The healing encounters
may be much more dramatic on occasion. Often they involve the use
of such unusual props as human bones, and take place in the middle
of the night in the setting of graveyards and cremation grounds,
which enhance the impression of the tantrik's close liaison with
supernatural powers and acquaintance with beings who exist in
realms other than the human one.

According to *some* tantriks (it is difficult to get a widespread
agreement on any tantrik matter), this view of tantric healing is not
so much false as it is limited. They claim that the "production
values" of tantric healing dramas—the use of burning embers from
a fresh funeral pyre to bake bread (to heal epilepsy), human skulls
as drinking vessels—should not obscure the fact that there is a
well-defined model of the body-mind system on which tantric healing is based.

The cornerstone of this elaborate and complex system which can
be sketched here only in outline and which we will consider later in
detail (chapter 7) is what the tantriks (and other Hindus) call the

"subtle body," with its thousands of "nerves" *(nadis)* or conduits of energy, and its six "centers" *(chakras)*. The subtle body, neither a psyche nor a soma but a kind of protopsyche-soma, is an imaginative construct, though, most Hindus would claim, it is clearly "visible" to an advanced yogi or a tantrik adept. The subtle body both links and lies at the root of physiological and psychological processes. Its central location is along a line running from a spot *(muladhara)* halfway between the genital organs and the anal orifice, corresponding to the sacrococcygeal plexus, via the spinal column to a spot on top of the skull. This is the line of symmetry that divides the body into two balanced halves. Along this line there are three major "nerves" which are the channels of subtle energy. The most important of these channels is the *sushumna,* located in the hollow of the cerebrospinal axis, extending from the *muladhara* to the cerebral region and whose opening at its base in the *muladhara* is normally closed. On *sushumna*'s left and coiling around it is the "masculine" *ida,* which has its exit in the left nostril. Similarly, on its right and coiling around *sushumna* is the "feminine" *pingala,* another channel for subtle energy.

Along the line of symmetry on the *sushumna,* there are six "centers" or *chakras* which are said to represent different states of consciousness. Fundamentally, the goal of all Indian mystical-spiritual practices, ranging from the tortuously physical to the ineffably contemplative, is to gather the energy that normally flows through *ida* and *pingala* and get it flowing through the central channel, the *sushumna.* As this energy—the famed kundalini—travels upward, it energizes and pierces each of the six *chakras* in turn. The particular "lotuses" associated with these centers then "open," a metaphor for mental transformation and the opening up of the psyche to hitherto inaccessible psychic experiences and "knowledge." The energy travels upward till it reaches the *sahasrara,* the seat of "cosmic consciousness" which precedes birth and survives death, and where the *unio mystica* takes place. The "nerves," "centers," "lotuses," are, of course, metaphors derived from the body and the natural world to describe perceptible (though admittedly uncommon) mental processes which would otherwise remain ineffable.

Each of the six *chakras* is said to be related to certain natural and cosmic phenomena on the one hand and to specific mental and physiological functions on the other. The details of the former relationship—between the "centers" of the human body and the cosmos—are not our concern here. Each *chakra*, however, is also said to be associated with specific physiological processes and psychological attributes and states which are loosely spoken of as being controlled by that particular *chakra*. The malfunctioning of a *chakra*, then, produces typical mental and physical disturbances. To give a few examples: the malfunctioning of *muladhara* is said to produce anxiety and jaundice; the malfunctioning of *svadhisthan chakra*, located at the base of the penis (sacral plexus), produces delusion, infatuations, sexual disturbances and fainting fits; the malfunctioning of *manipura*, situated in the lumbar region at the level of the navel (epigastric plexus), gives rise to anger, eye problems, swellings and pleurisy; a disturbance in *anahata* produces asthma and other respiratory disorders.[47]

In the tantric system the severe forms of mental disorder, where one completely loses touch with reality, are attributed to an unplanned and unprepared rising of energy through the central channel. Under severe bodily or mental strain, it is claimed, this energy may accidentally make contact with the *sahasrara* in the brain—with disastrous results. Similar to an ancient tradition, found in many other cultures, which links madness with holiness and equates the lunatic with the saint (as also with the lover and the poet), tantra posits a common underlying "physiological" mechanism for both madness and mystical states. The difference lies in the vastly different conditions under which the two states come about; a short circuit and blowing of the fuse in one case and illumination in the other.

How does a *chakra* get disturbed? The major underlying cause is undigested karma. When the disturbance of a *chakra* passes a certain level, a *bhuta* (lit.—and interestingly—a has-been) is generated. The term *bhuta* is a generic name for a host of spirits—male and female—which can take hold of a person and against which the dramatic treatment rituals described earlier are directed. Between undigested karma and mental illness, then, are two intermediate levels of *chakra* malfunctioning and *bhuta* generation. A tantric healer must "know" the *chakra*s, especially his own, and also be a master of *bhuta-vidya*, i.e., of "demonology." Once again we must remember that *bhuta* in the Indian context does not have the pejorative connotations with which Christianity has invested the word "demon." The Indian *bhuta* is closer to the Greek *daimon,* which can be good (obedient) or evil (disobedient), but is always a passion. As Coomaraswamy remarks, "We nowadays look back on all these things as 'superstitions' and such indeed they are, in the literal sense of 'survivals'; but that we now call the demons within us 'instincts' changes nothing in the nature of the 'ruling passions' to which we are subjected until we have learned to master them and use them for ourselves. . . . By whatever name we call the 'horses,' the problem remains the same, to drive or be driven by them."[48]

Before embarking on the treatment, a tantric healer then attempts to diagnose the particular malfunctioning *chakra* and the nature of the *bhuta* controlling the patient. This diagnosis is based on the patient's overt behavior *(achara),* his expressed thoughts and ideas *(vichara)* and his specific behavioral disorder *(vikriya).*

The malfunctioning of the *chakras* can also be determined by the more direct method of "feeling" them, a method which requires the healer to "know" his own *chakras* thoroughly. A well-known Bengali writer, Samaresh Bose, gives an instance of this kind of diagnosis that took place when a tantrik examined Bose's suitability for undergoing the tantric discipline: "Then he put his hand midway between my anus and penis (at Mooladhara). Then, feeling me from my anus to the base of my spinal column, he told Pabitri Ma almost unintelligibly, 'Ma, this fellow has the ability. If he tries he can put up a good fight. But his stamina is not good. He suffers from cough right round the year and smokes too much.'

"I was surprised, I do not know how by putting his finger just at one spot of my anatomy he could detect that I smoked too much and suffered from a bad cough."[49]

Once the diagnosis is made, the treatment consists of not only the dramatic rituals described earlier, through which an afflicting *bhuta* is conquered, but is also directed toward bringing back normal functioning to the upset *chakra.* For acutely disturbed, hyperactive patients, the first step would be to neutralize or "freeze" the *ajnya chakra,* located between the eyebrows, which is the gateway to the *sahasrara* in the brain. Mantra, hypnosis and cannabis-based drugs may be all used for this purpose. For the pacification of other *chakras,* music, oil massages, hot-water baths, prayers and other devotional rituals, besides the all-pervasive mantra, are employed. Let me here illustrate tantric diagnostics and treatment through a brief, ongoing case history reported by a tantrik.

The patient was a thirty-year-old clerk in a government office. He was losing weight for some time, was generally anxious, and had also become impotent. Ayurvedic and modern medicines had not helped and he was brought to the tantric healer by his father's elder brother. The healer proceeded as follows:

1. Observation of *achara*: The patient does not approach closely, makes a perfunctory gesture of obeisance and sits in a tense posture. He avoids eye contact and speaks in a low, mumbling voice.

2. Observation of *vichara*: On being asked what is wrong, the patient replies, "Nothing." On further inquiry he admits to a feeling of weakness and being run down and also expresses anxiety as to whether he would be able to hold on to his job. Discreet queries concerning "relations with wife" create anger and the observation that women are tigresses. No overt behavior disorders, *i.e.*, no *vikriya*, are observed.

3. Preliminary diagnosis: Loss of weight, impotence, fear of women, clearly shows affliction of the *svadhisthan chakra*. *Ajnya chakra* has also been weakened (loss of job feared) and tense posture, mumbling tone, show some minor affliction of *manipura*.

The possessing *bhuta* was identified by the healer as a fairy sorceress *(dakini)* of a weak type. For the pacification of the *chakras*, regular oil baths, the eating of rice with milk and sugar *(payasa)* once every other day and cutting down on chewing of betel nut were advised. The patient was also advised to abstain from sex, even if he felt up to it, for the four to five weeks till the pacification of the *chakras* was completed. After this period, the healer planned to exorcise the *dakini* through a ritual involving a sacrificial fire and felt fairly confident of success.

COOLING BREEZES

The Cult of Mataji

M y first encounter with Mataji and her cult was unplanned. On the inside page of the morning newspaper which carries announcements of plays, music concerts and other entertainments offered in the capital, there was the grainy photograph of a good-looking middle-aged woman with an imperious expression. She had a full face with high cheekbones, her forehead punctuated in the middle by a large round dot *(tikka)*, the face strikingly framed by long black hair that hung down loosely to below her shoulders. The text of the accompanying ad announced that the Primal Power *(Adishakti)* Mata Nirmala Devi was back in town from London for a week's stay. She will, it went on to say, hold discourses for her devotees every evening from seven to nine and grant mass self-realization—an instant awakening of the kundalini—to all newcomers.

The offer of an instant awakening of the kundalini, the goal of all Indian mystical-spiritual practices since time immemorial and supposedly attained by very few persons in a single lifetime, was certainly intriguing. I vaguely recalled having heard of Mataji as a dispenser of miraculous cures and quick mokshas, and suspected her of using these ploys to break into the increasingly competitive market for the supply of spiritual wares. Though she had traveled a long way from her beginnings as a faith healer, I knew that Mataji had not quite yet made it to the top rungs of gurudom. In the spiritual business, in which India is a leading producer and exporter and where the advent of a Western guru such as Werner Erhard of est is a rarity, Mataji's cult, though a steady performer, lagged far behind the established enterprises of the first rank. As far as influence, fame, number of devotees and capital assets are concerned, Mataji's is still a middle-sized undertaking, trailing by far such leading multinationals as the TM of Maharishi Mahesh Yogi, the Poona Ashram of Bhagwan Rajneesh, the Sathya Sai cult of Sai Baba, and even the Radha Soami Satsang of Maharaj Charan Singh. This underdog aspect made me feel more sympathetic to Mataji's particular message and mission than would have otherwise been the case.

I wish I could report that I went to Mataji a skeptic and came out a believer—thus fulfilling the alluring fantasy of a sudden, self-transcendent transformation that lurks in many of us. The fact, however, is that though my later experiences with the cult were to be quite different, that first meeting with Mataji yielded more Chaplinesque farce than mystic bliss.

I had reached the hall of the New Delhi school in which Mataji's program was held late, delayed by a hearty dinner with friends. Mataji's discourse and the group session of kundalini raising were over and most people had already left. Mataji sat on an ornately carved, thronelike chair. A big, handsome woman, she looked tired but relaxed, flushed with the characteristic glow that mass adulation brings to the face. She was surrounded by thirty-odd devotees, of varying ages and both sexes, and half a dozen others who betrayed their status as newcomers by the shy way they stood at the edges of the group, poised to take flight if the supernatural they expected also threatened to become unconventional. Most of the cult members squatted in front of Mataji. Eyes closed in meditation, their open hands extending toward her in a peculiar gesture combining supplication and grasping, these devotees, as I learned later, were gathering in her "divine vibrations," while they waited for the cool breeze on their fingertips and the palms which is supposed to herald the rising of the kundalini. Two Western devotees, in the white *kurta-pajama* uniform favored by many young European tourists of the occult, were loudly chanting Mataji's mantra, "Om Shri Mataji Nirmala Ma!" Another small group of four to five cult members, led by an officious-looking young Sikh, was busy raising the kundalini of two young women. Each woman lay prostrate at Mataji's feet, cradling a well-formed foot in her clasped hands while she pressed her eyes against it. With their left hands extended toward Mataji and the right hands making odd sweeping gestures along the length of the girls' spines, the helping devotees resembled less realized souls than harassed traffic policemen at busy intersections as they tried to hurry the kundalini flow along. Except for an occasional and abstracted laying of a hand on the back of a girl's head, Mataji ignored the goings-on in front of her, as she did the clamoring of a devotee for her attention. She was animatedly conversing with a slim young man dressed in a loud bush shirt and tight drainpipe trousers who sat at her feet, looking at her in adoration and gently massaging her plump knees.

Suddenly, Mataji seemed to have decided that the kundalini of one of the young girls was not going anywhere, at least on this particular evening. Removing her foot from the dazed girl's hands, she directed her to one of the assistants for further instructions with the cryptic remark, "You must have frequented graveyards when you were a child, daughter." Her glance then swept over the newcomers and came to rest on my face.

"What about you?" she asked in Hindi. "Do you want to cross over [*par*]?" referring to the crossing over of the river of life and death into immortality. Though the offer was sudden and I doubted my readiness for the journey, I still managed a "yes" with suitable show of enthusiasm. As I made my way to the empty place in front of her and was about to lie down on the floor, she asked, "What is your profession?"

"A psychologist," I answered.

"What kind? Freudian?"

I nodded my assent.

"That is bad," she said. "The left side of Freudians is normally very weak; Jungians are better."

She turned toward the young Sikh disciple—a college student, to judge by his appearance—who seemed raring to have a go at my kundalini, and confided disapprovingly, "Freud was a tantrik, you see!"

Lying down on the floor, my closed eyes pressed against Mataji's foot, which was still damp from the sweat (it could also be tears) of its previous clasper, I felt cocooned within myself—helpless to be sure, yet quite unafraid. The group above me conferred with Mataji on the state of my *chakras* and my kundalini and the voices came wafting down from a great distance. The conversation was esoteric —about "a catch in the *manipura*," "the needed cleansing of the

ajna"—a practiced, almost routine surgical conference held over a
patient drifting off into anesthesia. Suddenly, I felt a couple of sharp
taps at the base of my spine at the coccyx, where the kundalini is
normally supposed to be resting. I was suddenly aware that I had
overindulged in the delicious butter chicken curry at my friend's
house and had ignored the distended feeling in my stomach. The
young Sikh's attempt at jarring loose the kundalini reminded me
that any other unexpected taps in that general region could lead to
a loud mishap which could be highly embarrassing, especially at a
spiritual function. From that moment, my attention was concentrated on my sphincter muscles and I ceased to take any further
interest in self-realization.

Mercifully the session ended soon afterward. The kundalini, I was
told, had made good progress but could not pierce the "balloon of
the superego" in my brain. I was given Mataji's photograph, asked
to look at it every morning and evening through a candle flame while
I bathed my feet in warm, salty water. This would remove the
impurities from the "nerves" and "centers" of my subtle, psychic
body. I went home feeling quite ashamed of myself that I had let
the state of my stomach select the farcical aspects of the encounter
and suppress its earnest core.

The next time I met Mataji was at a friend's flat in Bombay. It
was a private gathering of only a few devotees, all of them determined that I should obtain self-realization on that very day. As I
waited outside in the foyer, sitting with some other aspirants in front
of a gilded throne on which there was a photograph of Mataji, three
of her disciples waved their hands around my back while they tested
the kundalini's progress through the vibrations they received in their
own fingers. "The third finger in my left hand is showing a block,"
said one. "Yes, yes," the others chorused. "The middle finger in my
right hand is giving out hot vibrations," said someone else. "Yes, yes,
I too can feel it," the others repeated. Each time they were unanimous in their different opinions. Obviously every one of my *chakras*
had a minor but decided flaw. Before I could feel either irritation
or disappointment, I was called to the other room, where Mataji was
waiting for me together with a few other advanced disciples. She
pointed to her feet and once again I was lying prostrate on the floor,
my closed eyes pressed against her feet.

Mataji seemed to be in a bantering good humor as she and the disciples began the process of raising my kundalini. I felt my back gently kneaded by anonymous hands and a feather-light touch going up from the base of the spine to its top. Gradually, I felt my body begin to relax. The sea breeze coming in through the open windows and gently ruffling my hair seemed to be part of Mataji's ministrations. I felt myself drifting off into a long-forgotten, pleasant sensation that was slowly suffusing throughout the body. After all, it is rare in adulthood that our bodies are fondled by strangers in a cherishing way, without expectations or demands. My thoughts too were losing their discursive moorings as they began to be replaced by visual images of my mother's soothing hand over the child's flushed brow, of her bending down to pick the child up and the child's awareness of her full breasts, which she had in common with Mataji. "He thinks too much," someone said above me, just when thought had disappeared and regressive imagery had taken over. "Look at his left side," Mataji said. "It is weak. See that block?" There was an answering chorus of "Yes! Yes!" "It is because he is a Freudian," she continued. "Freud approached the psyche through the left, forbidden side. The only mantra against Freud is 'Om Sakshat Mokshadaini Sakshat Nirmala Devi! [Om, verily the giver of moksha, verily Nirmala Devi]' " The devotees began to chant the mantra as they exorcised Freud.

"You too repeat it, son," Mataji said.

With a silent apology to Freud and my colleagues of the International Psychoanalytical Association, I repeated the mantra after her.

"It is getting balanced now," she said. "See?"

"Oh, yes!" came the chorused confirmation.

"Forgiveness, forgiveness," Mataji's voice intoned above me as her hand pressed down on my head. "You must forgive everyone. You don't have that in your psychology, do you?" Suddenly, she began saying *"Han! Han!* [Yes!, Yes!]," slapping her thigh each time for emphasis, the full-throated *"Han*s!" coming from deep within her chest. Every *"Han!,"* accompanied by a gasping withdrawal of the breath by the onlookers, was intended to spur along my kundalini to a final effort to make it to the *sahsrara*. After a final *"Han,"* Mataji grandly announced, "He is realized."

"Sit in meditation for some time," she told me as I sat up. "Do

you feel a cool breeze on the top of your head and on your palms?"
Indeed I did, though I could not distinguish the coolness due to the
rising of the kundalini from the gusty breeze coming in from the sea.
I felt well, though, calm and deeply relaxed. As she went out to the
foyer, to help speed up the recovery of a patient who had just been
discharged from the hospital after major surgery, I sat quietly in a
corner, resolved that I would find out more about Mataji's system
before I approached her again.

Essentially, Mataji's model of the human psyche is comprised of
the traditional tantric and hatha yoga notions of the subtle body,
with its "nerves" and "centers," and fueled by a pervasive "subtle
energy" that courses through both the human and the divine,
through the body and the cosmos. Mataji's contributions to this
ancient model are not strikingly original: as a former medical student
she has sought to give it a scientific, neurological veneer; as a former
faith healer, she has elaborated upon those aspects of the model that
are concerned with sickness and health; as someone born into an
Indian Christian family she has tried to introduce notions of traditional Christian morality into an otherwise amoral Hindu view of the
psyche.

I have already mentioned this model in the chapter on tantra,
which also shares this view of the human psyche and its evolution.
Indeed this model is the cornerstone of many Hindu cults and
schools aiming at self-realization—with healing as an important
by-product of this effort. The model itself, to be described below,
is the culmination of Hindu psychology and provides the basis for
its psychotherapy. Its scientific status, however, is still undetermined. This is chiefly due to the fact that in the Indian scheme of
things, empirical proof, which is the touchstone of modern scientific
thought, is only one kind of admissible evidence, and of late (I am
thinking of the last one thousand years) the search for this kind of
evidence has tended to be relatively neglected. In the Indian
scheme, the "centers-nerves-energy" model is taken to be true because its correctness has been and can be perceived by the "inner
vision" attained by anyone who has successfully gone through the
required yogic discipline. Moreover, its truth or "reality" is attested
to by the *authority* of tradition, which in India does not take second
place to empirical verification as a category of proof.

Hindu psychology places the birth of human consciousness at the time when the fetus is two to three months old. In the visual imagery, preferred by ancient Hindus to represent abstractions, a column of primordial energy that pervades the universe and which is identical with consciousness, passes through the top of the head —Mataji identifies the location as the fontanel bone—and is refracted into three main channels, our familiar *sushumna, ida* and *pingala.*[1] The bulk of this psychic energy passes through the *sushumna,* the central channel within the spinal column, and settles down in the triangular bone at the end of the spinal cord. In visual imagery, this event is represented by the serpent kundalini resting in three and a half coils at the base of the spine. On its way down, the psychic energy activates the seven *chakras,* or "centers of psychospiritual consciousness," which are placed on the central channel and control our physical, emotional, mental and spiritual "bodies." The unborn child is therefore connected to the Infinite, to the universal "divine consciousness," through the *sushumna.* Mataji, following the theories of Vasant Rele, equates *sushumna* with the parasympathetic nervous system, *ida* with the left and *pingala* with the right sides of the sympathetic nervous system and the *chakras* with the plexuses.[2] Such efforts to find physiological equivalents for the "organs" and processes of the subtle body are reminiscent of the French philosopher Descartes's attempt to identify the pineal gland (which in *chakra* language will correspond to the *sahasrara*) as the seat of the soul and the rendezvous for mind and matter. (Besides being patently confusing and probably wrong, I doubt whether the efforts to equate the mystical channels with the autonomic nervous system and the use of neurological language constitute any improvement on ancient metaphors.)

With birth and the cutting of the umbilical cord, the connection between the resting kundalini and the universal consciousness outside the human body is severed by the appearance of a gap within the *sushumna* in the region of the navel; the notorious "navel gazing" of the East is then literally a contemplation of this gap, called "void" in Zen Buddhism and "maya" in Hindu thought, which separates the individual consciousness from its universal roots. After birth, the infant's emotional reactions to distressful experiences, primarily of deprivation and separation, begin to be retained in the subconscious and lead to the development of what Mataji calls the superego. The "superego," very unlike its Freudian namesake, is located on the left side of the body, at the termination of the *ida* channel at the back of the brain. Besides passively storing reactions to distressful experiences, the infant also takes an active role in separating himself from the environment and becoming an individual. The process of establishing a separate identity and building up an individual "ego," located at the end of the *pingala* channel on the right side of the brain, is accelerated with the development of mental faculties. The scream of protest at birth, simultaneously a reaction to distress and an affirmation of nascent individuality, marks the beginning of both the superego and the ego structures, in which henceforth passive and actively generated karma will be respectively stored. Swelling up like balloons in the hind part of the brain, these structures cut the *sushumna* off from the entry point of universal consciousness at the apex of the head. The fontanel bone calcifies and a new microcosm, isolated from the surrounding macrocosm, has come into existence (p. 199). Here, the central "myth" of Hindu tradition, of the original divinity within each human being cut off from its fountainhead by man's active or passive interactions with a "polluting" world, is expressed in terms of body symbolism. Let me once again note that this conception of a mental-spiritual body is part of a widespread folk consciousness which is also shared by Indian medicine as well as by the mystical traditions.

As long as the *sushumna* is closed at both its ends and the kundalini rests at *muladhara,* the only psychic energy available to the human organism courses through the *ida* and *pingala,* through the left and right sides of the body. When psychic energy as attention passes to the left side, to the superego, we tend to become absorbed in affects and moods, in the whole realm of feelings and emotions and in recollections of the past. Indians, Mataji feels, are particularly susceptible to this kind of overindulgence of the left side. The stressing of this channel builds an overload on the "emotional body" and leaves a person open to all kinds of psychopathology ranging from relatively benign mood swings to instances of full-blown spirit possession. Spirit possession in this scheme takes place because the superego on the left side is open to a "seven-layered" realm of existence—the Hindu "hell"—which Mataji with her penchant for

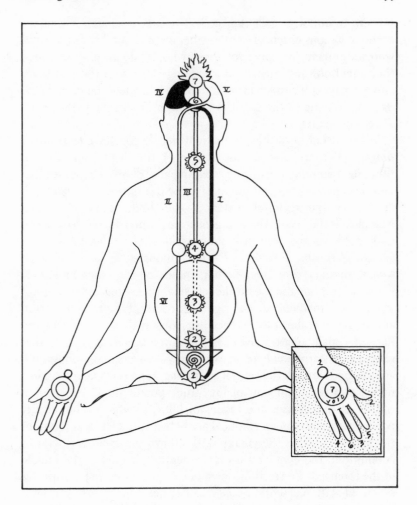

1. *Muladhara chakra*	I. *Ida nadi*
2. *Svadhisthan chakra*	II. *Pingala nadi*
3. *Manipura chakra*	III. *Sushumna*
4. *Anahata chakra*	IV. Superego
5. *Vishuddha chakra*	V. Ego
6. *Ajna chakra*	VI. Void
7. *Sahasrara chakra*	

modern terminology calls the "collective subconscious." This is the home of various orders of demonic beings, our familiar *bhuta-preta*, who are usually the spirits of those who, while alive, exaggerated their emotions and carried on a lifelong affair with their passions. Anyone paying too much attention to the left side is therefore in the danger that one of these spirits may enter his psyche with the aid of his superego.

When attention swings to the right side, it uses the energy of the *pingala*. We are then in the sphere of the "ego"—involved in thinking, planning, organizing, creating and all other activities that seek self-aggrandizement and mastery of the future. The ego too is open to another realm of existence—the Hindu "heaven"—which Mataji calls the "collective supraconscious" and which is basically as undesirable as the collective subconscious. Here dwell the lesser gods, the spirits of yogis and other "monsters of egotism" who sought mastery over their bodies, minds or the environment. If Freud's spirit has a home on the left side, then Adler's driven ghost roams the firmaments on the right. Of course, for a Hindu, heaven and hell, the realms of existence approached through *pingala* and *ida*, are equally unattractive. They are evolutionary dead ends that lead to a reincarnation here on earth; only "universal consciousness," approached through the central *sushumna*, represents man's original nature and the fulfillment of his "true" potential.

Due to the stresses and strains of life, the vital psychic energy normally oscillates in an elliptical arc between the left and the right sides. It is rare that the energy settles down on its proper point of equilibrium, the *ajna chakra* on the central channel in the middle of the forehead. The settling down of energy on the *ajna* constitutes a desired state of mental peace and balance which, Mataji claims, is the natural heritage of only the simple and the innocent at heart; the rest of us must struggle to decrease the pendulum swings of psychic energy. If the swings from the ego to the superego and back again are extreme, there is an acute danger of losing mental balance. To bring the psychic energy to a relative rest at the *ajna chakra*, or at least to reduce the arc of its swing, which we saw was also a preliminary step in tantric healing, is an essential part of Indian systems of mental hygiene.

In their proper state, that is, when the kundalini is flowing through them, the seven *chakras* are visualized as whirling wheels rotating clockwise on their axes on the *sushumna*. Through a network of subtle channels in the body, the *chakras* disseminate vibrations of the gods that preside over them. Though normally the god of each *chakra* represents a particular state of consciousness, in Mataji's system the *chakra* divinities stand for certain basic virtues. Ganesha, the presiding deity of the *muladhara chakra*, symbolizes the innocence and wisdom of the child; the divine couple of Brahma and Sarasvati, presiding over the *svadhisthan chakra*, stand for the creative and aesthetic principles; Vishnu and Lakshmi at the *manipura* send forth the vibrations of *dharma*, or righteousness. Shiva and Parvati at the left side of *anahata* represent existence, Durga in the middle is the source of a mother's protection and security while Rama and Sita at the right side provide fatherly protection and ideals of behavior. Radha and Krishna at the center of *vishuddha chakra* send forth the vibrations of conscience while they are flanked on the left and right by Mahavira and Buddha, who represent the virtue of nonviolence. *Ajna chakra* in the middle of the forehead has Jesus and Mary as its presiding deities, representing the virtue of forgiveness, while Mataji has reserved the seventh *chakra*, the *sahsrara*, for herself and for the last reincarnation, the god-to-come—Kalki; both Mataji and Kalki represent self-realization and individual integration into universal consciousness.

The *chakras* begin pouring their respective virtues into the human body-mind system when they become energized by the kundalini rising through the central channel. Upset *chakras*, on the other hand, are responsible for much psychic and physical distress and Mataji spells out the *chakra* pathology in detail.

The first *chakra*, *muladhara*, becomes upset when the individual's understanding of sexuality is defective or limited. Both repressed sexuality and puritanism can upset this *chakra* as much as promiscuity. Constipation is one of the physical disorders associated with *muladhara*.

Svadhisthan is strained when an individual's activities are dominated by the ego. Too much thinking, planning and so forth upset this *chakra* and cause diabetes and pain in the loins. The *chakra* may also be broken down by sexual perversions.

Manipura becomes heavy and disturbed by the ingestion of alcohol and drugs. It is also affected by misdeeds relating to money and by a lavish and opulent life-style. Predictably, liver trouble arises from a stress on the *manipura*.

Anahata gets disturbed on its right side by emotional problems in relationship to the father and on the left side by similar problems in relationship to the mother. Overactivity and a disrespect of ideal patterns of behavior prescribed for a son, husband, father, and a citizen, are other causes for *anahata*'s malfunctioning. Excessive disturbances of the *anahata* lead to heart problems and breast cancer.

Vishudhi is upset by the lack of self-respect, by self-denial and by dominating or being dominated by others. The physical symptoms of an upset *vishuddha chakra* are a pain in the throat or in the ear. As gateway to the *sahsrara, ajna* is an especially sensitive center. It is affected by the "wrong" use of eyes, wandering attention, erratic thoughts and—a particular preoccupation with Mataji—"by demonic gurus." A demonic guru such as Rajneesh (with whom Mataji in her apprenticeship years was once closely associated) can turn the *chakra* toward the left side, putting the person into the "collective subconscious" and thus making him or her vulnerable to domination by dead spirits. Burning sensations on the forehead and splitting headaches are the physical manifestations of an upset *ajna*.

Once the channels are cleansed, the centers freed of their "catches," and attention no longer fluctuates but is centered around the *ajna*, the stage is set for the kundalini to rise through the central channel. Mataji calls this process, of which the *unio mystica* is an end result, "the mobilization of parasympathetic nervous energy." Concentration, intellectual striving or any other forms of willed effort to raise the kundalini are of little use since they operate with the energy of the sympathetic nervous system. Only the traditional notions of God's grace, of "letting go" and "letting happen" and a complete surrender to Mataji and her "cosmic vibrations" can make the kundalini cross the gap around the navel and rise to the *sahsrara*. As the kundalini gently rises, she caters to the needs of each *chakra* on her way, curing the diseases caused by their constriction and the subsequent withdrawal of the gods. Mental disorders as well as organic malfunctions, hysterical paralysis as well as cancer, all get cured as kundalini wends her way upward.

With its right and wrong channels, *chakras* turning like ancient water wheels to distribute the flow into a network of channels, the hydraulic model of Indian mysticism is also the basis for healing in Mataji's system. Anyone who has become Mataji's follower and has received self-realization is simultaneously credited with the potential of becoming a healer. It is claimed that a cult member develops an acute sensitivity to the "vibrations" emitted by other people as well as to the state of their *chakras* and channels. By paying attention to the sensations of pain, burning and other discomforts on the tips of his fingers (each finger tip corresponds to a specific *chakra*), or in his own *chakras*, the healer can determine the patient's center of affliction and its probable cause. If, for instance, the healer has a burning sensation on the right thumb, it indicates that the right side of the patient's *svadhisthana chakra* is affected due to mental or physical overexertion; if the right thumb shakes, it means the patient is possessed by an evil spirit, and so on.

The healer's use of his own bodily and emotional reactions to the patient as an input for the purposes of diagnosis is not an idea that is wildly fanciful or inherently impossible. After all, the feelings aroused in the analyst by the patient in the initial interview—the monitoring of his countertransference—is important for understanding the patient's central conflict. Many psychiatrists informally learn some rule-of-thumb (and only partly tongue-in-cheek) aids for reaching a diagnosis: obsessional patients make the doctor yawn, strongly homosexual male patients cause a tightening of the anal sphincters, a young schizophrenic's account of his strange bodily feelings will often raise the hair at the back of the doctor's neck, while the so-called Hendrick's signs, namely what young female hysterics convey to the doctor's penis, have been the subject of many an embarrassed student's case report to his supervisor. Indeed, an influential school of Indian medicine considers the development of acute subjectivity, based on an inner, yogic vision, the highest skill that a physician can possess. As with other elements of her system which are often caricatures and occasionally vulgarizations of traditional Hindu ideas, Mataji's diagnostic notions also derive from a corpus of ancient "truths" whose empirical status is undetermined.

The ways of clearing the *chakras* and balancing the channels are many. If a person is agitated or excited, the healer raises the energy of the *ida* by making ascending movements with his hand along the right side of the person's spine; if the patient is apathetic and depressed, the healer similarly raises the energy in the *pingala* with one hand while pushing down the *ida* energy with the other. A *chakra* can be cleared by simulating its clockwise rotation with the fingers of a hand and by asking the person to put his right hand toward a photograph of Mataji and the left hand on the afflicted *chakra* so that the energy from Mataji is channeled directly where it is needed. Another method to remove a "catch" is by worshiping the deity of that particular *chakra*. For instance, knowing that Jesus resides in the *ajna chakra*, the healer and the patient turn their attention toward him and ask for his assistance and forgiveness. Elements of nature, which are related to the *chakra*, also play a part in the healing process. Sitting on the ground and looking at the earth is supposed to help in clearing up *muladhara* problems; bathing the feet in water—rivers and sea are preferred—clears the three lower *chakras*; looking at Mataji's photograph through a flame helps in clearing *manipura* and *ajna*, while gazing at the sky makes it easier to correct the malfunctioning of *vishuddha* and *ajna* centers.

In summary, besides the overactivity of the left and right channels, which creates mental tension, gives rise to psychopathological conditions and may connect an individual to the world of dead souls, upset or clogged *chakras* are held to be a second root cause of mental and physical disease. If the *chakras* are not linked together by the flow of energy, there is no "integrated" personality, while a "catch" in a *chakra* prevents its presiding god from sending out his particular "virtue" into the body-mind system. Balancing and cleansing of the channels and the removal of constrictions from affected *chakras*, then, are the preliminary steps in self-realization as well as in all healing. According to Mataji these preliminaries can only be carried out through dharmic living, a life lived according to the tenets of traditional Indian morality. Besides saying "Yes, sir" to your elders and paying taxes honestly, Mataji's vision of dharmic life is based on the familiar beliefs about the innocence of children, the chastity of women and the wisdom of the old. Dharmic life has that bygone, mythical society as its setting where there were no conflicts between the sexes, generations or social classes, and where everyone was content with his assigned karmic station in life—the rich to make money and the poor not to. A deeply conservative sexual morality is always a cornerstone of such utopias and Mataji's "dharmic life" is no exception. Sexual relations are permitted only within the marriage bond and complete fidelity between the partners, in thought, word and deed—the latter only in the missionary position—is expected. Rama and Sita are Mataji's ideal pair and an emulation of their pallid virtues is mandatory for her followers. For Mataji, Krishna's amorousness, Mahabharata's virile men, spirited women and amoral gods, and even Rama's father Dasharatha with his four wives lie beyond the Hindu pale. As in most utopian visions, Mataji's "dharmic way of life" is also threatened by a deep conspiracy and is beset by subversives. In the Indian case, the conspiracy is religious and not political, not modern but something that has been going on for hundreds of years. The conspiracy against dharma is tantric and tantriks are Mataji's version of cryptocommunists against whom she hurls splendid invective in almost every meeting. We'll come back to this pronounced paranoid element in her cult later.

The stories about Mataji's healing prowess are legion. Tales of curing incurable cases of cancer, making the blind see and the lame walk are avidly told and retold among her followers. Indeed, as with many other gurus and cults, the hope of obtaining relief from a physical ailment or a distressful emotional condition is one of the two primary motives for becoming a member of the cult; the other being a hidden wish for *siddhis*, or magical powers, which are interminably talked about by her followers even while they are being overtly decried. The gurus themselves would look at healing of sickness as a necessary bait for their proper task of leading a person toward self-realization. Perhaps they regret the fact that skepticism is a child of well-being and deplore the perversity of man who is otherwise so little interested in mystical bliss, even when it is so easily and so painlessly provided as by Mataji.

As a healer, Mataji is undoubtedly effective, though again, as with other healers, a number of her cures are little more than provision of temporary relief. A typical example is a woman who suffered from excruciating "back pains." After exhausting the resources of modern medicine she went to see Mataji at a friend's house. At that time Mataji was still developing her mystical technology of kundalini raising and had yet to complete the transition from healing to holiness. Mataji asked the woman to put her head on her lap and be still. After a few minutes the woman felt the pain leave her while at the same time there was a strong scent of jasmine flowers in the room. The pain came back when she returned home and though she faithfully attended Mataji's discourses on the following days, that first experience of a sudden disappearing of pain was never repeated.

The cult members of course consider such temporary cures as showing a lack of faith in Mataji and her divinity. Given their premise that faith in Mataji can permanently cure the most intractable disease, a patient's persisting symptoms "prove" that he lacks faith, which in turn "proves" the correctness of the premise. As Paul Watzlawick and Leon Festinger, among others, have pointed out, once a tentative explanation has taken hold of our minds, information to the contrary may produce not corrections but elaborations of the explanation.[3] The explanation becomes self-sealing, a conjecture that cannot be refuted, while in true human fashion we proceed to distort reality to fit our explanation rather than sacrifice the explanation that has been purchased at considerable emotional cost. This is not to say that I discount Mataji's claims of having cured many organic diseases, including perhaps even a few cases of cancer. Inexplicable cures of serious organic diseases occur in everyday medical practice and it is well documented that a number of unquestionable cases of cancer have disappeared without adequate treatment.[4] It is important to note that occasional cures of advanced organic diseases represent only a minute fraction of those who come to Mataji for help, the majority remaining unchanged or obtaining temporary psychological relief. It is quite likely that every village healer could boast of as many cures as Mataji if the patients came in the same numbers and in the same state of heightened psychological expectancy colored by faith and hope.

Cures, of course, say little about the truth or falsity of the underlying assumptions of a healing system. Jerome Frank, in writing about the miraculous cures at Lourdes, puts the whole matter in perspective when he writes:

> Rivers of ink have been spilled in controversy over whether or not the cures at Lourdes are genuine, based on the erroneous assumption that one's acceptance or rejection of them is neces-

sarily linked to belief or disbelief in miracles or in the Catholic faith. Actually, it is perfectly possible to accept some Lourdes cures as genuine while maintaining skepticism as to their miraculous causation, or to be a devout Catholic while rejecting modern miracles. The world is full of phenomena that cannot be explained by the conceptual schemes current at a particular time. Today these include inexplicable cures of fatal illnesses, in secular as well as religious settings. Depending on one's theoretical predilections, we may choose to believe that all, none, or a certain class of these are miraculous. The mere fact of their occurrence leaves the question of their cause completely open.[5]

The apparent success of different healing methods based on all kinds of religious faiths and secular ideologies compels the not improbable conclusion that the healing power resides primarily within the patient's mind rather than in the tenets of these faiths and ideologies. Like the hypnotic state, which occurs fundamentally as a result of the subject's imagination and expectation rather than because of what the hypnotist actually does, it is the tremendous outpouring and channeling of a patient's emotions and faith rather than a healer's person or methods, which seem to be responsible for dramatic cures.[6]

It is one of the premises of this book that the faith in spiritual healing and susceptibility to spiritual healers are particularly strong in India; but I do not mean to imply that Indians are especially gullible or of "weak intellect." A truly suggestible Indian, like his counterpart elsewhere in the world, probably shares the same underlying personality pattern of being someone above average in intelligence, responsive to vivid imagery, trusting and conventional, emotionally open yet dependent. I am referring here more to a matter of cultural inclinations. Compared, for instance, to the higher susceptibility in the West to everything that can be labeled "scientific" and packaged in a scientific-sounding patter, the Indian suggestibility is toward all that can be couched in the idiom of transcendence and traced back to its Vedic antecedents. As a people who are so strongly moved by ceremony and ritual—the setting in which most dramatic cures occur—Indians do not generally tend to interpose a detached,

critical intellect between themselves and the higher powers (especially when these powers are on a healing mission)—something they
are quite capable of doing in other areas of life; for example in their
response to political exhortation or advertising seduction.

What is miraculous, then, is not the cures but the power of what
we call the unconscious to direct and planfully intervene in extremely complex and still little-understood physiological processes.
Lewis Thomas succinctly captures this sense of awe at the capability
of the unconscious part of the mind when he examines the well-
known phenomenon that warts, which look so tough and durable,
can be made to disappear by "simple" suggestion.[7] The placebo
treatment of warts by painting them with a colored but inert dye and
telling the patient that the wart will go away when the color wears
off is as effective as any form of treatment, including surgical exci-
sion. On receiving the suggestion, whether from Sai Baba, who rubs
holy ash on a devotee's warts, or from a doctor in the hospital, the
"unconscious intelligence" needs to carry out quite complicated and
rather precise operations. If immunologic mechanisms are involved,
then various cells would need to be deployed in the correct order for
tissue rejection; if it is a matter of shutting off the blood supply
locally so that the wart is strangulated, then a selective turning off
of the precapillary arterioles is needed—both of these processes
being extremely complex and still little understood. The carrying out
of such unconscious operations in response to "mere" suggestion is
truly astonishing and in this special sense the cures effected by the
participation of Mataji (and other healers) may well be called miraculous. Authoritative suggestion also figures prominently in Mataji's
sessions of mass kundalini raising. At the end of each public meeting,
lights are dimmed, and everyone is asked to close the eyes and
stretch out both the palms toward Mataji, who demands a full and
continuous attention from the audience. Mataji's deep voice, amplified by the loudspeaker, begins what can be easily compared to the
process of hypnotic induction.

"I am your mother," Mataji's soothing voice comes drifting in
through the darkness. "Leave all your problems and worries in my
lap. Become thoughtless. Concentrate all your attention on me."
Then, in the fashion of a typical hypnotic operator who diverts the
subject's attention to his ideosensory or ideomotor responses with

such suggestions as "I'd like you to shift your attention to your hands. Notice how heavy your hands are getting. Your hands are getting heavier and heavier," Mataji repeats a similar routine. "Now you'll start feeling a cool breeze on your fingers and palms," she whispers through the microphone and then blows through it to simulate the rustling of a breeze. "Relax and it will happen. The breeze will come. A cool breeze is blowing on your palms." Like the hypnotic subject who invariably becomes aware of the heaviness in his hands and begins to build up the conviction that the hypnotist's suggestions are producing changes in his body, thus increasing his susceptibility to further suggestions, most members of Mataji's audience indeed feel a cooling breeze on their palms and fingertips. While the others keep sitting in meditation with their eyes closed, the few who have not felt the cool breeze are asked to open their eyes and look at Mataji. On the darkened stage, Mataji has lighted an oil lamp in front of her and the "unrealized souls" are asked to stare at the flame—Mataji's version of the hypnotic eye-fixation technique—while she repeats her earlier suggestions. Needless to add, because of the emotional pressures created in a group setting, the tendency to identify with the experience of other group members and the intense desire to please the leader, only a handful of people hold out against the power of this mass suggestion. Aware that a critical attitude works against suggestibility, Mataji rightly dismisses the holdouts as followers of other gurus, destined not to attain self-realization till they denounce the "false" guru and get rid of the "internal noise" the guru is creating.

Until now I have oscillated between *understanding* on the one hand, wherein I sought to comprehend Mataji's healing system in its own terms, and *explanation* on the other, which by its very nature lies outside the phenomenon being studied and must be couched in a language different from the one used by Mataji and members of her cult. Whereas explanation produces distance and makes a critical attitude possible, understanding seeks an identification with the experience of others without which no true interpretation is possible. This to-and-from movement between explanation and understanding, between a critical stance governed by a psychological (psychoanalytic) theory and an empathic understanding without condescension, evaluation or judgment, has been the methodological leitmotif of this study. I am acutely aware that because of limits to my own powers of empathy and critical intelligence, there will be unavoidable shortcomings on both sides of this two-pronged strategy. I have particular difficulty in maintaining the empathic stance when I look at some other aspects of Mataji's cult, especially its messianic thrust and its self-understanding as an embattled outpost of the "good" in a hostile, evil world.

In a book called *The Advent*, an official account of Mataji, her cult and its teachings, which is sold at Mataji's meetings together with her photographs and other literature, the author, a young Swiss disciple, writes: ". . . I discovered how the forces of evil have been able to spread unnoticed. How they permeate modern norms and criteria of references, how they condition the behavior of huge crowds of innocent people. I was shocked! I was frightened! Yet HH [Her Holiness] Mataji told me to expose the truth. So, in this chapter, I want to take you with me in the basement of the house of men to show you the threat to our race. It is a threat to our body, mind, awareness and evolution. Its essence must be denounced now."[8] The threat that Mataji denounces so passionately is what she calls "tantrism." "The tantrikas have acquired, through occult practices and black magic, the ability to control spirits. Such spirits are eager to accept the tantrika's control and they enjoy their unfulfilled desires by entering into someone's body . . . they first send forth their host of entities, to gather information about the history and the character of human beings who come to them. This invisible network of spies finds out the potential victims: hypocrites, licentious, self-indulgent, the naive and the rich. . . ."[9]

The tantric forces are not exclusively Indian, though they have been operating for a long time in this country, ever since they took over the world of art in the medieval period, "befooling simple, innocent craftsmen to make erotic sculptures" and managing to "defile Hindu cosmology and mythology by charging them with sexual connotations . . . a satanic shift of meanings in which all values are turned upside down."[10] In the West too, tantrism has been rampant, especially since Freud, who, like the Indian tantriks, "tried to exploit human beings in all aspects of human life, to connect every human endeavour with sex activity and to reduce human awareness to the animal one."[11]

An emphasis on sexuality and eroticism is only one, though a major, aspect of the tantric conspiracy. Tantrism actually incorporates all the forces of modernism and "as a life style appeals so cleverly to our weakness that it has become a universal feature of this Kali Yuga." Tantrik ideologues are disguised as "atheist theoreticians, scientists, psychologists . . . they penetrate the world of newspapers, show business, media, arts and publicity. They can be movie-makers, actresses, writers. Modern media technology directly helps them to spread their demonic vibrations all over the world."[12] It is in this period of crisis, when tantrism is flourishing in a "money-conscious, entertainment-hungry, sex-mad urban consumer society" with fluctuating population and unstable traditions, that Mataji offers herself as the savior against "All the demonic forces that have clubbed together."[13] Because of her efforts "quite a few people today are aware of the coalition between the forces of the dead, the fornicators and the sorcerers"[14] and "under the leadership of HH Mataji, Sahaja Yogis are daily repelling the onslaught of the forces of Darkness."[15]

The conjuring up of a desperate crisis and a battle against a resourceful enemy who lurks everywhere, represent both a contribution to and an activation of the cult member's paranoid potential. However harmful such an encouragement of the paranoid stance may be to the follower's (and the leader's) sense of reality in the long run, it certainly gives rise to shared feelings of triumph and euphoria while at the same time it is a vital source of the group's cohesion and strength. As Robert Waelder has remarked, "It gives strength through the polarisation of all tendencies in one direction and the complete intellectual conviction which eliminates doubts and ambiguities; here, clearly, the native hue of resolution is not sicklied over with the pale cast of thought."[16]

The drama of the threat of Evil, the appearance of the Savior, the initiation of the threatened into a dedicated army of the Good, are ritually reenacted in Mataji's public meetings. A meeting generally starts with a disciple, often a foreigner, berating the modern urban Indian's lack of spirituality while he praises its abundance in India's past. After the listeners are in a suitably penitent frame of mind, he offers salvation for the guilt over betrayed cultural ideals. Mataji, he says, the embodiment of caring and power, the nemesis of evil forces

and the protector of all who seek shelter with her, has finally arrived
to bring them back on the path of dharma, to get them in touch with
the core of their identity as Indians. The underlying mythological
imagery is of Durga, the goddess who is both a slayer of demons and
the compassionate loving mother. In her own speech, Mataji is
indeed Durga. There is a fierce passion in her voice as she talks of
the threatening forces of tantrism, denounces the false gurus and
asks each member of the audience to "take out" the guru he or she
believes in and beat him with a stick. A woman in the front row gets
up to leave.[17] "Sit down," she thunders. "Attention is a delicate
affair. You are disturbing it."

"Don't criticize," says someone from the audience. Mataji turns
toward the new threat to her authority like the tigress who is Durga's
mount.

"Get out if you don't want to stay here," her angry voice rolls over
the cowed audience. "I shall say whatever I want to, for I speak the
truth. I *shall* be listened to. Do you know Christ took a whip to drive
out people like you from the temple? What do you know? Do you
know you can get cancer of the throat by doing what that girl did?
Who'll cure her then? Only me. I have cured leukemia and other
cancers. Then you won't say, 'Don't criticize!' You'll come running
to me.

"Oh, children," she continues in a calmer voice. "I am your
mother. Give up all thought, only give me your faith and I'll take
you across the waters. Who else will or can do that for you? Only
I, your mother."

The eyes of the disciples in the audience shine with pleasure and
excitement. They are a part of her, not vulnerable to feelings of
helplessness but sharing the omnipotence of someone who appears
fully capable of repulsing every threat. In identifying with Mataji,
they have incorporated a part of someone who is supremely self-
confident and self-contained, utterly free from the human needs and
social restrictions that shackle the rest of us.

If I were to classify the gurus in terms of their "parental style"
—the combination of love and control that is characteristic of a
particular parent's behavior—then Mataji is obviously the "posses-
sive" mother. Offering a great deal of warmth and affection to her
"children," she is equally firm in making and enforcing rules, curb-

ing impulses and setting up standards of conduct. If we compare the parental styles of some other gurus, then Maharaj Charan Singh appears to be a gently loving and yet somewhat detached patriarch, neither fiercely loving nor overly strict. Bhagwan Rajneesh, on the other hand, is wholly indulgent, encouraging freedom without limits, giving a seeker the feeling that at last he is being loved and understood to the deepest core of his being and not being trained or socialized to meet goals or standards set by others. It seems to me that a well-developed model of parental styles might contribute to an understanding of the puzzling phenomenon of guru selection; namely, why one guru leaves a seeker quite cold while another arouses such intense emotions that his very life may be transformed. Let me give a brief illustration.

Amita, a thirty-year-old woman who is a lecturer in Hindi in a local college, is one of Mataji's closest disciples. Born into an orthodox, middle-class Brahmin family, she has been engaged in the "search" ever since childhood. "My mother used to worship five hundred and sixty million gods every day," she says in a bitter, contemptuous voice, "but it didn't change her a bit. She was a hot-tempered, dried-up woman with little human sympathy or kindness. So what was the use of observing all the rites and praying to the gods?" As Amita talks of her past, it is clear that she has been in a hostile encounter with her mother all her life. Amita went to see many gurus but was dissatisfied with every one of them till one day, a few years ago, she attended one of Mataji's public meetings. Her conversion was instantaneous and she has remained a devoted disciple ever since. "Mataji is like the cloud that gives rain to everyone," she says. I am struck by the juxtaposition of her imagery in which Mother is dry while Mataji brims over with the rain of love. For Amita, then, Mataji's parental style has elements of both the familiar and the strange. The familiarity is in Mataji's fierceness, the "hot temper"; the difference, and this is indeed crucial, is in the preponderance of warmth and love in Mataji as compared to Amita's early experience of the indifference of her mother's "style." A guru like Charan Singh, I would suggest, is too remote from Amita's central conflict, while Rajneesh would be too threatening to the moral values of a girl brought up in an orthodox, middle-class Brahmin family. Mataji's parental style, on the other hand, dovetails with

Amita's psychological needs and her social experience. Thus while an individual is being "reborn" through initiation into a cult, he is at the same time giving birth to a new parent, the guru, whose parental style will heal the wounds inflicted by the old one and free him from the burdens of his life history, just as the mystical experience itself is supposed to free him from the conditioning of history.

The people who come to hear Mataji and some of whom stay on to become her followers, generally belong to the newly urbanized, emerging middle classes. They are first-generation college students, clerks from government offices, low-level administrative personnel from industrial and commercial concerns, school and college teachers and others who have been exposed to the winds of change of what is loosely called "modernism." Lying somewhere between the vast traditional majority and a minuscule minority of the highly modernized which looks toward the West for all its models, this transitional sector of the population, living in India's towns and metropolitan areas, is the natural reservoir of the cults. Membership in a cult provides an individual with a new group identity to replace the village or caste community from which he has psychologically only recently emerged. Standing between the individual and the impersonal institutions of an urban society, the cults also offer substitutes for community and professional associations. The mutual obligations inherent in cult membership are not limited to an unclogging of each other's *chakras* but also extend, say, to the clearance of a fellow Sahaj yogi's income tax return or getting him a permit for bags of cement that are in short supply.

The transitional sector I speak of consists of many who have recently learned the language of modernism but are still uncertain as to its correct usage. Mataji's dressing up of ancient theories in "scientific" language—her talk of autonomic nervous system rather than of *nadis*, ego and superego instead of *ida* and *pingala*, collective subconscious rather than *preta-loka* ("the world of spirits")— is reassuring to an audience desperately trying to reconcile the modern world view with a core Hindu self. To hear such sentences as "We can be likened to a computer with tremendous potentialities. Self-realization has put the computer onto the mains"; "God's telecommunication system is very dynamic"; "The parasympathetic nervous system is a system which is like a petrol pump through which the petrol of divine love is filled in," is to find a satisfying modern terminology for ancient concerns. To say that a "UPI [Unit of Psychic Interference] is active at the Sixth Vertebra" instead of admitting the presence of a *bhuta* in the *manipura chakra* is not only to put old wine in new bottles but to drink the old wine without feeling that one is offending against the table manners of modernism. This homage to the technological world through an imitation of its language goes hand in hand with a rejection and denigration of the West, not as a geographical entity but as a source of modernity that includes the Soviet Union as well as Japan. Both Mataji and her followers point to Western divorce statistics, alcoholism, crime rates and sexual promiscuity, to self-congratulatorily convince themselves of the superiority of an Indian "dharmic" way of life that emphasizes balance, chastity, renunciation and obedience to tradition. To them, and to many other Indians (including a large number living in the West itself), the West is a gigantic whorehouse, whose cities have "truly become Babylon the great, a nest of harlots and prostitution."[18] They try to dismiss the challenge of Western ideas in arts, sciences, social and political thought by defensively bolstering an uncertain conviction that the eternal Hindu verities will ultimately prevail over an antimetaphysical godless civilization. Though Mataji and other cult leaders may well be right in underlining, however crudely, the importance of the metaphysical for the sustained health of a civilization, their lopsided stress on the sacred has its own problems. True renunciation, for instance, can only be carried out by those who are in a position to do so, who can exercise a real choice. In the absence of productive capacities and artistic and scientific creativity, which, yes, has also made the excesses of consumerism possible, the renunciation advocated by Mataji can only be a beggar's renunciation. Without an awareness and transcendence of crippling inhibitions and sexual hypocrisies that may well also lead to promiscuity, chastity, however laudable a goal in itself, is experienced as an imposition. Obedience to norms and authority, without a consciousness of equality and a critical stance toward received wisdom that admittedly can tilt toward anarchy, is little more than ritualism. Human freedom and choice are as much conditions of "self-realization" in the sacred as they are of "fulfillment" in the profane.

III

MEDICAL
TRADITIONS

8

INDIAN MEDICINE AND PSYCHIATRY

Cultural and Theoretical
Perspectives on Ayurveda

I t is a curved strip of silver, each rounded arm of its U-form about
four inches long while the bridge of the U is flat and has smooth
edges. The object is a tongue scraper, which I have used since my
childhood after brushing my teeth, to remove the filmy layer that
sometimes coats the tongue. I have not seen the silver tongue scraper
used in any other country I am familiar with, and I have accepted
the fact that my own use of a tongue scraper, as perhaps my particular way of oiling my hair or cleaning my rectal orifice with water and
the fingers of my left hand are Indian ways; a part of the culture that
adheres to me as it does to other Indians and needs little reflection
on either its origins or its functions. It was only recently, while
reading the *Caraka Samhita,* one of the three main source books of
the traditional Indian system of medicine, Ayurveda, that I encountered the silver tongue scraper outside my own private morning
rituals. There, in verses 74 and 75 in the chapter "Quantitative
Dietetics" of the first book of *Caraka Samhita,* sandwiched between
other verses on the proper ways of gargling, chewing, oiling the hair
and ears and paring the nails, and on the importance of footwear,
I read, "Tongue scrapers, which should be curved and not sharp
edged, are to be made of metals like gold, silver, copper, tin and
brass. The dirt deposited at the root of the tongue obstructs expira-
tion and gives rise to a foul smell: so the tongue should be scraped
regularly."[1]

As I delved deeper into Ayurvedic literature and became increasingly familiar with its lore through interviews and conversations with
its practitioners, I often encountered the now metaphorical tongue
scraper with repeated "Ah-has!" of recognition. In Ayurveda, I discovered the source of my unvoiced suspicion that the twig from the
neem tree with which I brushed my teeth as a child and which I later
sacrificed at the altar of modernization to the brush and the paste
did infinitely more than just clean the teeth. Here I found the source
of my reluctance to eat radishes and guavas at night, the origin of
my reverence for the beneficial properties of honey and clarified
butter, and of my secret respect for many herbs and roots, especially
if they come from (or are said to be from) the Himalayas. Reading
the Ayurvedic texts, I cannot help but marvel at the process which
has transformed instructions from ancient doctors on the grooming
and care of the body, dietary prescriptions for different seasons and
times of the day, on proper exercise and conduct, as unquestioned
and unquestionable articles of faith for countless generations of men
and women who were born, grew up and died in the fold of Indian
culture.

Ayurveda, of course, is more than dietetics or a system of physical
medicine based on a quaint humoral theory of disease. Its treatises
are as much dissertations on correct behavior as they are descriptions
of pharmacological potencies and physiological equilibria. From the
psychological point of view, what makes the study of Ayurveda
essential is its role as the principal repository of the Indian cultural
image of the body and concept of the person. As we shall see later,
these ideas of the person are often different from those that dominate Western consciousness and form the bedrock of the modern
sciences of man. The Ayurvedic notion of the constituents of the
person, his limits and extensions in time, the nature of his connection with the natural environment on the one hand and with the
psyche (and soul) on the other, the nature of the body's relationship
with the psyche but also with the polis and the cosmos in determining health and illness, may not always be at a conscious level. Yet
these ideas constitute the cultural prism through which men and
women throughout India have traditionally viewed the person and
his state of well-being. Indeed, at the level of cultural images of the
person and the body, Ayurveda provides us with a uniform pattern

within the many-hued weave of Indian society. Since Ayurveda has dominated the medical traditions of all South Asia and, to a lesser extent, Southeast Asia, Gananath Obeyesekere has suggested that this unity may extend beyond the geographical boundaries of India and that "Without some awareness of the theory of Ayurvedic medicine it is not possible for us to understand much of what goes on in the minds of men in the South Asian world."[2]

Ayurveda is not unique in its intimate connection with the culture and society from which it springs. Medical theories, opinions, practices, in any society, tell us as much about social beliefs as about the art and science of healing. For instance, open-heart surgery for cardiovascular disease and radiation and chemotherapy for cancer *after* the diseases have run their destructive course may tell us something about the high valuation placed on technology in solving problems whose causes are unknown, the importance of the individual vis-à-vis the community (especially if the therapy has been financially ruinous for the family), the mechanical conceptualization of the body, and so forth.[3] In contrast to Western medicine, however, Ayurveda has been less a mirror of the cultural belief system than one of its chief architects. Its contribution to the shaping of Indian consciousness derives from its overwhelming monopoly of the theory and practice of healing for scores of centuries till it was recently challenged by Western medicine. Its importance springs from the claim, accepted by generations of ancestors, that Ayurveda, the science of longevity, has no beginning and no origin since it partakes and reflects the laws of nature inherent in life and living beings and thus mirrors their unchanging essence.[4]

The belief that the storehouse of true knowledge is located in a remote golden past was firmly held by almost all the Ayurvedic doctors we interviewed. Discussion of their system often meant flat assertions; evidence for the assertions was usually the recitation of a Sanskrit verse from an old text and their concept of research was the location of verses in obscure texts that supported the doctor's position. A famous *vaid* (as the Ayurvedic physician is called), replying to my question about the basis of Ayurvedic knowledge, characteristically framed his answer with a mythological occurrence: "Parvati too asked Shankar [Shiva] the same question. 'O Lord,' she said, 'Kali-yuga [the last, dark age of the cycle of creation] is about to come. In this age there won't be any true gurus available. So the false gurus will reign. What should someone desirous of obtaining true knowledge do under these circumstances?' 'Such seekers,' Shankar replied, 'should go to the ancient texts, for in the dark age only these texts can be regarded as the true teachers.' " The patients and their relatives sitting around the learned doctor had nodded vigorous agreement.

In contrast to Ayurveda in India, the West has lacked a single medical system with the required weight and authority of the past. Characterized by a rapid turnover in theories of disease—from the Greek humoral theory to hostile spirits as principal pathogens, from disease as a consequence of a faulty distribution of bodily fluids to the theory of autointoxication, from the concept of focal infection to the bacterial and viral origins of disease—Western medicine could not have the same degree of impact on the formation of the cultural images of the body and person as Ayurveda has had in India.

I must admit with a sense of shame that my inquiry into Ayurveda has been long overdue. Trained in the Western therapeutic tradition and absorbing its implicit premise that other healing traditions are antiquarian leftovers of magical world views, of interest only to the historian of medicine or to the anthropologist, I could not quite summon the required scientific attitude of combined respect *and* skepticism, an open-eyed wonder *and* the beady eye of critical doubt which are perhaps essential for any serious inquiry. Many modern writings on Ayurveda, especially by the *vaid*s, appeared to be aggressively defensive, essentially continuing a chapter in the saga of nineteenth-century Indian revivalism. In their tortuous efforts to find modern equivalents and translate Ayurvedic concepts into those of Western physiology and psychology[5] and thus "prove" that ancient sages "knew it all"—akin to the efforts of many Indian mystics who seek to identify physiological locations for the mystical *chakra*s—the revivalists seemed to me to be prisoners of a cast of mind that derives ultimately from the colonial experience. Defensiveness, however, in relation to the modern Western intellectual and scientific tradition is only one aspect of the colonization of the mind. I must admit that, preoccupied with the mote in the revivalists' eye, I did not notice the beam in my own; I failed to see that identification with the Western tradition, however coolly sophisticated, is but another defense against the same deep-rooted feelings of cultural inferiority. It seems I could not explore Ayurveda without an a priori idealization or denigration, till a change in the Western theories of healing took place which in a sense accorded me "permission" to pursue an objective inquiry. I refer here, of course, to what Lewis Thomas has called the reemergence of "magic in medicine," the belief that, microbial infections apart, most of today's human illnesses are multifactorial in nature, caused by two great arrays of causative mechanisms: the influence of things in the environment and one's personal life-style.[6] This, of course, allows diverse healing practices, designed to change life-styles, to flourish. Many kinds of diets and jogging, yoga and biofeedback, transactions and primal screaming, all jostle for healing positions in a market where the imported healing practices of non-Western cultures have begun to command special interest and premium. When one further reads that the latest scientific medical opinion, promising to add eleven years to the life span, recommends the eating of breakfast, regular exercise, not eating between meals, not smoking cigarettes, not drinking excessively and sleeping eight hours each night, then we are squarely in the realm of Ayurveda. In the rules of personal conduct for longevity, Ayurveda appears infinitely more sophisticated; the observations of ancient Indian doctors are full of subtle differentiations.

Consider, for example, the matter of sleep. There are verses on the sevenfold classification of sleep, the role of sleep in obesity, good and bad sleep, methods and measures to induce good sleep, and indications and contraindications for day sleep. "Sleeping during the daytime in all seasons," the text says, "is prescribed for those who are exhausted by singing, study, alcoholic drinks, sexual acts, elimination therapy, carrying heavy weights, walking long distances; those suffering from phthisis, wasting, thirst, diarrhoea, colic pain, dysponea, hiccups, insanity; those who are too old, too young, weak and emaciated; those injured by fall and assault, those exhausted by journey by a vehicle, vigil, anger, grief and fear; and those who are accustomed to day sleep."[7] Generally, however, sleeping during the daytime in seasons other than summer is not advisable and the text goes on to mention the kind of people for whom day sleep is especially proscribed, listing various diseases that can be caused by violating this prescription, and concluding, "So we should keep in view the merits and demerits of sleep in various seasons and situations in order that it may bring happiness."[8]

I have suggested above that Ayurveda is a principal architect of the Indian view of the person and the body. The question arises how this part of the edifice, deriving from medical science, which by its very nature is more "earthy" and practical, fits together with other building blocks of the Hindu world view, especially with the metaphysical cluster of ideas around the theory of liberation, i.e., the moksha-dharma-karma complex. The meeting of medicine and metaphysics in the Ayurvedic texts can only be described as "correct" though sometimes formal and strained because of unvoiced reservations—on both sides. As Debiprasad Chattopadhyaya in his scholarly study of the Caraka Samhita points out, the sometimes confusing and peculiar appearance of the extant text of the Samhita derives from the fact that the metaphysical and religious views introduced into it—including those of karma and adrishta (unseen causes)—are on the whole loosely superimposed on its genuinely scientific content.[9] The doctors certainly display attitudes that often seem placatory toward conventional Hindu piety though these attitudes have little impact on the theories they need for their practice. Good health, the goal of their profession, they write, is the only means to fulfill the scripturally posited four "ends" (purushartha) of life, namely, virtue (dharma); material goods (artha); sensual pleasure (kama); self-realization (moksha).[10] Therefore, Ayurveda is the most sacred of all the Vedas since it does good to mankind not only in respect of the life beyond but also in the present life.[11]

Yet the enthusiasm for virtue (dharma) and liberation/self-realization (moksha) seems muted in contrast with the exuberant affirmation of this-worldly ends of gathering wealth and the enjoyment of sensual pleasures. For instance, in the chapter on the three basic desires of life we read, "A person of normal mental faculty, intelligence and energy, desirous of his well-being pertaining to this world and the world beyond has to seek three basic desires, viz., desire to live, desire to earn and desire to perform virtuous acts."[12] After the commentator has assured us that sensuality has been omitted only because "the desire to satisfy passion constitutes the natural instinct of mankind and as such it is too axiomatic to be discussed,"[13] the text goes on to assert that "out of all these desires, one should give priority to the desire for longevity." Why? Because "with the end of life there is the end of everything" and "one must have a desire for wealth because there is nothing so miserable as a long life without wealth. So one must try to tap the various sources of wealth."[14] As for the third desire, the living of life in "virtue" to attain happiness in future life, the text says, "This desire is in fact shrouded with some doubts. There is doubt, whether one will have a life [rebirth] at all after his death. But why doubt? There are people who believe only in things which are perceptible and as such do not believe in rebirth because of its imperceptibility. On the other hand people believing in rebirth simply rely upon the evidence of scriptures. There are contradictory opinions also: 'parents,' 'nature,' 'impersonal soul' and 'free will' are considered as causes of birth by different schools. So the question remains whether there is rebirth after death."[15] A string of verses then follows on the "evidence" in favor of rebirth, giving the impression that skeptical medical students needed a lot of convincing on a dubious issue.

The struggle of ancient doctors against traditional Hindu metaphysics may seem pathetic to their modern counterparts till we remind ourselves that this struggle, or, better, this dialectic, has characterized Indian society since time immemorial. In ritual as in art, this dialectic has taken the form of asceticism versus eroticism and has been the conflict-laden theme pervading many Hindu lives —Gandhi being the most prominent example of recent times. The ancient doctors were Hindus too, and if they often seem to choke on some of the doctrines of the Hindu world view which they could neither spit out nor swallow, they deserve sympathy rather than censure. One can imagine that for them the doctrine of karma would be especially difficult to accept, and, as Chattopadhyaya has pointed out, this is indeed the case as far as the medical texts are concerned.[16] In some sections of the *Caraka Samhita,* there is talk of diseases resulting from the actions of previous lives and the futility of curative efforts till the effects of the individual karma have been exhausted after taking their own predetermined course. On the other hand, a whole chapter of the *Caraka Samhita,* pointedly silent on the karma of previous lives, confidently proclaims and explains the notion that successful medical treatment depends on four and *only* four factors—the physician, the medicament (drug or diet), the nursing and certain qualities of the patient.[17] Openly listing a number of diseases that are incurable, the *vaids* do not make the indefensible claim that they can cure all diseases. They *do* assert that given the right kind of nursing, a curable disease can always be cured by the right doctor, applying the right therapy and, they might have added, "to hell with the patient's balance on the karmic ledger!" It is the confident scientist, sure of the efficacy of his knowledge and techniques, where there is little room for chance or luck, who writes: "To say that patients adopting the therapeutic measures having the sixteen qualities [of the four factors of medicine] die is not borne out by facts; therapeutic measures can never be ineffective in curable diseases. . . . As an archer having the knowledge and practice [of archery] shoots arrows with the help of his bow and does not err in hitting a massive body nearby, and thus accomplishes his object, so a physician endowed with his own qualities and other accessories proceeding with the act [of treatment] after proper examination will certainly cure a curable patient without fail. So it is not correct to say that there is no difference between the application and non-application of therapeutic measures."[18]

Ayurveda's disbelief in, or at least contradictory attitudes toward, Hindu metaphysics also extends to other facets of Hindu orthodoxy. The cow is rarely mentioned in the venerable company of gods, Brahmins and ancestral spirits, but is discussed where it actually belongs—in the class of animals called *prasaha* that grab and tear off their food—and the text blithely proceeds to discuss the merits of eating beef, especially for those suffering from "rhinitis, irregular fever, dry cough, fatigue, heightened digestion and metabolism *(atyagni)* and wasting of muscles."[19] It is the same with the drinking of alcohol. Hindu lawgivers have often strongly disapproved of alcohol[20] and, as we saw earlier, drinking is frowned upon by most mystical cults that aim at individual self-realization. Ayurveda marches to a different drummer. Though it warns against alcoholic excesses, the attitude toward liquor is generally approving, and occasionally lyrical: "(Wine is) the aid of affectionate embraces of women's bodies full of warmth of youth, the warm clasp of their waists, thighs and full-grown breasts."[21] There is a whole section on the beneficial aspect of the various types of liquor, which ends with the considered conclusion, "Wine in general is exhilarating and nourishing. It eliminates fear, grief and exhaustion. It promotes confidence, energy, intelligence, contentment, nourishment and strength. If taken by good people observing all the rules, it works as an elixir."[22]

I am not suggesting that ancient doctors were dedicated hedonists who took care that their patients' religion never got in the way of their pleasures. I doubt whether Hindus could be or ever have been as unswerving in their pursuit of hedonism as, for instance, the ancient Egyptians or even the Romans. Yet as a modern clinician, intimately involved with his patients, who—quite apart from their individual conflicts—seem to enter the psychotherapeutic situation with the myriad inhibitions of a society whose collective psyche seems to be under the constricting sway of its mystics and saints, I like to build my own private mythology of the "Indian Past." Peering into this past through the haze of centuries to contemplate the professions and practices of my colleagues of antiquity, I see little of the public myth of the piety and spirituality of the Satyuga—the golden age of spirituality—that beguiles so many of my countrymen today. Instead I behold the Hindus as a cheerful, energetic and erotic people. They are respecters of death, yes; they are involved in the metaphysical questions that death arises, certainly. Yet they do not let the search for answers to these questions dominate the living of their lives; neither do they withdraw from the possible joys of life because of the probable sorrows.

The Person in Ayurveda

Ayurveda is steadfast in insisting that medicine should always be centered on the person rather than on the disease. It believes that the twin goals of maintaining good health and deliverance from disease in ill health can be reached only if the doctor has a thorough understanding of the person. The person in his wholeness is called the "asylum" *(asrya)* of disease and constitutes the main subject of medical science. In the words of an oft-quoted verse, "Mind, soul and body—these three are like a tripod; the world is sustained by their combination: they constitute the substratum for every thing. This (combination) is the person *(purusa)*: this is sentient and this is the subject matter of this Veda (Ayurveda): it is for this that this Veda (Ayurveda) is brought to light."[23]

The philosophical emphasis on the *wholeness* of the person is reflected in the *comprehensiveness* of the diagnostic examination prescribed for the Ayurvedic physician. Besides the thorough physical checkup to discern any pathological condition, the tone of the system, age, compactness, proportions, digestive power and capacity for work, the medical examination includes the patient's emotional and social spheres. The doctor is directed to infer the patient's "understanding from the nature of his actions, his passion from the intensity of his attachments, his infatuations from the lack of his understanding, the degree of his anger from the violence of his actions, his grief from his despondent mien, his joy from his exuberance. . . ."[24] The knowledge of the patient's present mental state and his more enduring personality traits must be further supplemented by gaining a thorough familiarity with his familial, social, geographical and cultural context, by ascertaining his caste, lineage and "land examination" *(bhumi-pariksha)*. In the latter, "the doctor has to know the region in which the patient is born, grew up or has developed the disease. The peculiarity of the land should be noted, the food habits of its inhabitants, their way of life, physical vitality and character. The doctor must also note the general conditions of the health of the region's inhabitants, the special features of their habitat, their inclinations, the kinds of diseases that they most often contract and also what is generally considered wholesome or unwholesome in this region."[25]

The collection of such a large number of facts is not for the sake of any compulsive notions of thoroughness. Before he makes his diagnosis, prescribes a therapy or ventures on a prognosis, the physician is expected (again ideally, since present Ayurvedic practice is quite different) to collate and compare this information against his knowledge of the different orders of being—physical, mental, social —in which a person lives and which both constitute and circumscribe his wholeness. Some of this knowledge, especially nonphysiological, is often organized in terms of categories of triads: the three types of land (arid, marshy and ordinary); three types of temperament *(sattva, rajas, tamas)* with their sixteen subtypes; three bases of physical differentiation with twenty subtypes; the three ages of man-childhood *(bala)*, middle years *(madhya)* and old age *(jirna)*— with their further subdivisions, and so on. Whatever the limitations of these categories and of practices rooted in category-based thought, the attempt at categorization in diverse fields of knowledge reflects the determination of ancient Indian doctors to invest the otherwise vague notion of "wholeness" with concrete content.

The person in Ayurveda, then, is conceived of as simultaneously living in and partaking of different orders of being—physical, psychological, social and, one must add, metaphysical. A systematic knowledge of all the orders and their interrelationships is considered essential for the education of a doctor. I should further add that the boundaries between these orders are considerably fluid; or, in other words, the separation between psyche and soma or between soma and natura is much weaker—when it is made at all—than is the case with modern Western concepts of the person. This is an inevitable corollary of the fact that in the monistic Indian world view the person is seen as a microcosm; all that is part of the cosmos has its homologue within the person.[26]

This equivalence of man and creation leads to a fundamental postulate of Ayurveda, namely the identity of the physical part of the person—the body—with the physical part of the cosmos—nature. The locus of this identity is in "the five root forms of matter" *(pancha-bhuta)*, and the theory of the *pancha-bhuta* is a cornerstone of the Ayurvedic system.

Body, Nature and Health

According to the *pancha-bhuta* theory, everything in the universe, animate or inanimate, is made of five forms of matter—earth, fire, wind, water and *akasa* (roughly translated as ether). Under certain favorable conditions, matter becomes organized in the form of living creatures. These living creatures constantly absorb the five elements contained in environmental matter (nutrition), which is transformed by the fires in the body into a fine portion *(prasada)* and refuse *(kitta or mala)*. Successive transformations of the fine portion of food produce the seven physiological elements of "organic sap" *(rasa)*, blood, flesh, fat, bone, marrow, semen, as well as the substance constituting the sense organs, body joints, ligaments, etc. Nutrition, then, is of critical import. "Food sustains the life of living beings. All living beings in the universe require food. Complexion, clarity, good voice, longevity, genius, happiness, satisfaction, nourishment, strength and intellect are all conditioned by food. Professional activities leading to happiness in this world, Vedic rituals leading to abode in heaven and the observance of truth, *brahmacharya* leading to salvation are all based on food."[27] The body, like nature with its ceaseless transformations of matter, is in a state of perpetual flux, for "nothing about the body remains the same. Everything in it is in a state of ceaseless change. Although in fact the body is produced anew every moment, the similarity between the old body and the new body gives the apparent impression of the persistence of the same body."[28] As far as the body is concerned, death is the reversion of matter constituting the organism to its original state; the term death—*dehanta* (end of body)—is synonymous with "end of activities," "impermanence," "cessation."

The Ayurvedic assumption of the identity of body and nature is a logical consequence of the leitmotif of the Indian world view that asserts an underlying unity in the apparent multiformity of creation and strives for a transcendence of dualities, oppositions and contradictions. Since time immemorial the siren call of this "mystical" leitmotif has continued to exercise a powerful hold on the Indian intellectual and scientific imagination. The plant physiologist Jagdish Chandra Bose, for instance, echoes the scientific philosophy of Ayurvedic doctors when he writes: "There is no break in the life-processes which characterise both the animate and [the] inanimate world. It is difficult to draw a line between these two aspects of life. It is of course possible to delineate a number of imaginary differences, as it is possible to find out similarities in terms of certain other general criteria. The latter approach is justified by the natural tendency of science towards seeking unity in diversity."[29]

Within the context of a ceaseless flux of body and nature, the ancient physicians believed health to be a state of dynamic equilibrium of the bodily elements. The Ayurvedic theory emphasizes especially the equilibrium of the three humors *(tridosha)*—wind, bile and phlegm. Of the three humors, wind occupies a prominent position. Food is said to be moved into the stomach and blood circulated through all parts of the body by the power of the *prana* kind of wind. The *apana* wind in the anus region acts downward to expel flatus, urine, feces, semen and fetuses. The *samana* wind, located in the region of the navel, helps in the digestion of food and transforms it into blood, semen, feces and so forth. The *udana* wind in the throat, acting upwards, produces speech and song (as well as belches) while the *vyana* wind, pervading all parts of the body, circulates the nourishing sap. Bile and phlegm too are each of five kinds, distinguished by their specific functions in the body system. For instance, the *pachaka* bile in the stomach is a source of physical strength through its action in digesting four kinds of food, while the *alochaka* bile in the eyes accomplishes the act of seeing. Taste is experienced in the tongue with the aid of *bodhaka* phlegm, while the *sleshmaka* phlegm in the joints adds to their articulation.

Illness occurs when any one of the three humors becomes excessively "agitated" and increases disproportionately in relation to others. The imbalance of humors occurs (and this is the general theory of the causation of disease in Ayurveda) due to the *excessive* use, *deficient* use or *misuse* of (1) the objects of the senses, (2) action (consisting of the actions of body, mind and speech) and (3) time, *i.e.*, the different seasons.[30]

The restoration of the balance of bodily elements and thus of health rests on the consumption of environmental matter in the right form, proportion, combination and at the right time. After ascertaining the nature of any imbalance in the body, the doctor identifies a substance (or a combination of substances) in nature—drug or diet—which, when transformed within the body, will correct the humoral disequilibrium. This is why "there is nothing in nature without relevance for medicine" and why Ayurveda has collected an enormous amount of data on the therapeutic efficacy of all kinds of natural substances. Here seasons, plants, natural substances and constituents of the body are all integrated in a complex yet aesthetically elegant theory of physical health as an equilibrium of somatic and environmental elements.

The Body Image

The human body occupies a unique position in creation as the only object that is part of both our inner and our outer worlds.[31] The body distinguishes itself from other parts of the universe by the fact that it is perceived simultaneously through two types of sensation. On the one hand we perceive our bodies through the inner, "proprioceptive" sensations of depth sensibility while on the other hand the body is also perceived by external, "sensoriperceptive" sensations, mainly tactile and visual. Our earliest inner sensations, the beating of the heart, the contractions and expansions of the lungs as we breathe, the abdominal sensations associated with feeding and evacuation, are the central crystallization point for the "feeling of self" around which a "sense of identity" will be later established. The external perception of the body's central and peripheral parts will help the infant gradually work out the distinction between the self and the not-self and contribute to the differentiation of the self from the world of objects. The integration of these two kinds of processes, of our bodily feelings and the unconscious fantasies about the body's processes and contents on the one hand with the relevant visual, auditory and kinesthetic data on the other, yields our individual *body image*. Shimmeringly hazy at the beginning of life, the contours of the body image in our "prehistory" change ceaselessly like the bed of a capricious monsoon stream. Sometimes its parts are surrealistically distorted, while at others a part may disappear altogether like the extra-smile anatomy of the Cheshire cat. It is only after the quasi-bodily experimentation starting from the end of the first year of life, when touching and the visual taking in of the bodily parts —one's own and those of others—help the child in the construction and drawing of the body together in a central gestalt, that the body image gradually becomes stable, its boundaries differentiated more firmly from all that is not the self.

Of course, this body image, the nucleus of an individual's identity and the guarantor of his separation from the object world, does not coincide with the objective body. The proportions of different limbs are apt to be distorted, while the images of bodily processes can be truly fantastic. In certain psychotic episodes, we find the regressed individual expressing the feeling that his body has expanded (or contracted) or that his face has become "different"; sometimes he might feel that one of his organs does not belong to him or even that it is inexplicably absent. In other, more "normal" cases, the body image may include articles of clothing or even an amputated limb. There are mature women whose body image consists of the vagina of a little girl that will get torn and damaged in the sexual act, while the fat man or woman with a sylphlike body image has been a familiar and poignant object of many literary efforts, both tragic and farcical.

Perhaps, as Phyllis Greenacre has suggested, each individual needs constantly to reinforce the sense of his own body through an association with others of predominantly similar appearance.[32] Even at a mature age, the individual may need at least one other person similar to himself, to look at, speak to and to "take in," in order to accentuate his own body image and thus safeguard the core of his sense of identity. The isolation and avoidance of human contact sought by many aspiring and adept yogis—the "withdrawal to the Himalayas" syndrome—may indeed have its roots in a systematic effort to diminish the clarity of the personal body image. In turn, this diminution temporarily dissolves the laboriously built up sense of identity and undoes the differentiation of the self from the nonself. Little wonder that the body—"the temple of the living god"—is of such vital significance in mystical rituals, practices and symbolism, since it is preeminently our body (or more precisely our body image) that holds us back from the mystical goals of nonduality, nonseparation and dissolution of individual identity in a larger "cosmic" identity.

I have discussed the body image in terms of individual development and emphasized both its universal and idiosyncratic elements. Each person's body image, however, also has a strong cultural component. I would go so far as to suggest that, given the body's central position in human life, the cultural variations in the body image lead to radically different ways of experiencing the world and organizing this experience. Let me illustrate this through a comparision of some aspects of the Indian body image with my impressions of the "modal" body image in Western—mainly North American and northern and central European—societies.

The Indian image of the body, I have pointed out earlier, emphasizes its intimate connection with the cosmos. As a nineteenth-century Bengali text on the body puts it, "In this universe a great wheel of transformative power *(maya-chakra)* is spinning ceaselessly. The small individual wheels of transformative power in the bodies of living things are connected with that wheel. Just as, when some great steam-driven wheel turns like the prime mover, then all of the components of the machinery move together in coordination and smoothly accomplish their tasks, similarly the small wheels of transformative power that turn through their connection with the great wheel, within the bodies of individual living things, help accomplish such bodily activities as regulating the flow of blood in the body, digesting food, inhaling and exhaling, and moving back and forth."[33] The Indian body image stresses an unremitting interchange taking place with the environment, simultaneously accompanied by ceaseless change within the body. As Francis Zimmermann writes, "There is no map nor topography of the body but only an *economy,* that is to say fluids going in or coming out, residing in some *asrya* (recipient) or flowing through some *srotas* (channels)."[34] It is the imagery from the vegetable kingdom, such as the plant's drawing of nourishment through the roots, the rising of the sap, and the milky exudation of the resinous trees, that provides models for the image in Ayurveda. Indeed, as Wendy O'Flaherty has shown in her discussion of some Vedic and post-Vedic myths, fluidity and the transaction of fluids—between humans, between gods and between humans and gods—are central Hindu preoccupations.[35]

The Hindu body imagery gives rise to a whole class of diseases, which Obeyesekere has called *cultural diseases,* where a person falls ill because of his conviction that an inordinate loss of a bodily substance—essentially a fluid—has taken place. The most obvious example of such a cultural disease is *svapanadosha* (lit. "dream fault") in which young men complain of body aches and headaches, increasing enervation and feelings of unreality about the body scheme because of the loss of semen in nocturnal emissions. Clinically, the complaint involving substance loss may resemble the hypochondriacal sensations at the beginning of schizophrenia where the body image is perceived to be altered and the body, or some of its parts, are felt to be not quite the same as usual. Substance-loss anxieties, however, are clearly not schizophrenic but the natural (though pathological) outcome of a cultural vision of the body in ceaseless flux.

I do not mean to imply that such a vision protects the members of the culture against the universal anxiety felt at the threat of loss of individual boundaries and identity. In fact, the presence of this cultural body image, though increasing the tolerance of the anxiety associated with the danger of identity dissolution, also keeps this anxiety closer to the surface of consciousness. The traditional preoccupation of Hindu culture with the question of identity, with "Who am I?," then needs to be viewed against this backdrop, *i.e.*, the Hindu stress on the vision of an unchanging human core—the *atman*—may (among other things) also be a cultural defense against the fundamental anxiety aroused by an image of the body in unflagging transformation.

The Western image is of a clearly etched body, sharply differentiated from the rest of the objects in the universe. This vision of the body as a safe stronghold with a limited number of drawbridges that maintain a tenuous contact with the outside world has its own particular cultural consequences. It seems to me that in Western discourse, both scientific and artistic, there is considerable preoccupation with what is going on *within* the fortress of the individual body. Preeminently, one seeks to explain behavioral processes through psychologies that derive from biology—to the relative exclusion of the natural and the metanatural environment. Let me give an illustration.

For many years, research on child development has focused on what is happening within the child as it grows up. There has been much interesting work on the "unfolding" of a child's capacities and the construction of a number of sophisticated tests and benchmarks of intellectual and cognitive development. In contrast, the work done on a systematic conception and differentiation of the environment in which the child's development takes place has been minimal. At most, the environment has been conceived of in nutritional and human terms; for instance, in finding out the effects of maternal deprivation on the development of the child. The natural aspects of the environment—the quality of air, the quantity of sunlight, the presence of birds and animals, the plants and the trees—are a priori viewed, when they are considered at all, as irrelevant to intellectual and emotional development. Given the Western image of the body, it is understandable that the more "far-out" Indian beliefs on the effects of the natural world on the human body and psyche, for example, the effects of planetary constellations, earths, magnetic fields, seasonal and daily rhythms, precious stones and metals—are summarily consigned to the realm of fantasy, where they are of interest solely to a "lunatic fringe" of Western society.

Similar to the Indian body image which holds out the threat of a dissolution of individual identity and thus encourages a cultural preoccupation with questions of identity and the unchanging part of the self, the Western body image too contains an intrinsic threat. The danger here is of a complete isolation and the cutting off of the self from its human and natural moorings. This, in turn, encourages a (defensive) cultural preoccupation with the question of man's "alienation" and the ecological issue of man's relationship with his environment.

Another central aspect of the Indian body image is the very high amount of emotional investment in the body. To a Westerner, the attention that the texts expect a person to devote to his body appears more appropriate to a doting mother's care of her newborn infant than to an adult's relationship with his body. The efforts to increase the body's strength, beauty and grace and to preserve its youthfulness against the ravages of age may even be seen as an expression of "bodily narcissism" in a neutral and relativistic sense since the rejection of the body in the West for long periods of its history has loaded the word with a negative value orientation.

Beginning with the eyes, the *Caraka Samhita* recommends the application once in every five nights of a collyrium made of copper and a daily application of a collyrium of antimony to soothe the eyes and enhance their natural luster.[36] Nasal drops made from *anu taila* (an oil made by boiling twenty-four different herbs and plants with rainwater and then with goat's milk and oil) are to be administered three times a day for seven days during the autumn, spring and rainy seasons. This ensures that "his (the user's) hair and beard never become white or grey; he never experiences hair fall; they grow luxuriantly. . . . His face becomes cheerful and plump; his voice becomes sweet, stabilised and stentorious."[37]

I have already mentioned the tongue-scraping part of oral hygiene. In addition, chewing of various spices and nuts is recommended for the clarity, taste and good smell of the mouth, and gargling with *til* oil for the strength of the jaws, depth of voice and —a peculiarly Hindu ideal of masculine beauty—"plumpness of the face."[38] Regular oiling of the hair and the ears and periodic oil massages are a part of the normal body care; the latter is suggested to make the physique smooth, strong and charming and to prevent the onslaught of aging.[39] The use of scents and garlands of flowers "stimulate[s] libido, produce[s] good smell in the body, enhance[s] longevity and charm," while the "wearing of gems and ornaments adds to prosperity, auspiciousness, longevity, grace, prevents dangers of snakes, evil spirits, etc."[40] Even sexuality is pressed into the service of bodily narcissism; frequent intercourse is recommended in winter to keep up the body's vigor, while complete sexual abstention is prescribed for the duration of the summer.[41] Somehow, it seems quite appropriate that India's national bird is the peacock!

In contrast, the legacy of rejection of the body in the West persists in the unconscious fantasy of the body as a dirt-producing factory. As Lawrence Kubie has pointed out in an original and stimulating paper, there exists an unconscious image "of the body as a kind of animated, mobile dirt factory, exuding filth at every aperture and that all that is necessary to turn something into dirt is that it should even momentarily enter the body through one of these apertures."[42] Kubie's remarks on this ubiquitous fantasy perhaps apply more to the North American and northern and central European societies than to Mediterranean ones, and he may well be correct in identifying a widespread Western assumption that the insides of the body are in fact a cistern, that all apertures of the body are dirty avenues of approach, dirty holes leading into dirty spaces, and that everything which comes out of the body, with the possible exception of tears, is for that reason alone dirty.

Speaking as an Indian, I must say that I too have been struck by the North American and European taboo on body apertures, a taboo which at the most permits the wiggling of an itching ear but not a digging into it with a finger; nasal acrobatics but not a boring in the nostril with a finger to remove an uncomfortably lodged mucus. In contrast to the relative unconcern in India with public hawking, belches and farts, the Western taboo forbids noises or smells to emanate from an aperture that may draw attention to the opening and thus to the dirt factory humming behind it. By extension, a cavity, a cleft or a pit in the body carries the presumption of dirt, whose smells must be disguised—to the considerable satisfaction and profit of the deodorant industry and the media that thrive on the dirt fantasy. I do not mean to imply that the dirt fantasy is absent in the Indian context. There is certainly a horror of the dirt of others (though perhaps a great tolerance of one's own dirt) that is expressed in the preoccupation with purity and pollution. What makes the dirt fantasy in India different is its relatively greater access to consciousness; the fascination and revulsion with dirt, as we saw in the Tantra chapter, are neither disguised nor displaced to the extent they are in the West.

Psyche and Soma

In an earlier section, I have attempted to sketch the Ayurvedic view of the transactions between the body and the environment—in illness and health—and the principle of soma-*natura* identity which governs these transactions. We must remember that in the Hindu view, the person consists of two other bodies besides the gross physical one, namely the "subtle body" *(linga sharira)* and the "causal body" *(karana sharira)*. The causal body is purely a metaphysical construct, the "pure self" of Hindu philosophy, and thus of limited interest as far as medicine is concerned. We need to look more closely at the subtle body and its relationship to the gross one *(sthula sharira)*, again both in illness and in health, and a convenient point of departure is provided by Ayurvedic embryology.

The physical development of the fetus depends on three main factors: the "seed" of the father, the "seed" of the mother and the *rasa*, or "organic sap," which nourishes the embryo. The "father factor" is responsible for the growth of hair, nail, teeth, bone, blood vessels, ligaments and sperm; the "mother factor" for the skin, blood, muscle, fat, heart, pancreas, liver, spleen, kidney, bladder, stomach, intestines, colon, rectum and anus. Besides these determinants, of the physical body, Ayurveda—following the dominant schools of Hindu philosophy—also discusses the role of the subtle body in the constitution and development of the person.

The subtle body, visible only to the Yogic vision, can be conceived of as the core of the person which "adheres" to the individual soul. As we have noted earlier, since birth and death are not regarded as the beginning and end of the person but as mere changes of state, then it is the subtle body, the "core person," which maintains a continuity of personal identity through many cycles of birth and death till the time of final liberation. Essentially, the subtle body consists of (1) *buddhi* (lit.), intelligence and the individual counterpart of the cosmic intelligence; (2) *ahamkara* or "I-ness," the individuating principle which is responsible for the manifestation of individuality in the person and for limitation, separation and variety in the cosmos; (3) *manas*, which has been roughly but inadequately translated as mind and should include "heart"; (4) the *indriyas*, the five potential sensory organs of ear, skin, eye, tongue and nose, and the five potential motor organs of speech, touch, walking, evacuation and reproduction; (5) the *tanmatras*, which are forms of subtle matter or potential energies, namely the potentials of sound, touch, color, taste and smell that later evolve into the five basic elements of matter constituting the gross physical body. Body and the mind are then two different aspects of the subtle body. The identity of the somatic and mental planes is also expressed in the notion that the food consumed by a person gets divided into gross and subtle elements; the gross elements nourish the body while the subtle part of food builds up the mind and fuels mental processes.

Entering the conceptus at the moment of fertilization, the subtle body brings the capabilities of transmigration into different orders (*yonis*) of living beings, potentials for consciousness and self-realization. It incorporates essential life processes governed by the different forms of *vayu*. It contains within it the predetermined life span of the individual, his capacity for individuation, understanding, recollection and a host of emotional and behavioral predispositions which reflect the psychic constellation reached at the end of a previous life. Difficult to translate exactly into any one of the Western concepts related to the person, it seems that the essence of the subtle body (minus the *tanmatras*) comes closest to the ancient Greek meaning of the "psyche." As the animating principle in man and other living beings, the psyche too was the source of all vital activities and psychic processes—rational or irrational—and considered capable of persisting in its disembodied state after death.

Because of the inclusion of the *tanmatras*, the subtle body is more than the psyche and in fact becomes the locus of identity of body and mind, the subject of both physiological and psychological predicates. The concept of the subtle body constitutes the Indian solution —of a thoroughgoing psychophysical monism—to the mind-body problem. As we know, though the metaphysical dispute in Western philosophy surrounding the nature of the relationship between the body (*i.e.*, the brain and the nervous system) and the mind (*i.e.*, certain mental events) has a long history and appears to be formidable, there are only a small number of proposed solutions. The first is that the body and mind are ontologically distinct and cannot affect each other, *i.e.*, the answer lies in a psychophysical parallelism. This, however, dismisses the "unity of science" hypothesis from the very outset and is thus intolerable to many scholars. The second proposed solution is of interactionism, which holds (like the dualism of Descartes) that mind and body are separate but affect one another. This thesis is perhaps the dominant one in current Western thought. Even though it is not known exactly how brain and mind interact, the interactionist position is considered methodologically the most fruitful.[43] The third hypothesis, that mind and body are identical, whether as different modes of one and the same x, or as x described from two different standpoints in two different languages, is at the center of controversy in Western philosophy but an accepted part of Indian thought.[44]

The Indian thesis of psyche-soma identity is also underlined by the location of the mind in the heart. In Ayurveda, the heart *(hridaya)* is not an organ but is conceived of as the center of a network of channels within the body which carry the flow of vital fluids. The localization of consciousness and thought at this nub of somatic, vital activity emphasizes the psyche-soma continuity of being that marks the beginning of life. Here, I should note that different localizations of the mind can be of considerable interest from the viewpoint of a comparative cultural psychology.[45] For instance, the general Western location of the mind and thus of *conscious* thought in the head leads to an unavoidable placing of dreams, fantasies and other psychic activity somewhere "down below" in the body—in the "subconscious," and therefore to the notion of a *somatic* base to such activity, as in the Freudian theory. It also leads to (or perhaps reflects) a distance (if not an opposition) between the mind and the psyche-soma. In the Hindu imagery, the fount of unconscious psychic activity—the *chitta*—is located below the heart in the region of the perineum. Since it is below the center of somatic activity, the unconscious *chitta* has not a somatic but a metaphysical base in the psychic traces, the *samskara,* from a previous life. The head, on the other hand, becomes the container of a potential "supra-" or "above-consciousness" for which there is no place in the Western body scheme since the head is already otherwise occupied.

The identity thesis, the traditional Indian solution to the body-mind problem (except, of course, that it was never an *Indian* problem!)—also underlines the Ayurvedic theory of "psychosomatic" illnessess. Psychosomatic medicine in Ayurveda differs in significant respects from its counterpart in Western medicine, which has been preoccupied with one particular type of interactionism, namely the "mysterious leap from the mind to the body," or, more prosaically, with the problem of somatization.

We know that Freud's early formulations emphasized the role of emotional factors in certain somatic *conversion* reactions, most notably in hysterical conversions. Closely allied with the hysterical conversions are inhibitions of certain bodily functions, such as constipation, impotence, frigidity, psychogenic sterility, anorexia and insomnia, whose symptoms are also symbols. In each case the symbol tells a story, most often, as Joyce McDougall puts it, of "the sufferer-hero being a guilty victim of forbidden wishes, who has met with setbacks on the pathways to desire."[46] The conversion disorders are psychogenic without an evident physiological lesion or infection, and can be understood mainly in psychodynamic terms—perhaps a uniquely modern achievement without peer in Ayurveda or indeed in any other traditional system of medicine.

The other kinds of bodily disorders in which the mind seems to be involved—bronchial asthma, essential hypertension, peptic ulcer, ulcerative colitis and neurodermatitis among others—demonstrate a clearly physiological dysfunction. Here, symptoms are *signs,* without symbolic significance, but are nevertheless related to the patient's personality structure, life circumstances and life history. These are the *psychosomatic* illnesses, more mysterious and certainly more intractable than the conversion disorders, though there have been many interesting attempts to connect the mind with the body in their etiology. Perhaps the best-known attempt is by Franz Alexander, who linked the damming up of specific emotions with specific cell and tissue damage.[47] Thus, for instance, Alexander linked asthma to the dammed-up urge to cry out to the mother for succor, and viewed ulcer as an outcome of the chronic desire to be fed— opposed by shame and guilt. These earlier formulations have now widened out into theories that invoke the whole personality rather than one specific emotion. There is the competitive, restless, time-haunted, so-called Type A person supposedly bound for a coronary; there is the cancer-prone personality who represses and denies emotional stress and depression. Most of these theories, though still controversial, nevertheless lie in the mainstream of current Western psychosomatic medicine.

Ayurvedic psychosomatics has taken a different, and relatively untraveled, road. Consistent with its thesis of the identity of mind and body, Ayurveda posits that any disturbance, physical or mental, must manifest itself both in the somatic and in the psychic spheres, through the intermediary process of the vitiation of the "humors." Let us take some scattered examples from literature.[48] Lust, grief and fear increase wind, and anger increases bile. If the wind active in any bodily substance gets disturbed, then it destroys the power of the "mental organs [*indriya*]" and gives birth to fear, grief and infatuation. Bile clears the mind and makes it capable of action. The weakness of phlegm induces lethargy, infatuation, greediness and indiscrimination.

Physical and mental disturbances can *both* upset the humors and in turn produce different diseases with either (predominantly) mental or physical symptoms, depending upon the manner in which the intervening humors have been upset. Thus, besides diseases of primarily physical origin and with predominantly physical symptoms, Ayurveda recognizes three other classes of disease. They are: (1) diseases of primarily mental origin with predominantly mental symptoms such as *unmada,* a generic term for all mental disorders in which an individual loses the power of regulating his actions and conduct according to the rules of his society: *unmada* includes almost all the psychotic disorders as well as what we would today call impulse neuroses and obsessions; (2) diseases of primarily mental origin and predominantly physical symptoms such as epilepsy *(apasmara)*, hysterical fits *(apatantraka)*, diarrhea from grief and fear *(sokaja* and *bhaya atisara)*, insomnia *(nidranasa)*, "fever from grief and sexual desire" *(sokaja* and *kamaja jvara)*; and (3) diseases of primarily physical origin and predominantly mental symptoms, *e.g.*, certain delusional states *(attatvabhinivesa)* and alcohol or drug intoxication *(mada)*.

In principle, Ayurvedic therapy for these—and in fact *all* diseases —cannot be other than a blend of the psychological and the physiological. In practice, though, the psychological part of the treatment rarely goes beyond suggestion, exhortation, consolation and a recommendation of meditative procedures. The language of emotions has remained primitive and the grammar of feelings rudimentary. Ayurvedic treatment, as we shall see later, even for diseases of primarily mental origins and with predominantly mental symptoms, is overwhelmingly a physiological therapy for the psyche. Its value for the modern clinician does not lie in the sophistication of its psychological theory, but in its modes of physical treatment of the psyche, as well as in its intriguing notions on the relation of food to emotions.

Mind and Mental Illness

Manas, often translated as "mind," has in fact a more concrete and limited meaning than the corresponding Western concept. As part of the subtle body, *manas,* together with "intelligence" *(buddhi)* and "I-ness" *(ahamkara),* is a part of the "internal organ set"—the *antahamkarna*—in contrast to the set of external organs *(bahamkarna),* i.e., the five sensory organs of perception and the five motor organs.

Manas is different from the mind in other ways too. As an "atomic" entity made of subtle matter that becomes conscious and capable of performing its assigned tasks only through the power of the underlying *atman,* the imagery of *manas* seems more concrete than that of the mind. Psychologically a mediator between the "inside" and the "outside," metaphysically, *manas* is also the barrier between the two, the sheet covering the "true" nature of reality.

The functions of *manas* have been described as: (1) activation, direction and coordination of the sensory and motor organs *(indriya bhigraha);* (2) self-regulation *(svasya nigraha);* (3) reasoning *(uha);* and (4) deliberation, judgment and discrimination *(vicara).* "Mental illness" primarily refers to the impairment of these functions. Considering the nature of the mental functions, the closest counterpart of *manas* in Western psychology would seem to be the ego of psychoanalytic theory with its very similar list of functions and processes, rather than the psychic apparatus which we call the "mind."

Given the Ayurvedic thesis of a psyche-soma identity, *manas* is naturally influenced by the humoral imbalance that also disturbs the gross body. There are, as we shall see later, different types of insanity linked with the disturbances of wind, bile and phlegm. The specific humoral connection of *manas* is said to be with the wind, while its intimate cosmic connection is with the moon, which is the counterpart of *manas* in creation. Besides being affected by disturbances in the bodily humors, *manas* is permeated by the three "qualities" *(gunas)* of purity, light *(sattva),* activity, passion *(rajas)* and inertia, darkness *(tamas).* These qualities wage a constant struggle for supremacy and therefore keep *manas* in an ever-changing state of restlessness. Of the three "qualities," *rajas* and *tamas* are called the humors of *manas.* They are, so to say, the mental humors whose excitation and disturbance lead to mental illness or, more exactly (remembering the principle of psyche-soma identity), to illnesses whose origins are chiefly mental. Of course, the vitiation of the mental humors will also be reflected and expressed in the bodily sphere. In the etiology of epilepsy *(apasmara),* for instance, it is pointed out that the vitiation of the heart and sense organs by the mental humors leads to an obstruction of the bodily humors, which can no longer travel in their accustomed channels, thus giving rise to the morbidity typical of epilepsy.

What are the reasons for the disturbing increases in the mental humors of *rajas* and *tamas*? The answer in Ayurvedic texts is consistent with that of traditional psychological theory and singles out desire *(ichha)* and repulsion *(dvesha)* as the twin causes. As a category, desire is defined as the wish to obtain an object which has pleased the body or the "mind" and includes the emotions of lust, elation and covetousness. Of course, to be desirous of certain objects is natural. It is only when desire steps over the bounds of propriety *(maryada)* inherent in the *object* and becomes a slave that the humors get excited. The second category, repulsion, is defined as the avoidance of an object that has caused pain to body or "mind" and is associated with the emotions of anger, fear and envy. Obstructions on the pathways to desire and roadblocks on the escape routes of pain will inevitably excite the mental humors and lead to mental and bodily symptoms.

So far these are also more or less straightforward Freudian propositions. Where Hindu psychology differs from psychoanalysis is in attributing to desire and repulsion a power and a kind of eternal fixity in human affairs which even the most dour of psychoanalysts contemplating the human condition is hard pressed to match. For in Hindu psychological theory, desire and repulsion are not only the products of individual life experience from birth onward but have two other roots. One of these roots goes down to the prenatal stage, specifically the *dauhridaya* ("bicardiac," where one heart is of the fetus and the other of the mother) period of pregnancy around the third and fourth months. In this period, the unfulfilled longings of the mother as also her unrelieved fears are said to be transmitted to the newly activated psyche of the fetus, to be stored there and thus build the fount for its eventual suffering. In a sense, this is the simplest yet deepest of depth psychological statements which starkly maintains that every person carries within him the wishes and fears of the mother as the essential core of his or her psyche. The other root of desire and repulsion goes back even further in time to a previous existence. It is postulated that the unfulfilled longings and unresolved traumas at the end of a previous life enter the conceptus as a "memory-trace" *(samskara)* of the subtle body which, in time, will rise to the surface, demanding completion and closure, and increase both *rajas* and *tamas*.

One of the ways the physician gains knowledge of a person's

mental humors is through an examination of his dreams. Of the various categories of dreams—dreams that repeat what has been seen in waking life, dreams that enact what has been heard, dreams that dramatize what has been experienced, dreams that foretell the future and dreams that occur in conjunction with the disturbance of a particular bodily humor and thus have diagnostic significance, Ayurveda also enumerates two other kinds of dreams that are important for the estimation of a person's mental state. These are (1) the *prarthita* dreams, which gratify those desires that could not be gratified in the waking state and (2) the *kalpita* dreams, which are the *mise-en-scène*, the dramatization of individual fantasy.[49] Both the latter types of dream reveal Ayurveda's concern with the "mask of desire" in the human psyche. Of course, this is also the concern which, at the beginning of this century, both sparked and lay at the core of psychoanalytic undertaking.

The Ayurvedic dream theory is remarkable in many other ways. The *vaid*s maintain that the widely held belief that we are in the waking state ("consciousness") during the daytime is delusionary. In fact, even while awake, dreaming is the predominant psychic activity. Here they seem to be preempting Jung's important insight that we continually dream but that consciousness while waking makes such a noise that we do not "hear" the dream. Another important Ayurvedic idea in which further research may prove fruitful is the connection of dreams not only with psychic life or clairvoyance, but also with the physiological events in the body. To illustrate through clinical vignettes: A woman came to a well-known *vaid* in Delhi, hoping that he would confirm her pregnancy. It was, however, a case of delayed menses. She narrated that the night before she had dreamed of a bride, standing still in the traditional red apparel of marriage. The *vaid* told her that she would get her period the next day and the period would be without any pain or discomfort. If there was going to be pain, the *vaid* said, then the woman would have been dancing or moving in some other way. In another case, a man's vision of different snakes in a dream was not invested with any symbolic significance but was indicative of fluctuations in blood pressure and medicated accordingly.

The Ayurvedic insights into the working of man's psyche and the causation of mental illness are remarkable achievements, for any century. Unfortunately, the genuine psychological content of Ayurveda is limited to this, a skeletal edifice at best. It was never fleshed out with the kind of detail that makes a collection of scattered insights grow into a body of disciplined knowledge. It seems to me that the reason for this failure lies partly in the Hindu penchant for *wholeness,* which precludes a preoccupation with only one aspect of a phenomenon, thus eschewing specialization and even looking askance at the experimental method, whose hallmark is the isolation of variables. In its explanation of mental illness, Ayurveda would not (or could not) pursue detailed investigations into the role of the psyche (or even of the body) in the etiology of mental illness. It had to simultaneously bring within its framework the social and the metaphysical aspects, thus diluting its clinical thrust and dissipating the force of its psychological insights. Mental illness became the province of many kinds of healers, of shamans and exorcists, mystics and astrologers. As a *vaid* in assessing the present status of the treatment of mental disorders has remarked, "The science of mental illness has become scattered among the *ojhas, sayanas,* tantriks, *saddhus* and illiterates of the lower castes. There is no single volume where the whole of ancient knowledge is available. The methods of treating some kinds of mental disorders are passed from the teacher to the student orally and, not being scientifically collected, they too are disappearing."[50]

THE COSMOS IN MENTAL ILLNESS

Ayurveda's use of the metaphysical factor may be seen in its diagnostic procedures as well as in the etiology of certain types of insanity supposedly caused by spirit possession. To take the diagnostic aspect first:

One of the chief tools for the diagnosis of the mental humors as indeed for the diagnosis of the bodily humors has been the monitoring of the *nadi,* a word which stands for the pulse but also for the nerves. In the "science" of the *nadi,* one sees the material body of traditional Ayurveda supplemented or even transmuted into the symbolic body of the tantric tradition. The expert physician, it is claimed, can feel the heaviness and steadiness of the phlegm *nadi,* indicating the dominance of inertia or *tamas*, through the tip of the third finger; or know of a *manas* permeated with activity or *rajas* through the feel of the bile *nadi* in the middle finger.[51] The knowledge of *nadi*s is said to be as much a spiritual *(adhyatmic)* science as a material one—an adept needing to be both a yogi *and* a clinician. With the proper spiritual imagination, developed through the use of an inner ascetic-vision rather than relying on the ordinary eye-vision *(netra-chaksu)* alone, the adept can "see" the state of a person's five *bhutas*, three humors and the three mental qualities through the examination of a single *nadi*.

The metaphysical factor is also represented in a whole class of *unmada* which is said to be due to possession by the gods, ancestral spirits and various heavenly and demonic beings, such as the *gandharva, yaksha, Rakshasa* and *Pishacha*. Mental illness due to spirit possession and its treatment through various magical means and exorcism rituals, of course, belongs to a much older tradition that goes back to the *Atharva Veda* and, as we saw in the earlier chapters, still flourishes in all parts of India. Unrelated to the Ayurvedic theories of the body or mind, the descriptions of the *unmada* due to spirit possession and their treatment seem to stand out as foreign and unassimilated elements in the text of the medical treatises, being witness to an uneasy meeting between medical and priestly concerns. This is in contrast to Tibetan medicine, which, as we saw earlier, though it originally derives from Ayurveda, has exuberantly affirmed the metaphysical, cosmic aspects of illness and accorded them a central position in all mental disorders.

THE POLIS AND MENTAL ILLNESS

Besides the use of dreams and examination of *nadi* to determine the state of a person's mental humor, the dominance of one or the other of the three mental qualities can also be inferred through his diet, character and conduct. A person whose *manas* is dominated by inertia, for instance, prefers stale, smelly, half-cooked food and food devoid of its natural juices. Laziness, dullness and mental unsteadiness mark his personality. An "active" *rajasic manas*, on the other hand, prefers spicy, sour and bitter foods: pride, impatience, sensuality and anger are his chief psychological characteristics. The person dominated by the purity of *sattva* prefers sweet and agreeable-tasting food that "brightens the intellect and spirit." The list of *sattvic* traits is a long one—purity, devotion to truth, self control, freedom from anger, conceit, greed, infatuation, envy, etc.

It is evident that these personality types, based on the dominance of one or the other mental qualities, have little to do with the complexities of human psyche or with the various shades of behavior and the ambivalence of emotions that normally characterize an individual. The types are more the expression of what the Brahminical tradition considers socially desirable or undesirable qualities in a person. They are akin to the castes (in the *varna* sense) in their hierarchy from the pure to the impure—the *sattvic* type is the Brahmin, incorporating the ideals of traditional morality, the *rajasic* type being the passionate and impulsive *kshatriya*, while the inert *tamasic* type represents the *shudra* and all the other lower orders, who have always appeared sullen and dull to the ruling elites. Mental illness in Ayurveda is then a deviance from the social, *sattvic* ideal of mental health—the *tamasic* deviates from this ideal in his impurity and the *rajasic* in his unbridled impulses. The social definition of mental illness is emphasized even more clearly by a modern *vaid*: "When we call certain conditions mental illness we only mean that the person's thoughts, speech and actions have become unnecessary or harmful to society."[52]

The equation of the socially desirable with "health" is also reflected in Ayurvedic prescriptions for the maintenance of positive mental health and the prevention of mental disorders. Besides the more than three hundred "noble acts" that are prescribed in relation to eating, natural urges, studying, social relations, sexual intercourse, social manners ("one should not laugh loudly, nor release wind with sound; one should not indulge in yawning, sneezing or laughter without covering the mouth, nor scratch the nose, grind the teeth"), there is a general behavioral prescription for achieving the ideal, "healthy" personality.[53] Such a person should not be impatient or overbold. He should neither trustingly rely on everyone nor should he be oversuspicious of others. He should not demand too much of his intellect or of his senses. He should neither be conceited over his achievements nor become despondent over his loss. He should not act in a fit of anger or of rejoicing . . . and so on and so forth.[54] Lying in the mainstream of the Hindu moral traditions, the Ayurvedic notion of the healthy personality is pervaded by the ideals of moderation, control and responsibility and the preponderance of the Apollonian "golden mean." Its guiding principle for mental health is perhaps best expressed by the Latin hexameter *Quidquid agis prudenter agas et respice finem* ("Whatever you do, do it with prudence and consider the consequences")—a principle that also seems to govern the prescription for mental health in many Western psychotherapeutic systems.[55]

THERAPY

I have already mentioned that there is no specific Ayurvedic psychotherapy for illnesses of predominantly mental origin. The *satavavajaya* therapy mentioned in the texts actually refers to the methods of mind-control and "restraining the mind from unhealthy objects"[56] in the different schools of yoga. The average *vaid*'s knowledge of these techniques and their rationale is no different from the average Western doctor's knowledge of psychoanalysis, *i.e.*, it exists at the level of what can be called "the rumor about psychoanalysis." The *daivavyapasra* treatment, comprising ritual and magical elements—chanting of appropriate mantras, use of precious stones and gems, penances and atonements, wearing of charms and amulets, visiting sacred complexes or pilgrimage—has its roots in the *Atharva Veda* (especially the *Kausika Sutra*) and does not derive from any systematic theory of mind and mental processes. The treatment of mental disorders in Ayurveda therefore follows along the same lines as the treatment of bodily illnesses, namely according to *Caraka*'s well-known and concise dictum "Purify, pacify and remove the cause." The individual *vaid* generally selects some elements from the standard therapeutic repertoire according to the precepts of his school or the practices prevalent in his particular region. Briefly, this therapeutic repertoire consists of the following treatments:

Purification: The set of "purifying" treatments has traditionally consisted of purges, emetics, enemas and bleeding. The purifying treatments have lately fallen into disuse except in certain parts of the country, such as Kerala.

Here, the purifying treatment, which lasts for seven days and often for several weeks, is inaugurated and concluded by two preliminary proceedings: oily massages and sudorifices. In Kerala, both these preliminary treatments have acquired the status of independent therapies. Rejuvenating properties are ascribed to special techniques of oily massages, affusions of oil, sudorific and nourishing massages with boluses of rice, etc.,[57] and are practiced in cases of stress-related disorders and general physical and mental exhaustion. Even in Kerala, purges and emetics are seldom used because of their "violence." Enemas—and especially the "oily enema"—are the main method of purification. The only purge still in wide currency all over the country, particularly in the treatment of mental disorders, is the "purge to the head" administered through specially prepared nasal and eye drops.

Pacification: The pacification treatment consists of the application of external unguents or the taking in of internal decoctions derived from plants and metals. Besides a number of compounds used as tranquilizers and antidepressants, there are specific pacification medicines that pacify by "strengthening the nerves" in case of epilepsy, hysterical convulsions and some types of *unmada.*[58]

Removal of cause: Since one of the major causes for any illness lies in a perverted use of the acts of the body-mind-speech entity, the diet and conduct therapy is an important part of the whole treatment. In the treatment of mental disorders, the *vaid* takes an active role in the patient's life as he endeavors to make him follow the rules of "proper conduct" (in the socially desirable sense), through a stream of advice, suggestions and exhortations to stop a particularly harmful activity or to start an especially desirable one.

In the following chapter, we shall see how the Ayurvedic theory of mental illness and its therapy are applied in concrete cases by an eminent practitioner.

9

THE GOOD DOCTOR
OF JHARSETLI

Jharsetli, a medium-sized village forty kilometers northwest of Delhi, lies in the heart of the prosperous farm belt of Haryana. Similar to other villages in the area in most respects, a part of Jharsetli, because of its proximity to the main highway, has acquired a semiindustrial façade. Here, at the edge of the highway, there are small repair shops with an antique lathe or grinding machine resplendently ensconced in the middle of the cluttered premises, while old and worn-out truck tires stacked in heaps outside announce the arrival of the village in the industrial era. There are also a couple of dingy roadside eating places—the *dhabas*—serving long-haul truck drivers with hot cups of tea and spicy *samosas* as the men sit around on rope cots, animatedly discussing the prospects of the availability of diesel oil, the alcoholism of a colleague, the high-handedness of an excise inspector and the latest political scandal from the capital. In contrast to the apparent placidity of the rest of Jharsetli, there is an oddly appealing air of grubby vitality in this part of the village, a seediness not of decay but of impending birth.

The *dharmashala* in which the doctor—Guruji, as he is commonly and respectfully known—works and lives was constructed many years ago by some pious rich people as an inn to provide poor travelers and pilgrims with shelter. The original purpose of the inn disappeared long ago, in 1963 to be exact, when Guruji took over the building and hung out a simple shingle with the inscription *Manasik Chikitsa Kendra*—"Center for the Treatment of Mental Illnesses."

The inn-hospital is a decrepit, single-storied structure, its rows of small, ill-ventilated and unfurnished rooms arranged in an L-shaped complex. Lying almost at the outer edge of the village, a couple of hundred yards off the highway, Guruji's domain is isolated from the rest of the village and has an aura of self-sufficiency. There is a gnarled but sturdy pipal tree in front of the main complex and, a few yards beyond the tree, there stands a small temple, much older than the inn and in a correspondingly worse state of neglect. A narrow, unpaved path from the temple leads down to a large pond. Behind the pond one can see miles and miles of lush green fields (at least they were lush during our first visits in winter) stretch into the distance, the shimmering grass-shoot greenness immensely soothing to the eye. If one can shut out the faint purr of the truck traffic from the highway and blot out the slight whiff of exhaust fumes that scents the air, then the inn with its temple, the pair of pie dogs taking their ease under the pipal tree, the pond with a bathing water buffalo and the surrounding fields, have the quality of a stage village —a colored postcard for tourists depicting the changeless vista of rural India.

Guruji seems very much at home in these surroundings. He is a sixty-odd-year-old man with humorous eyes that belie the apparent strictness of his manner. Dressed in a freshly laundered *dhoti*, a clean white turban wrapped neatly around his head and wearing a rough *khadi* coat buttoned up to the collar, Guruji walks with the upright stance and the self-assured, unhurried gait of a man accustomed to command respect and to expect deference; not unlike the *Klinik-Chef* of a provincial German hospital before the student unrest of the sixties shook up the belief of all *Chefs* in their God-given authority. When he is not on his seat diagnosing patients and dispensing packets of medicinal powder, Guruji is constantly on the move within the small complex of the inn-hospital. Often, he may be seen in the verandah, with his hands clasped behind his back, supervising squatting assistants and members of the patient's families as they grind and mix herbs into medicines. Two or three times a day, he goes into the temple, where he personally prepares his more expensive medicines, which use precious metals and metallic compounds as ingredients and which take three to six months before they are ready. He can often be seen talking to the ten or so of the severely disturbed patients and their relatives who live with him on the inn's premises. Resolving medical problems, admonishing the

transgressors of rules, arbitrating disputes, cracking jokes with a
deadpan expression on his face, Guruji is clearly the hub of the small
community and the force that holds it together.

Although Guruji is consulted by a few patients with minor physical ailments, the bulk of his clientele consists of severely disturbed
psychotic patients from nearby villages and towns. To watch Guruji
interview these patients is to watch a master at work. With a remarkable economy of words and gestures and with a superb sense of
timing, Guruji often succeeds in establishing the beginning of a
relationship with the patient in the very first interview. This is done
without an expression of a professional "caring" in his words or the
jarring chord of insincere concern in his voice. Let me reproduce the
opening scenes of some encounters between Guruji and his patients
to illustrate.

Two men walk up to Guruji with the patient in their middle. He
is a middle-aged man who drags his feet as he walks and supports
his weight by putting his arms around the shoulders of his companions. His hair is unkempt, the eyes bloodshot and the face haggard
from weakness and exhaustion.

Guruji: "Where do you come from?"

The men mumble the name of a village near Rohtak.

Guruji: "What is wrong?" He addresses the question to the patient. The three men start to speak at the same time. The patient
has great difficulty in being coherent. As he talks he gestures with
his hands as if his spreadeagled fingers are knitting isolated syllables
into complete words and then separating the words from each other.
Guruji is listening with concentration, trying to make sense of his
garbled speech. One of the companions interrupts: "Don't believe
what he says, Guruji." Guruji turns toward him with a start, anger
flashing across his face. "Why shouldn't I believe *him*? Because you
think you are normal and he is mad? 'Don't believe what he says,
Guruji,'" he mimics the man. He turns back to the patient, his
expression again gentle. "Yes, what is wrong with you?"

Patient: "Don't fight with me. I . . ." His speech is again jumbled.

Guruji: "Brother, I haven't understood you. Is your throat dry?"
The patient nods. Guruji asks one of the companions to get the
patient a glass of water. The man drinks the water but is still unable
to speak. Guruji looks inquiringly at the companions. They explain

that the patient is engaged in a litigation with his brother on account of some land. Recently, he has started to become uncontrollably excited in the court, shouting, screaming and ready to hit anyone who tries to restrain him.

Guruji (smilingly to the patient): "So you have come to me after fighting so much!" Then in a feigned scolding voice: "I won't keep you here. Tomorrow you'll also fight with me. Will you?" The patient is visibly relaxed. He nods his assent and then, realizing his mistake, vigorously shakes his head in denial. Guruji (to all of them): "Go and sleep inside. I will check his pulse tomorrow morning."

There are many other such vignettes which make it abundantly clear that Guruji considers it his (in Szasz's words) "moral mandate"[1] to aid the patient's struggle, not only against his illness but also against those who by their conduct either "cause" or perpetuate the illness. Here, Guruji may be considered to be a radical modern, for it was one of Freud's distinctive departures from the psychiatric tradition of his time to consider himself solely the individual patient's agent and thus to repudiate any obligations (when they were conflicting) to the patient's family and society. This radical strain in psychoanalysis, carried to its logical (some would say, illogical) extreme in the "antipsychiatry" movement associated with the names of R. D. Laing and David Cooper, is still uncommon within the psychiatric profession. Most therapists, though paying lip service to the adage of "in the best interest of the patient," do not really consider themselves the agent of the patient but rather that of his family and society since it is economically and professionally imprudent for them to do otherwise. Guruji, who sees many patients who have been through the mill of psychiatry departments of hospitals, is well aware of this facet of Western psychiatry. "In your tradition," he once remarked to me, "Largactyl* is given and the patient made to sleep. As long as he is asleep he won't trouble anyone. The patient's family is satisfied and so too is the doctor. As far as the patient is concerned, he is too drugged to complain. How convenient for everyone!" Let us look at some more scenes from interviews that convey other aspects of Guruji's therapeutic style.

---

*A major tranquilizer prescribed in cases of schizophrenia and often called "the chemical equivalent of a straitjacket."

This patient is a *gurkha* from Nepal around forty years of age, and he is brought to Guruji by his cousin. The patient's movements are dull and retarded, his face often contorting in involuntary grimaces. He appears oblivious to his surroundings and is letting himself be led docilely by his escort. The cousin tells Guruji the history of the patient's illness. The patient was employed for nineteen years as a night watchman in a factory in the nearby town of Faridabad. Two months ago, his services were abruptly terminated. The patient sank into a deep withdrawal, unable to take care of himself and refusing to speak to anyone except in an incoherent mumble. He has "had electricity" (the local expression for electroconvulsive therapy) in the hospital but there was no change in his condition. Guruji looks at the patient gravely for a moment before he bends toward him and shouts: "So you are a thief, eh? You stole!"

The patient lifts up his eyes toward Guruji. He has become agitated, his throat moves convulsively and strangling sounds come from deep within his chest. I marvel at Guruji's psychological acumen, for obviously in the present labor situation a factory management will not dismiss an old and trusted watchman for a lesser offense.

"If you did not actually steal yourself then you helped the thieves to break in," Guruji persists, but he is smiling now, his voice gentle and forgiving the accusation contained in his words.

"But, son, in these days of big thieves, you are only a small fry, so why suffer so much?" Guruji says and looks around for confirmation. The men and women milling around him smilingly nod their agreement, savoring his allusion to the financial morals of India's political leadership. Guruji is all paternal and forgiving now as he takes the patient's right wrist between the thumb and fingers of his right hand for the diagnostic examination. The patient's facial expression is visibly brighter and he is looking up at Guruji—a human connection, though still tenuous, definitely established.

The next patient is a young peasant who is accompanied by his father. The young man is tense, giving the impression of a spring coiled under great pressure. When their turn comes, the father nudges the son's elbow, indicating that he should step nearer the doctor. The son frees his arm with a jerk and glares back at the father, an interaction that Guruji misses. The patient then sits on the bench, buries his arms deeper into the blanket wrapped around his shoulders and stares stonily at Guruji.

Guruji: "So, my son, have you come here to look at my face? What is the matter?"

The father: "He is like this all the time. If anyone wants to come near and talk to him, he gets violent and lashes out. Do something, Guruji, he is all the wealth we have."

Guruji is unmoved by the father's appeal and addresses the patient: "Come, stand up."

The young man does not move.

Guruji: "No, my friend, this won't do at all. I have so much other work and, unlike you, my father is no longer alive to bear all my sulks. My son"—his voice is gentler—"I am glad you came to me early. Let me feel your pulse."

This time the young man does as he is told.

Guruji (affectionately): "What happens to you, son?"

The patient: "They don't let me work. Whenever I work someone comes and stops me and I get angry." He is on the verge of tears.

Guruji (to the father): "Don't do that. Let him work as much as he wants to. How much land do you have?"

The patient: "A hundred and ten acres."

Guruji: "Ah, then you are quite a landowner! Where are you from?"

The patient (now quite responsive): "From Rohtak."

The father intercedes: "We feel someone has done something to him." He is alluding to sorcery. Guruji (sarcastically): "Yes, no one has any other work to do. Everyone is just sitting around, waiting to perform sorcery. No, brother, this is a kind of illness. The blood pressure increases in the temple artery and his temper climbs up. There is no sorcery or black magic involved." He gives the medicines to the father and asks him to bring the son back after three months. "Let him work as hard as he likes and take him for long walks in the morning," he says to the father, "but you shouldn't accompany him, let him go with someone else."

My purpose in reproducing scenes from interviews is to highlight Guruji's expertise in establishing and handling his relationship with the patients. Many psychotherapists would perhaps agree with Szasz's contention that the conduct of the human encounter is the only special skill that a therapist needs.[2] If we psychoanalysts also add the therapist's self-awareness and self-discipline, his critical and inquiring attitude, the ability to understand the patient's communications and the "meaning" of his illness, then these additions describe the "tools" of the psychotherapeutic trade; they are, in a sense, the superstructure built upon the foundation of the primacy of the human encounter. Of course much of the rest of psychotherapeutic paraphernalia—diagnostic tests of various kinds, administration of drugs to "facilitate" psychotherapy—belongs to the realm of gadgetry. They are pale imitations of the medical enterprise, designed to share in its prestige and lend scientific credibility to a basically human encounter which otherwise may not be considered "scientific" enough. In this sense they are little different from the chicken entrails, divining sticks and mystical squares and circles which lend metaphysical respectability to the encounter between a traditional healer and *his* patient.

Looking back at many of Guruji's interactions with his patients, I would say that his therapeutic style often reminded me of what Watzlawick calls "the playing of communication games," with the intention of changing the patient's interpersonal situation and freeing his relationships from the rut in which they have gotten bogged down.[3] This form of psychotherapy essentially emphasizes the art of *reinterpretation.* In a reinterpretation, the conceptual and emotional framework in which a situation is experienced by the patient is replaced by another framework that applies equally well, or even better, to the "facts"; therapy then changes the total meaning of an existing situation. A successful reinterpretation almost always takes the patient's opinions, expectations and assumptions into account, *i.e.,* the therapist uses the patient's own conceptual framework to provide new meanings to old situations. Reinterpretations do not try to teach the patient a new language in which he can formulate, express and then resolve his problems, nor do they give him new insights. What a reinterpretation does is to teach a patient a different "game" which makes it impossible for him to continue playing his old "game." Watzlawick gives the example of a pessimist who generally plays an interpersonal game that consists of first mobilizing the optimism of another person so that he can react to this optimism with increasing expressions of pessimism.[4] If the counterplayer falls into the trap, he either goes on increasing the expressions of his optimism or gives up his efforts to make the pessimist feel better, in which case the latter has scored another pyrrhic victory. The game changes dramatically the moment the counterplayer decides to react even more pessimistically than the pessimist. The new interaction is no longer an instance of *plus ça change, plus c'est la même chose,* since one element of the situation (pessimism) cannot be combined with its inverse (optimism) to maintain the desired invariance of the situation. A brand-new game—with prospects of behavioral change —has been introduced for which the use of the pessimist's language, *i.e.,* his pessimism, was of critical importance. Let me illustrate Guruji's intuitive use of the art of reinterpretation.

Surinder, a twenty-three-year-old watch repairer from a small town nearby, has been staying at the *dharmashala* for the last three months, together with his parents. Guruji's diagnosis for him is *kamonmada—unmada,* or insanity, due to *kama,* or sexual desire. Surinder has always suffered from unstable mood and heightened excitability, though his present "breakdown" occurred on his wedding night. "Listen, Doctor," he said, responding to a question that sought to elicit further details, "when does a man become mad? A man is like a balloon. If you go on squeezing it then after some time the balloon bursts. This is what happened to me. My parents have squeezed me so hard that my brain has burst. I got married but on the first night I discovered that my wife's hymen was torn. I know that the hymen can tear because of too much exercise, but I felt certain that she had been fucked before. I came out of the room and started screaming and couldn't stop. Now I couldn't care less about torn or intact hymens; I only want to fuck. But my pigfather refused to fetch my wife back from her parents' house."

Here Surinder was interrupted by his father, who approached him threateningly, a stick in his hand. Surinder is often beaten by his father when he gets into one of his excited states. Many inmates hold the opinion that the father is even madder than the son and in urgent need of Guruji's treatment. Surinder first attempted defiance of his father, "Try and hit me and I'll break your teeth!" Ignoring the threat, the father caught Surinder by the neck and dragged him back to their room at the rear of the inn. After a few minutes we heard people shouting and then Surinder came running in and fell at Guruji's feet. His father was following him, his stick raised and a torrent of angry abuse directed toward the son. Surinder was sobbing. "Guruji, save me! They'll take my life. Get them out of here, otherwise I'll run away."

"What happened?" Guruji asked.

"Nothing," Surinder replied. "The old ass just started hitting me."

"This dog shat in the middle of the room," the father fumed. "I'll call the bastard's wife back only when he gets well. In this state, even a bitch won't stay with him!"

"Can I help it if my bowels loosen by themselves?" Surinder asked rhetorically.

Guruji broke into peels of loud laughter.

"Congratulations, son! What a good solution you have found!" he said. "Who told you of this trick to get your parents out of here?"

The people standing around us also began to laugh and Surinder too was smiling through his sobs.

"Next time, shit in the kitchen!" Guruji continued. "Then you'll see how fast the old man and the woman take to their heels." Surinder, who was also laughing heartily, espied the basket of fruit in a corner and asked Guruji for an apple. "I'll give you an apple only when you shit in the kitchen," Guruji said. "Now get out of here!" The reinterpretation of Surinder's interpersonal situation was elegantly completed.

At any given time, there are generally eight to ten patients living in the *dharmashala* together with their family caretakers. These patients are severely disturbed, the most common presentation—from a Western psychiatric viewpoint—being catatonia, a schizophrenic disorder manifested in posturing, mutism, facial grimaces and mannerisms. In the acute excitement stages, when delusions of grandeur, loquacity and hyperactivity prevail, the patients require physical restraint. At such times, Guruji's two assistants, both of them former patients, handcuff the patient or tie him down to his cot with the help of his relatives till he calms down. Though a special medicine may be occasionally given to a patient, the medical regimen is generally uniform. It starts in the morning, with a "purge to the head." The effects of this *nasya* ("nasal") treatment, in which a medicine is administered through the nose and eyes, are dramatically painful; the patients report that it is as if their eyes and the nasal passage had been set aflame. The *nasya* is supposed to open the clogged *dhamanis* and *siras*—channels and ducts—leading to the brain. Before breakfast the patient drinks a glass of *thandai*, an herbal tranquilizer made from rose petals, lotus flowers, sandalwood, aniseed and leaves from certain trees. After each meal, the patient is given a spoonful of a digestive powder *(churna)*, and before retiring for the night he gets sleeping pills with a glass of milk. All the medicines—the nasal purge, the tranquilizer, the powder and the pills—are prepared on the premises by the patients (if they are well enough to do so) and by their relatives under the supervision of Guruji's assistants; the patients and their families participating, quite literally, in the process of their own cure.

An important part of the daily regimen in the clinic are the morning and evening walks with Guruji. Here is the description of one such walk by a colleague who spent many days at Jharsetli:

"One day, after Guruji was through with his consultations, he invited me for the evening walk with his patients. On our way to the main part of the *dharmashala* where the patients and Guruji's assistants were waiting for us, we were beckoned by a young man who was lying on a cot, his legs manacled and his hands tied together with a rope. Guruji took out a key from his pocket and shouted across to him, 'I am coming, I am coming! Don't be so impatient.' After he had been set free, Sanjay (this was the man's name) got up, rubbing his sore wrists and ankles, and addressed me in broken English, 'You what? I Sanjay. I no mental, my father was mental.' He then tried to embrace me, a maneuver which I deftly sidestepped. 'When will you ever get some sense!' Guruji sighed exasperatedly. 'Did you take your medicines today?' Sanjay ignored the question. 'He my brother,' he said, pointing toward me. Guruji had already gone ahead to collect the others. Sanjay ran up to him and said in Hindi, 'Please don't keep me tied up. I'll lecture about you, I'll make you a minister. I am not less than Sanjay Gandhi.' 'All right, all right,' Guruji said with a hint of impatience. 'If you keep quiet the whole way, I'll see what I can do.' Besides Guruji and myself, our small group now consisted of three patients—Sanjay, Surinder and a quiet, withdrawn middle-aged man whose name was never mentioned, Guruji's two assistants, and his five-year-old grandson, who scampered around the group and in and out of the fields, silently absorbed in his own secret games.

"Guruji seemed to be in a reminiscing mood this evening. Or, perhaps, taking advantage of my presence, he only wanted to have a dig at Western medicine and doctors. In any event, he told us of his own illness many years ago when he could not sleep at night, had acute indigestion and kept on worrying about inconsequential things. He suspected that the illness was due to the sheath of his liver getting thicker but one of his patient-cum-students insisted on taking him to a well-known internist in Delhi for a checkup. The doctor examined him and then wrote out the prescription. 'I was not a fool,' Guruji said, 'for I saw that all the medicines he had prescribed were for a mentally ill patient. I tore up the paper then and there and asked the doctor if he thought I was mad.' There was an appreciative laughter from our group in which Guruji joined and then Sanjay said, 'So you were also mad once! Tell me, were you also handcuffed?' Guruji ignored the question and continued with his story. 'I came back, treated myself with Ayurvedic medicines, and look at me today! If you ever race me you'll only see my back.' 'Guruji,' Sanjay interrupted, 'will you race me? You won't be able to touch me.' 'You are nothing,' Guruji replied. 'I'll even leave your sons far behind.'

" 'You'll be long dead by then,' Sanjay said. 'Tell me, where should I build a memorial for you, here or in Delhi?' Then, as if he felt guilty about his thought, Sanjay added in a more subdued tone, 'Everyone has to die sometime.' Guruji merely smiled.

"On our way back, as we entered the *dharmashala,* I saw another patient lying on his side on a cot, his hands tied behind his back. 'How are you?' Guruji asked him. 'Who has tied your hands?' The patient nodded toward his parents, who were sitting on the ground beside the cot.

" 'Untie him!' Guruji ordered the father and then asked, 'Have you brought milk?'

" 'Yes,' the father said.

" 'How much?'

" 'Three hundred grams.'

"Guruji was annoyed. 'So little! If you were short of money you could have asked me. Your son's mind may have become deranged but his body is still intact. It has to be looked after properly.' Angrily, he strode away toward his seat in the outer verandah.

"I did not follow him but let myself be led by Sanjay and Surinder toward their living quarters, where they had invited me for a cup of tea that was being prepared by Sanjay's mother.

" 'Sexuality is the biggest problem these days,' Sanjay said as we sat down on the cot. 'It spoils our thoughts.' His friend Surinder ignored this attempt at serious conversation and asked me bluntly, 'So what conclusions have you come to, Doctor Sahib? Please don't mind my saying so but you are a cunt [*chutia*]. Guruji is a clever one. He'll never reveal his secrets to anyone. You should ask the assistants or you should ask me. Bring some mercury tomorrow and I'll make you such a good medicine that you'll never become mad.'

" 'No one can save him from madness, child,' Sanjay interrupted. 'My secret powers tell me that one day he too will be tied up here. Anyone who wants to live honestly these days cannot save himself from madness. This Surinder here, all he wants is to fuck a woman, but they just stuff him full of medicines.' Sanjay's mother had joined us with the tea. As we drank our tea she said to me, 'It is the hospital electricity which has made him [Sanjay] worse. Please keep on visiting us. He looks upon you as his brother. Actually, he cannot get along with his elder brother at all.' As I got up to leave, I heard Sanjay say to Surinder in a matter-of-fact tone, 'My brother is going. How similar his ideas are to mine! He'll also become mad.' Surinder seemed to agree and I heard their laughter all the way to the outer verandah where I joined Guruji.

" 'Obsession [*dhun*], what else?' Guruji replied to my question as to what was wrong with Sanjay. 'In the last elections, he took part in all the processions, did a lot of slogan shouting without caring about eating or sleeping and went around the bend. Some of it is also due to heredity. His father too has been admitted here three times. The last time his father stayed here was when Indira Gandhi was defeated and he suffered from a kind of *aghatonmanda* [insanity due to shock]. Sanjay's own *unmada* has no name.' In the meanwhile, Sanjay had come out.

" 'Guruji,' he said, 'tell me, are you mad or not?' Guruji pretended anger. 'Give me my stick. Haven't I told you to keep quiet?'

" 'But I am fed up,' Sanjay said. 'I want to go back. I must start

my political work.' Guruji began to joke with him. 'Yes, yes, without
you politics will stop.'

" 'You are the guru of madmen,' Sanjay said. 'That means you are
the biggest madman around. This doctor is also going to be admitted
here soon. Instead of me, keep this doctor, or would you prefer to
have my uncle instead?'

" 'Go on, get away from here,' Guruji said.

" 'I am going,' Sanjay said, and then he added, 'Anyone who looks
after madmen just has to be mad himself.' "

It will be evident that I am attributing Guruji's healing success to
two sets of psychotherapeutic factors. I would locate the first set in
what for want of a better word can only be called Guruji's "personality." It is clear that Guruji has a well-defined professional identity
that does not suffer from a diffusion of roles. The way he has
incorporated his quick anger, ironic humor, genuine concern and
commitment to the patient in his therapeutic style accurately reflects his own personality, as does his need for a close personal
relationship with his patients and his "use" of patients as companions. Guruji's therapeutic style has very obviously evolved out of his
personal needs, thus lending it that particular "authenticity" which
often contributes decisively to the success of the psychotherapeutic
encounter.

Guruji's clear-cut professional identity and authenticity, it seems
to me, also have their roots in his strict adherence to his own
therapeutic tradition. For whereas many therapists in the West,
under the influence of a medical model, emphasize their "flexibility"
and eclecticism, the traditional Indian approach has always believed
that a clear-cut commitment to one school and an intense identification with its tenets are essential for any successful learning or practice.
Whether it be the different schools of yoga or of medicine, success
—either in achieving a full selfhood or in healing—is only possible
if the practitioner (after he has chosen a system or school in con-
formity with his own personal inclinations and needs) remains true
to his particular *gurukula* and *gurusthana*—*i.e.*, the traditions of his
school and the teachings of his own preceptor within that school.

Secondly, Guruji's treatment of psychotic patients fulfills most criteria for an ideal milieu therapy. Guruji's therapeutic institution is small and located near the population it serves. It is open and there is considerable communication and movement between the inside and the outside. Patients have many of their personal belongings and their own clothing available to them. Small groups of patients and their family members come together with the staff members in meaningful work (preparation of medicine) and social interaction (*e.g.*, the walk). We know that such a humane therapeutic community, providing predictability, certainty and continuity of experience, can gradually replace the patient's pseudo-reality with a new reality, promoting a resolution of painful tensions and enhancing self-esteem.

Guruji himself emphasizes the physiological rather than the psychological explanations for his therapeutic successes. "Talk is useless as long as the *nadis* [nerves] that carry the mind to the *indriyas* [the sensory and motor organs] are dry," he says. "In madness the mind's connection with the outer organs is broken or it has become tenuous and weak. The *indriyas*, freed from the mind's control, are uninhibited. How can talking remove the dryness of the nerves or strengthen them so that the mind again informs and pervades the senses? Impossible!"

"In Ayurveda," he continues, "the cure of mental illness takes place primarily on the plane of the body. First, we try to determine the bodily functions that have become disjointed. In *unmada*, for instance, we see whether the patient's blood pressure hasn't increased to an extent that he cannot even lie down. We check his heartbeat and other body signs to see how harmony can be restored to the disturbed functions.

"The most important areas we concentrate on are: the patient should have a good sleep, he should eat properly and his bowels must move regularly. If these three functions [*kriyas*] are put back in order then the patient is already half cured. Yes, after that, by all means encourage him to go for walks and spend as much time with him as you can."

From Guruji's viewpoint, his Ayurvedic system of treatment is closer to the sleep therapy tradition of older European psychiatry as well as to the Rauwolfia-induced sleep used by Yoruba healers for the treatment of psychoses,[5] rather than to any forms of psychotherapy. As practiced in the well-known clinic in Kerala, where oil massages, special diets and prolonged sleep of up to fifteen hours a day are central to the treatment of "nervous disorders," Ayurveda comes close to two other well-developed systems of therapy—the nineteenth-century "rest cure" developed by the American neurologist Weir Mitchell and the Japanese Morita therapy.[6]

I would have of course liked to say to Guruji that by concentrating on the restoration of particularly the three bodily functions of sleeping, eating and bowel movement, he is also simultaneously engaged in a therapy of the mind that goes beyond his conception of "strengthening the nerves" so as to achieve an uninterrupted mind flow. Guruji, according to my psychoanalytic *gurukula*, is also re-creating the maternal beneficence of infancy and early childhood, symbolically providing the patient with the good mother who so solicitously fussed over his eating and sleeping, bladder and bowels. But knowing Guruji's mocking attitude toward my *gurukula* and having had some experience with his tart tongue, I prudently decide to remain silent.

Consistent with his emphasis on the physiology of mental illness, Guruji begins his diagnostic examination by asking the patient about the regularity and "goodness" of his sleep, hunger and evacuation. He follows these questions by feeling the patient's pulse. He calls this "reading" the *nadi*—the word *nadi* standing for both nerves and arteries. According to Guruji, a good *vaid* can see the image of every important organ of the body reflected in the beat, movement and temperature of the *nadi*, a skill which like dancing or music can be acquired only through personal instruction combined with systematic practice. By making *nadi* examination a major part of his diagnostics, Guruji is following contemporary Ayurvedic practice where most *vaid*s begin—and end—their diagnostic efforts by examining the patient's pulse. This practice diverges sharply from the comprehensive examination prescribed in ancient texts that I have described in the last chapter. Typically, many *vaid*s defend their departure from the dominant textual concept of diagnosis by quoting one or another obscure verse in support of their present practice. How does *nadi* examination work?

In perhaps the oldest extant text on the science of *nadi*, Kanada's *Nadi-Vijana*, the human body is said to have thirty-five million *nadi*s

—the specific number in millions being an Indianism for the incalculable.[7] Of this vast number, seventy-two thousand gross *nadis* convey the "qualities" (touch, smell, etc.) of the sensory organs, while seven hundred subtler *nadis* are conduits of the "organic sap" *(rasa)* obtained from food, with which they "irrigate" the whole body. Though there are twenty-four "clear" *nadis* worthy of examination, the most frequently examined *nadis* are the radial artery in the right wrist, followed by the *nadis* in the fingers and thumb. Except in cases of emergency, the examination must be conducted in the morning—hence Guruji's morning consultancy hours. This is due to the belief that the beat of the *nadi* is in its "pure," natural state in the morning after the night's rest; in the afternoon because of heat, and in the evening because of the day's accumulated tensions, the natural beat of the pulse is likely to be contaminated. Of the three humors, an increase in wind makes the *nadi* unsteady; its movement like the "slithering of a snake"; an increase in bile is reflected in a "froglike hopping"; while increase in *phlegm* makes the *nadi* slow and steady "like the gait of a pigeon or hen." The text describes different combinations of beat and movement of the *nadi* —the pulse signatures for various diseases and emotional states. Moreover, in case of a long-standing serious illness, the state of the patient's *nadi* is believed capable of predicting the time of his death within a specified number of hours, or even days.[8]

After the *nadi* examination of the artery in the wrist, Guruji generally asks a patient to stand up; and, putting both his palms down on the shoulders at the base of the throat, he presses up laterally against the sides of the throat with his thumbs. Here he is feeling primarily the two *nadis* that take the *prana* wind to a spot called the "life center" *(jiva kendra)* located at the rear of the head. Going down the body, the *nadis* join together below the ribs, just above the liver—a spot which Guruji also examines by pressing his fingers against it. Since the *prana* wind is held responsible for the circulation of blood as well as the mind, Guruji speaks of the increase of blood circulation to the head interchangeably with an increase in the *prana* wind. According to his system, any mental disturbance or shock excites the "life center" and disturbs the normal circulation of the *prana* wind, which in turn disorganizes the bodily functions. In his further explanation of disturbances in the *prana* wind, Guruji uses the modern idiom by saying that a severe shock and increased blood pressure can break the yellow substance in the nerves (he is probably referring to the myelin sheath) so that the transmission of electric impulses *(vidyut tarang)* of *prana* also gets disturbed.

Whereas in insanity *(unmada)* the speed of blood circulation increases, in epilepsy *(apasmara)* the blood circulation to the "life center" diminishes sharply, leading to the disconnection of the *indriyas* from the mind and to the typical epileptic fits. In cases of *unmada*, the medicines prescribed are intended to slow down the blood circulation and sometimes Guruji also carries out a venisection in a vein in the temple. The main drug used in difficult cases of *unmada* is made from sulfur, mercury and gold and is prepared by Guruji on specific days and in a ritual manner on the premises of the temple, which Guruji also uses as his iatrochemical laboratory. The medicine given in epilepsy is made from copper sulfate and supposedly increases the speed of blood circulation. In addition, Guruji also gives a yellowish liquid which is to be used as a nasal purge during the epileptic fit.

In explaining hysterical fits or *yosh-apasmara*—the "epilepsy" of young femalehood—Guruji says that after the two main *nadis* join together below the ribs, a branch goes to the uterus. An increase in the blood circulation in this branch, *i.e.,* the increased rate of *prana* wind in the uterus, leads to hysterical fits. This is the reason, Guruji claims, that the flow of menstrual blood is greater in quantity and longer in duration in women suffering from hysteria. Diagnostically, he distinguishes hysterical fits from epileptic ones on two counts: first, there is no frothing at the mouth in hysteria, and second, hysterical fits do not exhibit the regularity of their epileptic counterparts.

Dietary instructions are another important element in the treatment of all mental disorders. Guruji expressly forbids the eating of jaggery, chilies and all sour substances. Jaggery, he says, is sweet only to the tongue; beyond the tongue it works as a poison that stirs up the blood and produces heat in the body so that the person is mobilized for acts of rage or sex. Sour foods increase promiscuity, especially in females, while red chilies and pepper activate a person's urge to dominate others. Instead he recommends a "pure," mostly bland diet. These instructions are based on the Ayurvedic notion that there is a mutual relationship between food and the "mind." Certain types of "mind" (or personality) not only prefer certain kinds of food—as discussed earlier—but also each item of food consumed enhances one or the other mental "qualities" of *sattva, rajas* or *tamas. Sattvic* foods, such as cow's milk, rice and green lentils, do not produce an inappropriate increase in any of the three humors, enhance the purity of the mind and are invariably recommended in all mental disorders. *Rajasic* foods such as tea and spices increase bile and make the mind restless, while *tamasic* foods such as meat and eggs tend to produce involuntary withdrawal.

This tripartite division of foods, corresponding to the three humors and three qualities of mind, is similar to the bipartite symbolic classification of food into hot and cold categories in Chinese medicine (or in contemporary Hispanic-American medical beliefs), where a cold illness is treated by a hot food and vice versa.[9] Whether *sattvic, rajasic* and *tamasic* foods have any pragmatic, instrumental value and a demonstrable psychophysiological effect is unknown; there is little doubt, however, that by linking ideas of illness with ideas of treatment, they provide reassurance to the patient and the family and have a definite placebo effect. One of the first questions asked of a doctor by a patient and his family pertains to what foods he should eat and what he should abjure—a question that has left me nonplused whenever it has been asked by a patient beginning or contemplating psychotherapy. We are, then, not surprised to learn that of the ten techniques in which the traditionally trained Ayurvedic physician was expected to excel, one was . . . cooking.

Whatever the actual merits of the prescribed *sattvic* diet, the cultural belief in its purifying power—symbolically purifying the insides of bad thoughts, feelings and fantasies—exercises a strong suggestive effect on the patient. However, going beyond its therapeutic implications, I am suggesting that the preoccupation with the qualities of various foods constitutes one end of a pervasive Indian cultural theme, at the other end of which lies an equal concern with the matters of defecation. As Margaret Egnor, an anthropologist studying medical notions and practices in the southern Indian state of Tamil Nadu, records: "Constipation is regarded as a much more serious disease in India than it is here. Stools are expected to be soft and even runny; purgatives are widely used. If a person fails to defecate one day, this is taken as seriously as a fever."[10] Psychologically, these heightened concerns with eating and defecation point to a cultural prominence of what Winnicott has called the "basic oral fantasy": "When hungry I think of food, when I eat I think of taking food in. I think of what I like to keep inside and I think of what I want to be rid of and I think of getting rid of it."[11] In making use of this cultural fantasy, Guruji's dietary instructions show how deeply Ayurvedic therapy is embedded in (and how well it fits in with) the central symbolic structures of the Indian universe.

10

EPILOGUE

Healing and Culture

This book has been an account of a journey through the world of Indian healing wherein I have described and discoursed upon the many sights and persons I encountered on my travels. The world I saw through the eyes of Indian healers and the tongue of their traditions was, at first, as different from my normal world as it is from the everyday world of most of my readers. Yet once I could reevaluate many of my own assumptions, both professional and personal, the encounters with the practices and practitioners of Indian healing did not appear strange after all. An awareness of the relativity of all healing approaches, together with a recognition of the universality of their concerns, helped me in lessening the imaginative leap required to understand the "mysteries" of this other world.

The journey was of value in other ways too. It made me more aware (in Heinz Kohut's felicitous phrase) of the "health and maturity moralities,"[1] ancient and modern, religious and secular, that pervade psychological healing and inform the work of psychotherapists as much as the rituals of shamans and the ways of gurus. At the same time, I also realized how much any health and maturity morality, received or acquired, can come in the way of understanding others—whether the others be individuals, groups or wider cultures; a constant questioning of the stubborn remnants of these moralities in one's own self seems to be a necessary precondition for all inquiry and understanding. Now, at the end of my travels, rather than summarize what has already been discussed, I would like to make a few personal observations on the contrasts between the Indian and Western views of the person and on the nature of psychotherapy itself, in both its traditional and its modern aspects. Let me begin with the issue of human freedom.

We saw that one of the aims of tantric exercises is to experience various inner states of consciousness through an identification with different gods and goddesses. The Radha Soami Satsang also stresses the experience of different psychic states—which it calls the "mansions of the soul"—as a major goal of its meditative practices. In the folk and local healing traditions, the dissociation states are neither alien nor frightening to Indian patients, who may, in fact, as in the case of Asha at the Balaji temple, positively welcome the experience. Human freedom in the traditional Indian context, then, seems to imply an increase in the potential to experience different inner states while limiting action in the outer world to stereotypes and unquestioning adaptation. The Indian emphasis has been on the pursuit of an inner differentiation while keeping the outer world constant. In contrast, the notion of freedom in the West is related to an increase in the potential for acting in the outer world and enlarging the sphere of choices, while keeping the inner state constant to that of a rational, waking consciousness from which other modes of inner experience have been excluded as deviations. Each culture, though, has consistently underestimated the strength and attraction of the other's freedom ideal.

In my travels, I was also repeatedly struck by the overwhelming role that the "therapeutic" occupies in Indian culture and society, the sheer number of healers and the variety of their healing offers being only one manifestation of this traditional Indian preoccupation. Elsewhere, I have suggested that Indian society is organized around the primacy of the therapeutic in the sense that Indians seem to emphasize protection and caring in their social (and political) relations more than the values of performance or equality.[2] This stress on the therapeutic is reflected in many facets of Indian culture, including its myriad gods and goddesses (three hundred and thirty million at last count, corresponding to the country's population at the time this figure was "calculated"), and the profusion of myths and legends that surround them. There is a god for every psychic season, a myth for every hidden wish and a legend for every concealed anxiety. For instance, if it is the "birth fantasy" that is someone's unconscious preoccupation, then the person has a choice between different myths—even about a single god—which canalize the fantasy and work it through to different and sometimes surprising resolutions. The elephant-headed god Ganesh is born solely due to the agency of his father Shiva in one myth, "proving" that his existence is indubitably masculine, while in another version he is created out of the impurities of his mother's body without paternal intervention.[3] Incorporating all possible fantasies around core human concerns—birth, love and death, body and bodily functions, relationships with parents, siblings and children—Indian myths, through a process of "creative" listening, reading or watching their enactment in folk plays and dance dramas, are readily available to the person for the lifelong task of strengthening psychic integration and maintaining continuity of the self. There are other aspects of Indian culture, including many of its rituals (especially those related to death and mourning), which also incorporate the therapeutic in a way that has largely disappeared from the everyday life of most Western societies.

A third cultural difference between India and the West lies in their ideals of mental health. In the West, there seem to have been two broad approaches to this problem. In the traditional biomedical approach, mental health is sought to be comprehended as analogous to the health of the body, namely as "that condition in which its functions are duly and efficiently discharged." As far as the body is concerned, such a definition is clear enough. There can be little argument about the beating of the heart, the bile secreted by the liver, the kidneys' work in producing urine and the labor of the pancreas as it maintains blood sugar. The notion of what constitutes the efficient discharge of mental functions, however, is much hazier than the corresponding knowledge about bodily functions—a fact which is not too surprising since the mind itself is a much more ambiguous entity; we still talk of *theories* of the mind in the plural and discuss different *models* of the mind. Given the difficulty in determining what constitutes the efficient discharge of such mental functions as intellect and thought, perception and fantasy, feeling and affect, will, volition and learning, the medical approach has retreated to a minimal perspective wherein mental health is seen as the absence of disabling symptoms that interfere with a reasonable functioning of the person.

The second approach to setting up ideals of mental health has come from psychotherapy. Though in its pioneering years psychoanalysis did not advance any explicit criteria of mental health, perhaps also because early psychoanalytic treatment took place in a social setting in which there was an unspoken consensus and homogeneity concerning values,[4] many later analysts as well as psychotherapists of other persuasions have been adding various details to the Western image of the "healthy personality." Most Western psychotherapists today would agree that a healthy adult has the ability to tolerate anxiety without being crippled. He has the capacity to experience pleasure without guilt and can distinguish between his fantasies and the objective reality, irrespective of the reality's painfulness and the intensity of his own needs. He has insights into his conflicts, an acceptance of his strengths and weaknesses, and can use his aggressive energies for achievement, competition and the protection of his rights. These and other similar notions of mental health are pervaded by the humanistic ideals of moderation and responsibility; of balance in short—a balance between inner needs and the demands of outer reality.

Balance, we saw earlier, also characterizes the ideals of many Indian therapeutic approaches: balance between the three humors (Guruji), balance between emotions and intellect, *ida* and *pingala* (Mataji). Even the tantric effort to enhance a man's receptivity and femininity can be seen as seeking to restore a balance between activity and receptivity, masculinity and femininity. What makes the majority of Indian approaches to mental health different from the dominant Western view on the subject, however, is their emphasis on the *relational.* In the Indian prescriptive lists (for example, in Ayurveda) one is struck by the number of ideals of mental health that prescribe the person's behavior in relation to others, especially family and community. A restoration of the lost harmony between the person and his group, we saw earlier, was one of the primary aims of the healing endeavors in the local and folk traditions.

An intriguing explanation for this difference is found in the work of the anthropologist McKim Marriott, who has suggested that the dominant Indian and Western concepts of the person are quite different, if not antithetical.[5] Whereas the modern Western sciences of man conceive of the person as an *individual* (indivisible) nature that is enduring, closed and has an internally homogeneous structure, Indian theories (as evidenced in astrological, biological, moral and ritual texts) hold the person to be a *dividual, i.e.,* divisible. According to Marriott, the Hindu dividual is open, more or less fluid and only temporarily in integration; he is not a monad but (at least) dyadic, deriving his personal nature interpersonally. Hindu persons, then, are constituted of relationships; all affects, needs and motives are relational and their distresses are disorders of relationships.[6] This dichotomy between the Hindu view of a dividual, interpersonal and transpersonal nature of man and the Western individual, instinctual and animal nature of man, though a suggestive and fruitful concept for the understanding of many cultural differences, should not be overemphasized. From my own experience of Hindu patients (and others), I find that in spite of the Indian cultural highlighting of the dividual and the relational, the patients are more individual in their unconscious than they realize and often seek out Western-style psychotherapy partly in order to be comfortable with their individual strivings and needs. Conversely, it is quite conceivable that in spite of the Western cultural emphasis on autonomous individuality, the Western patients are more relational in their unconscious than *they* realize.

Freud, who was tolerant of all psychotherapies, ancient or modern ("There are many ways and means of practising psychotherapy. All that lead to recovery are good."), characteristically used Leonardo da Vinci's contrast between sculpture and painting to distinguish the therapy he had originated—psychoanalysis—from all the other ways of mental healing.[7] Psychoanalysis worked *per via di levare,* chipping away at the surface till the statue contained within the stone appeared; it did not introduce or add something new but stripped in order to expose and crystallize. The other psychotherapies worked as painting does, *per via di porre,* putting paint (*i.e.,* suggestion) where a blank canvas existed before. Others have followed and elaborated upon Freud's distinction between uncovering and supportive-suggestive therapies,[8] but if we continue to use this distinction (at least for the moment) it is undeniable that the Indian psychotherapeutic traditions (perhaps with the exception of tantric *sadhana*—though not tantric healing) fall in the realm of supportive psychotherapy. This becomes quite clear if, for instance, we recapitulate the therapeutic elements of the cure that takes place in the healing temple of the Lord of the Spirit World. First, the patient is assured that he will be cared for and that his heightened need to depend upon others, whether the higher powers of the gods or the accompanying family members and the temple community, will be satisfied. Second, he is helped to look at his distress (the possessing *bhutas*), which is gradually made familiar (if not familial), thus diminishing its terror. Third, a catharsis—that purgative of pathogenic affects—takes place in the dissociation state of *peshi* (in the narration of dreams in the case of the *pir's* patients) in which unacceptable roles or impulses are acted out. Fourth, with the assistance of a large and partisan section of onlookers spurring him on from the stands, the patient is encouraged to employ the defenses of denial, projection and splitting to repress and suppress his conflicts. Fifth, the stress-producing circumstances of external life—the stress being initiated in the case of young men and women either by the imminence or as a consequence of marriage and manifested also as a disturbance in family relationships—are sought to be ameliorated by exposing the family members to the patient's conflict (and their own role in this conflict), thus encouraging a realignment of these stressful relationships. In a garb more suited to the symbolic universes of Western culture and the concrete stresses of life in Western societies, these five elements also characterize most modern psychotherapies. If life's difficulties are transitory and a real change in family and community relationship does occur, then the temple healing (as also cures by the *pir* or the *bhagat*), not unlike most modern psychotherapies, is sufficient to maintain psychic equilibrium. If the problems are deep-seated, then these healing systems, again like the modern psychotherapies, call for recurrent involvement on the part of the patient. In the Balaji temple, we saw this involvement manifested in a class of ex-patients who visit the temple at regular intervals while the few patients who stay on at the temple and, in a sense, are addicted to the healing system, have their counterparts in many of the modern psychotherapies.

The psychotherapeutic content of the "mystical" approaches of Maharajji and Mataji also belongs to the category of supportive therapy, though some elements of the supportive constellation the gurus choose to highlight may be relatively underplayed in the shamanic efforts. Of course, in most "mystical" traditions, instead of the cathartic techniques of possession trance or dream narration, the technology employed to deal with pathogenic affect is one or another form of meditation. However, as discussed earlier, a major psychotherapeutic factor in the healing by the gurus is the patient's (insofar as seeker or disciple is also a patient) emotional relationship with the guru. "Health via identification," as Jerome Oremland calls it (and which he distinguishes from the classical transference cure),[9] is the pervasive imagery of these cures. In identifying with the guru, the patient incorporates idealized images of the guru which he feels as genuine and valuable additions to his own personality. Looking at himself, at others and at his problems with new eyes (the eyes of the guru), the problems no longer seem as intractable as they did earlier. Better adjustments to the real-life situation can and do take place, the changes often being sustained over long periods of time. Psychoanalysis, with its characteristic notions of individuality and personal autonomy, will see the limitations of these approaches in the fact that these identifications and incorporations (and hence the personal changes) are ultimately defending against an underlying *fear*, the fear of the loss of the guru, and the most a patient can hope to become is a poor imitation, a smudged copy of the guru's idealized image. In the Indian culture, however, where the fear of separation and loss is considered the most legitimate of human anxieties,[10] and where the ideal model of learning and personal transformation stresses identification—the student being *proud* to be even a poor copy of the preceptor—it is precisely the limitations of the guru–disciple model that are seen as its virtues. It is therefore not surprising that some Indian psychiatrists consider the guru–disciple relationship as the most acceptable model of psychotherapy in the Indian setting.[11]

The differences between the supportive-suggestive character of the Indian traditions and the *per via di porre* of psychoanalytic therapy are, of course, not so sharp as they might appear at first glance through the use of this distinction. For even the "purest" of uncovering therapies—classical psychoanalysis—with its insistence that only the acceptance of truth in all its affective and cognitive aspects can lead to any true healing, has nonetheless some components of support and reassurance. It has also, in spite of the analyst's sustained and self-conscious effort to guard against the danger, occasions when covert suggestions may indeed be conveyed to the patient. Conversely, the Indian psychotherapies do address the origin of the illness, even though the uncovering of these origins is at the level of a group rather than individual fantasy. The *pir*'s system, for instance, is oriented toward the repressed sexual fantasies of his young Muslim women patients and the fantasy around the devouring female (and the dangerous mother with her poisoned milk) of his male patients. Similarly, Ayata's work with the Oraon tribals has envy and the defenses against envy at its core. Guruji's Ayurvedic ministrations "recognize" the basic oral fantasy of his patients, while Mataji's system seems to specialize in dealing with the paranoid fantasy of an open body being entered at will by malignant spirits. Instead of the painstaking uncovering of the individual's unconscious fantasies that takes place in psychoanalysis, a traditional psychotherapeutic system seems to start off with a primary fantasy that is assumed to fit the core unconscious conflict of *all* the patients involved with that particular system. In other words, it is assumed that given the homogeneity of various groups in a traditional society where individual divergence within the group is minimal, the mask of desire crafted by the group's culture will also fit a majority of its members.

Traditional psychotherapies, then, like their modern Western counterparts, also take into account—in *some* fashion or other, at their periphery or nearer the center—the core human preoccupations around man's biological destiny and his relationships with significant others. For me the encounter with the familiar, known afresh now and stripped of familiarity, was as much a part of my travels as the strange.

NOTES

CHAPTER 1 INTRODUCTION

1. For a detailed elaboration of the threefold individual functioning see Erik H. Erikson, *Childhood and Society* (New York: W. W. Norton, 1952), chapter 1.

2. See Erwin Ackerknecht, "Problems of Primitive Medicine," *Bulletin of the History of Medicine*, 11, 1942. See also Ari Kiev (ed.), *Magic, Faith, and Healing* (Glencoe: The Free Press, 1964).

3. Michel Foucault, *Madness and Civilization: A History of Insanity in the Age of Reason* (New York: Pantheon Books, 1965).

4. Clifford Geertz, "The Growth of Culture and the Evolution of Mind," in J. M. Scher (ed.), *Theories of the Mind* (Glencoe: The Free Press, 1962), p. 724.

5. See Bennett Simon and Herbert Weiner, "Models of Mind and Mental Illness in Ancient Greece," *Journal of the History of Behavioural Sciences*, 2, 1966, p. 308. See also Georg Misch, *A History of Autobiography in Antiquity* (Cambridge, Mass.: Harvard University Press, 1951).

6. An example of this, as A. K. Ramanujan points out in a personal communication, is U. R. Anantamurthy's justly acclaimed *Samskara*.

7. John Woodroffe, *The Garland of Letters* (Madras: Ganesh and Co., 1955), p. x.

8. M. Merleau-Ponty, *Phenomenology of Perception* (London: Routledge and Kegan Paul, 1962), p. 345.

9. Lionel Trilling, *Sincerity and Authenticity* (London: Oxford University Press, 1972), pp. 1–2.

10. Wendy D. O'Flaherty, *Asceticism and Eroticism in the Mythology of Siva* (London: Oxford University Press, 1973), pp. 317–18.

CHAPTER 2 SOUL KNOWLEDGE AND SOUL FORCE: THE PIR OF PATTESHAH DARGAH

1. See Wayland D. Hand, "The Folk Healer: Calling and Endowment," *Journal of the History of Medicine*, 26, 1971, pp. 263–75.

2. Sigmund Freud, "From the History of an Infantile Neurosis" (1918), in J.

Strachey (ed.), *The Standard Edition of the Complete Psychological Works of Sigmund Freud,* 24 vols. (London: Hogarth Press, 1953–72), vol. 17, pp. 7–104.

3.   Richard A. Scheweder and Edmund G. Bourne, "Does the Concept of the Person Vary Cross-Culturally?," unpublished paper, Committee on Human Development, University of Chicago, 1980.

4.   *Ibid.*

5.   T. K. Oesterreich, *Die Besessenheit* (Langensalzach: Wendt and Klauswell, 1922).

6.   Erika Bourguignon, "Spirit Possession Belief and Social Structure" in Agehananda Bharati (ed.), *The Realm of the Extra-Human* (The Hague and Paris: Mouton, 1976), p. 19.

7.   Deriving from the ancient Arabs, the belief and lore of the *jinn* were both modified and spread to other countries by Islam. See J. Hastings (ed.), *Encyclopaedia of Religion and Ethics,* 13 vols., Edinburgh: 1908–26, vol. 1, pp. 669 ff., for the ancient Arab beliefs, and vol. 4, pp. 615 ff., for a general description of Muslim demons and spirits.

8.   Sudhir Kakar, *The Inner World: A Psychoanalytic Study of Childhood and Society in India* (Delhi and New York: Oxford University Press, 1978), pp. 87–103.

9.   Katherine P. Ewing, *The Pir or Sufi Saint in Pakistani Islam,* unpublished Ph.D. dissertation, Department of Anthropology, University of Chicago, 1980, pp. 53–56.

10.   See Debiprasad Chattopadhyaya, *Science and Society in Ancient India* (Calcutta: Research India Publications, 1977).

11.   *Koran,* ii.96.

12.   See Ja'far Sharif, *Islam in India* (1832), G. A. Herklots (trans.) (New Delhi: Oriental Reprints, 1972), p. 218.

13.   *Ibid.,* pp. 228–29. Even today, the essentials of this ritual are the same as those described by Ja'far Sharif almost a hundred and fifty years ago.

14.   *Ibid.,* p. 228.

15.   *Ibid.,* p. 235.

16.   *Ibid.,* p. 231.

17.   Cited by Auden in "The Act of Healing," in *W. H. Auden, Collected Poems,* E. Mendelson (ed.) (New York: Random House, 1976), p. 627.

18.   *Ibid.*

19.   The existence of this "expectancy effect"—namely, that the patient's (and therapist's) expectations of change significantly influence the outcome of psychotherapy—has been well documented by a number of studies. For a summary of these findings see Jerome D. Frank, "The Role of Hope in Psychotherapy," *International Journal of Psychiatry,* 5:5, 1968, pp. 383–95.

20.   Erna M. Hoch, "Pir, Fakir and Psychotherapist," in *The Human Context,* 6:3, 1974, pp. 668–76; Gananath Obeyesekere, "The Idiom of Demonic Possession: A Case Study," *Social Science and Medicine,* 1970, 4, pp. 97–111.

21.   See also Obeyesekere, *op. cit.,* p. 104.

22.   I am indebted to Alan Roland for this insight. See his "The Familial Self,

the Individualised Self, and the Transcendent Self: Psychoanalytic Reflections on India and America," *The Psychoanalytic Review* (in press).

23. Ewing, *op. cit.*, p. 48.

24. See J. E. Cirlot, *A Dictionary of Symbols* (New York: Philosophical Library, 1962), p. 347.

CHAPTER 3 LORD OF THE SPIRIT WORLD

1. For a detailed description of various kinds of Indian spirits, see J. Hastings (ed.), *Encyclopaedia of Religion and Ethics*, 13 vols., Edinburgh, 1908–26, vol. 4, pp. 602 ff.

2. For the local legend of the temple and its deities see Anon., *Shri-Balaji-dhammahatmya* (Vrindavan: Matrapith, n.d.).

3. *Ibid.*, p. 48.

4. The classic work on the Asclepius cult is C. A. Meier, *Ancient Incubation and Modern Psychotherapy* (Evanston, Ill.: Northwestern University Press, 1967).

5. See, for instance, John A. Sanford, *Healing and Wholeness* (New York: Paulist Press, 1977), pp. 49–51.

6. For psychiatric and sociological views on spirit possession in India see Stanley S. Freed and Ruth S. Freed, "Spirit Possession as Illness in a North Indian Village," *Ethnology*, 3, 1964, pp. 152–71; Edward B. Harper, "Spirit Possession and Social Structure," in B. Ratnam (ed.), *Anthropology on the March* (Madras: The Book Centre, 1963), pp. 165–97; J. S. Teja, B. S. Khanna and T. B. Subhramanyam, "Possession States in Indian Patients," *Indian Journal of Psychiatry*, 12, 1970, pp. 71–87. For a cultural view of spirit possession see Peter Claus, "Spirit Possession and Spirit Mediumship from the Perspective of Tulu Oral Traditions," *Culture, Medicine and Psychiatry*, 3(1), 1979, pp. 29–52.

Of the twenty-eight patients interviewed at Balaji, ten were male and eighteen female. They ranged in age from sixteen to sixty-five years, with a median age of twenty-seven years. They hailed from large metropolises, small towns, and villages in almost equal number. All of them belonged to the upper castes and were predominantly of middle and lower-middle class status. Almost all had a few years of schooling and seven had even some college education.

7. On the concept of negative identity, see Erik H. Erikson, *Identity: Youth and Crisis* (New York: W. W. Norton, 1968), pp. 172–76.

8. See Colleen Ward, "Spirit Possession and Mental Health: A Psychoanthropological Perspective," *Human Relations*, 33(1), pp. 149–63.

9. Sigmund Freud, "Studies on Hysteria" (1895), in *The Standard Edition of the Complete Psychological Works of Sigmund Freud* (ed. J. Strachey), vol. 2 (London: Hogarth Press, 1958), chapter 2.

10. Alan Krohn, *Hysteria: The Elusive Neurosis* (New York: International University Press, 1978).

11. *Ibid.*, p. 188.

12. Erikson, *Childhood and Society* (New York: W. W. Norton, 1954), p. 36.

13. The link between spirit possession among women and their social powerlessness has been also emphasized by Harper, *op. cit.*, and Teja *et al.*, *op. cit.*

14. Thomas S. Szasz, *The Myth of Mental Illness* (New York: Harper and Row, 1974), p. 230.

15. Hastings, *op. cit.*, p. 604.

16. See chapter 4.

17. Gananath Obeyesekere, "Psychocultural Exegesis of a Case of Spirit Possession in Sri Lanka," in V. Crapanzano (ed.), *Case Studies in Spirit Possession* (New York: John Wiley, 1976), p. 289.

18. For whatever it's worth, eleven of the twenty-eight patients (and their relatives) reported "considerable improvement" in their condition at the end of their stay at Balaji. The breakdown of those reporting improvement was hysteria, eight; manic depressive, one; obsessive-compulsive, one; and undiagnosed (complaining symptom, white patches on skin), one.

19. Quoted in Virginia Adams, "Freud's Work Thrives as Theory, Not Therapy," in *The New York Times*, August 14, 1979.

CHAPTER 4 OTHER SHAMANS

1. W. G. Jilek, "From Crazy Witch Doctor to Auxiliary Psychotherapist—The Changing Image of the Medicine Man," in *Psychiatria Clinica*, 4, 1971, pp. 200–20.

2. G. Wissler, *The American Indian* (New York: Oxford University Press, 1931), p. 204.

3. P. Radin, *The Trickster* (New York: Schocken Books, 1972), and *Primitive Religion—Its Nature and Origin* (New York, Dover Press, 1957), pp. 131 ff.

4. See, for example, A. Metraux, *Voodoo in Haiti* (New York: Oxford University Press, 1959), p. 64; W. D. Hambly, *Origins of Education Among Primitive Peoples* (London: Macmillan, 1926), pp. 219 ff.; R. E. S. Tanner, "The Magician in Northern Sukumaland, Tanganyika," in *South-West Journal of Anthropology*, 13, 1957, pp. 344–51, all cited in Jilek, *op. cit.*, pp. 201–02.

5. G. Devereux, *Mohave Ethnopsychiatry and Suicide* (Washington: U.S. Government Printing Office, 1961), p. 285.

6. L. Bryce Boyer, "Notes on the Personality Structure of a North American Indian Shaman," in *Journal of Hillside Hospital*, 10, 1961, pp. 14–33.

7. See M. Eliade, *Shamanism: Archaic Techniques of Ecstasy* (Princeton: Bollingen Foundation, 1964); B. Myerhoff, "Shamanic Equilibrium: Balance and Meditation in Known and Unknown Worlds," in W. D. Hand (ed.), *American Folk Medicine* (Berkeley: University of California Press, 1976).

8. R. H. Lowrie, "Shamans and Priests Among the Plains Indians," in W. A. Lessa and E. Z. Vogt (eds.), *Reader in Comparative Religion* (New York: Harper and Row, 1965).

9. See, for instance, J. Halifax, *Shamanic Voices: A Survey of Visionary Narratives* (New York: E. P. Dutton, 1979); J. M. Murphy, "Psychotherapeutic Aspects of Shamanism on St. Lawrence Island, Alaska," in A. Kiev (ed.), *Magic, Faith and Healing* (New York: The Free Press, 1964); D. Sharon, *Wizard of the Four Winds: A Shaman's Story* (New York: The Free Press, 1978).

10. A. H. Leighton and J. H. Hughes, "Cultures as Causative of Mental Disorder," in *Causes of Mental Disorder: Review of Epidemiological Knowledge* (New York: Milbank Memorial Fund, 1961).

11. See Claude Lévi-Strauss, "The Effectiveness of Symbols" and "The Sorcerer and His Magic," in *Structural Anthropology* (New York: Basic Books, 1963), pp. 167–85 and 186–205.

12. *Ibid.*, p. 204.

13. The idealization of the shaman may be seen in the writings of the school of "antipsychiatry" of which R. D. Laing and David Cooper are the best-known proponents. See, for example, David Cooper, *The Language of Madness* (London: Penguin Books, 1980).

14. For a brief historical and anthropological account of the Oraon see R. O. Dhan, *These Are My Tribesmen—The Oraons* (Ranchi: G. E. L. Church Press, 1967); see also N. Prasad *et al.* (eds.), *Land and People of Tribal Bihar* (Ranchi: Bihar Tribal Research Institute, 1961).

15. An instance of a pacification ritual is *shringara* ("adornment"), generally carried out with female patients. The ingredients used in *shringara* are a mud pack, seven flowers, three red bangles, turmeric root, a silver and a copper coin and an earthen pot. "With *shringara*," Ayata says, "we give respect to the *shaitan* and at the same time bid him good-bye. We are telling him that we have no complaint against him and ask him to forget any grievance that he may have."

16. A. F. Davies, *Skills, Outlooks and Passions* (Cambridge: Cambridge University Press, 1980), p. 347.

17. George Foster, "The Anatomy of Envy," *Current Anthropology*, 1972, pp. 166–82.

18. *Ibid.*, pp. 175–82.

19. Helmut Schoeck, *Envy* (London: Martin Secker and Warburg, 1969), p. 247.

20. Davies, *op. cit.*, pp. 359–60.

21. O. Pfister, "Instinctive Psychoanalysis Among the Navahos," *Journal of Nervous and Mental Disease*, 76, 1932, pp. 234–54.

22. Raymond Prince, "Variations in Psychotherapeutic Procedures," in H. C. Triandis and J. G. Draguns (eds.), *Handbook of Cross-Cultural Psychology*, vol. 6. (Boston: Allyn and Bacon, 1980), pp. 314–21.

23. The relevant studies are: (for Ghana) M. Kilson, "Possession in Ga-Ritual," *Transcultural Psychiatric Research Review*, 5, 1968, pp. 67–69; (for Japan) T. Yoshida, "Mystical Retribution, Spirit Possession and Social Structure in a Japanese Village," *Ethnology*, 6, 1967, pp. 237–62; M. H. Herskovits, *Dahomey: An Ancient West African Kingdom* (New York: Augustine, 1938); (for Nigeria) R. H. Prince, "The Problem of Spirit Possession as a Treatment for Psychiatric Disorder," *Eth-*

nos, 1974, pp. 314–33; (for Pacific Micronesia) A. P. Leonard, "Spirit Mediums in Paulau: Transformations in a Traditional System," in E. Bourguinon (ed.), *Religion, Altered States of Consciousness and Social Change* (Columbus: Ohio State University Press, 1973); (for the Middle East) J. K. Kennedy, "Nubian Zar Ceremonies as Psychotherapy," *Human Organisation*, 26, 1967, pp. 185–94; N. Kline, "Psychiatry in Kuwait," *British Journal of Psychiatry*, 109, 1963, pp. 766–74, T. A. Bassher, "Traditional Psychotherapeutic Practices in Sudan," *Transcultural Psychiatric Research Review*, 4, 1967, pp. 158–60; W. Bazzoui and I. Al-issa, "Psychiatry in Iraq," *British Journal of Psychiatry*, 112, 1966, pp. 827–32; and (for the American Southeast) W. La Barre, *They Shall Take Up Serpents: Psychology of the Southern Snake-Handling Cult* (Minneapolis: University of Minnesota Press, 1962).

24. Prince, *op. cit.*, p. 316.

25. W. Sargant, *Battle for the Mind* (New York: Doubleday, 1957).

26. Prince, *op. cit.*, pp. 330–31.

27. Alexandra David-Neel, *Magic and Mystery in Tibet* (London: Souvenir Press, 1965), preface.

28. Rechung Rinpoche (tr.), *Tibetan Medicine* (Berkeley: University of California Press, 1976), pp. 49–51; see also Theodore Burang, *Tibetan Art of Healing* (London: Robinson and Watkins, 1957). The humoral system of Tibetan medicine borrowed from Ayurveda is discussed in greater detail in chapter 8.

29. Robert B. Ekwall, *Religious Observances in Tibet* (Chicago: University of Chicago Press, 1964), p. 24.

30. *Ibid.*, p. 26.

31. Perhaps Rainer Maria Rilke best conveys the Tibetan experience of the mantra as a center of force and reality and not a mere conventional medium of expression when he writes:

> Wo sich langsam aus dem Schon-Vergessen,
> Einst Erfahrenes sich uns entgegenhebt,
> Rein gemeistert, milde, unermessen
> Und in Untastbaren erlebt:
> Dort beginnt das Wort, wie wir es meinen,
> Sein Geltung übertrifft uns still—
> Denn der Geist, der uns vereinsamt, will
> Völlig sicher sein, uns zu vereinen.

> (Where slowly from the long-forgotten,
> Past Experience rises up in us,
> Perfectly mastered, mild and beyond measure,
> And realized in the intangible:
> There begins the word, as we conceive it,
> And its meaning quietly surpasses us—
> For the mind that makes lonely, wants
> To be sure that we shall be united.)

Cited in Lama Angarika Govinda, *Foundations of Tibetan Mysticism* (London: Rider, 1960), p. 21.

32. Lévi-Strauss, "The Effectiveness of Symbols," *op. cit.*

33. *Ibid.*, pp. 202–04.

CHAPTER 5 THE PATH OF THE SAINTS

1. Franz Alexander, "Buddhistic Training as an Artificial Catatonia (The Biological Meaning of Psychic Recurrence)," *Psychoanalysis*, 19, 1931, pp. 129–45.

2. Nathaniel Ross, "Affect as Cognition: With Observations on the Meanings of Mystical States," *International Review of Psychoanalysis*, 2:1, 1975, p. 90.

3. One of the most eloquent spokesmen of this position is Sayeed Hossein Nasr, who has protested against the "monolithic and monopolistic character of Western sciences of man," which he calls "pseudo-sciences." See his *Islam and the Plight of Modern Man* (London: Longmans, 1975); see also Ashis Nandy, "Subjects and Subjecthood in Contemporary Psychology: Politics, Ethics and Culture of a Science," unpublished lecture delivered at Department of Psychology, University of Allahabad, March 1978.

4. Sri Aurobindo, *Bases of Yoga*, cited in E. Servadio, "A Psychodynamic Approach to Yoga Experience," *International Journal of Parapsychology*, 9, 1966, p. 181.

5. Maharaj Charan Singh, *Light on Santmat* (Beas: Radhasoami Satsang, 1958), pp. 238–39.

6. See Agehananda Bharati, *The Light at the Center* (Santa Barbara: Ross-Erikson, 1976), p. 119.

7. *Ibid.*, pp. 91–92.

8. The historical details are based on the standard work on the subject by Agam Prasad Mathur, *Radhasoami Faith* (Delhi: Vikas Publishing House, 1974).

9. *Ibid.*, pp. 119–33.

10. This view has led individual Satsangis as well as their gurus to interpret, with indifferent scholarship but with passionate conviction, the message of other religious texts such as the Bible as being identical to their own. See, for instance, Randolph Stone, *The Mystic Bible* (Beas: Radhasoami Satsang, 1966); Shanti Sethi, *Message Divine* (Beas: Radhasoami Satsang, 1972); Maharaj Charan Singh, *St. John, The Great Mystic* (Beas: Radhasoami Satsang, 1975).

11. Mathur, *op. cit.*, p. 120.

12. For an account of the expansion of the Beas group see Katerine Wason, *The Living Master* (Beas: Radhasoami Satsang, 1966), pp. 52–84, and *Radha Soami Satsang Beas, Teachings and Brief History* (Beas: Radhasoami Satsang, 1977).

13. Phyllis Greenacre, "Crowds and Crisis," *The Psychoanalytic Study of the Child*, 27, 1972, p. 143; see also Andrew Peto, "On Crowd Violence: The Role of Archaic Superego and Body Image," *International Review of Psycho-Analysis*, 2:4, 1975, pp. 449–66. In contrast to Greenacre and Peto, who stress the potential for crowd violence in this regression, my experience is that when the crowds are

unified by a central spiritual idea and a leader, the psychological regression tremendously increases the potential for libidinal expression. This is of course also the original view of Freud in "Group Psychology and the Analysis of the Ego" (1921), *Standard Edition*, vol. 18, pp. 69–145.

14. The following condensed reproduction of Maharajji's discourse is partly from my notes but largely from a published version, *Truth Eternal* (Beas: Radhasoami Satsang, 1977).

15. The literature on the third category has been extensively reviewed by Graham Little, who has proposed an intriguing theory of leadership based on the three categories: see his "Leaders and Followers: A Psycho-social Perspective," *Melbourne Journal of Politics*, 12, 1980, pp. 3–29.

16. *Ibid.*, p. 8.

17. For a detailed discussion of the origins of this archaic narcissistic configuration see Heinz Kohut, *The Analysis of the Self* (New York: International Universities Press, 1971), pp. 83–84.

18. The literature on the physiology and psychology of meditation is vast. An excellent review from the psychoanalytic viewpoint is by M. Shafii, "Adaptive and Therapeutic Aspects of Meditation," *International Journal of Psychoanalytic Psychotherapy*, 1, 1973, and "Silence in Service of the Ego: Psychoanalytic Study of Meditation," *International Journal of Psychoanalysis*, 54, 1973, pp. 431–43.

19. See *Light on Santmat, op. cit.*, p. 120, pp. 163–64, and Maharaj Charan Singh, *The Master Answers* (Beas: Radhasoami Satsang, 1966), p. 276.

20. *The Master Answers, op. cit.*, pp. 41–45. See also *Thus Saith the Master* (Beas: Radhasoami Satsang, 1971), p. 191.

21. *Ibid.*, p. 205.

22. *Ibid.*, pp. 57 and 252–53.

23. McKim Marriott, personal communication.

24. *The Living Master, op. cit.*, p. 20.

25. *Ibid.*, p. 33.

26. *Ibid.*, pp. 43, 46.

27. This formulation, in a personal communication, is by McKim Marriott.

CHAPTER 6 TANTRA AND TANTRIC HEALING

1. Edward C. Dimock, Jr., *The Place of the Hidden Moon* (Chicago: University of Chicago Press, 1966), p. 106.

2. *Ibid.*, p. 246.

3. It is well known that the number of tantric texts and commentaries runs into the thousands and it is only a rare scholar who has an overview of even a major portion of this literature. Perhaps the most accomplished modern scholar of Hindu tantrism was the late Gopinath Kaviraj, whose *Tantrik Sahitya* (in Hindi; Lucknow: Hindi Samiti, 1972) lists over five thousand manuscripts and summarizes the contents of many of these works. Devadatta Shastri, *Tantra Sidhanta aur Sadhana* (Allahabad: Smriti Prakashan, 1976), provides a good Hindi introduction to tantra.

It can be supplemented by a more advanced text, Gopinath Kaviraj, *Tantrik Vadmaya main Shaktadrishti* (Patna: Bihar Rashtrabhasha Parishad, 1963). In English, the works of Sir John Woodroffe (writing under the pseudonym of Arthur Avalon) are still the best starting point; see especially his *Shakti and Shakta* (Madras: Ganesh and Co., 1956); *Tantra of the Great Liberation (Mahanirvana Tantra)* (New York: Dover Publications, 1972), esp. pp. i–cxlvi; *The Garland of Letters (Varnamala)* (Madras: Ganesh and Co., 1955). For more modern accounts, see the chapter on tantrism in Mircea Eliade, *Yoga: Immortality and Freedom* (Princeton: Princeton University Press, 1958), pp. 200–73; Agehananda Bharati, *The Tantric Tradition* (London: Rider, 1965); Herbert V. Guenther, *Yuganaddha: The Tantric View of Life* (Varanasi: Chowkhamba Sanskrit Series Office, 1976).

4.   For a concise statement on the historical origins of tantra and its relationship to other religious traditions in India, see M. Eliade, *op. cit.*, pp. 200–07.

5.   A. Bharati, *op. cit.*, p. 10.

6.   *Ibid.*, p. 19.

7.   The "Kritische Schule" of Frankfurt, associated primarily with the names of Theodor Adorno and Juergen Habermas, has highlighted the socially emancipative function of psychoanalysis: see Klaus Horn, "Die Gesellschaftliche Funktion der Psychoanalyse," in E. H. Englert (ed.), *Die Verarmung der Psyche* (Frankfurt: Campus, 1979), pp. 47–48.

8.   Ananda K. Coomaraswamy, "On the Indian and Traditional Psychology, or Rather Pneumatology" in *Selected Papers* (R. Lipsey, ed.), vol. 2 (Princeton: Princeton University Press, 1977), p. 335.

9.   Joyce McDougall calls them "absence" and "difference": see her "The Psycho-soma and the Psychoanalytic Process," in *The International Review of Psychoanalysis*, 1(4), 1974, pp. 437–60.

10.   See Melanie Klein, *The Psychoanalysis of Children* (London: Hogarth Press, 1932); *Contributions to Psychoanalysis, 1921–1945* (London: Hogarth Press, 1948); Klein *et al.*, *Developments in Psychoanalysis* (London: Hogarth Press, 1952).

11.   A. Coomaraswamy, "The Tantric Doctrine of Divine Bi-unity," in *Selected Papers, op. cit.*, pp. 234–40.

12.   Tantric texts, both Hindu and Buddhist, abound in passages such as the following: "Soon after he has embraced his female partner *(mudra)*, inserted his male organ into her vulva *(vajra-vesapravartna)*, drinks from her lips sprinkled with milk, makes her speak cooingly, enjoys rich delight, and makes her thighs quiver, King Cupid, (man's) adamantine nature *(vajra-sattva)* will become manifest." The passage is from a Buddhist tantric text, *Prajnopayaviniscayasiddhi of Anangavajra*, cited and translated by Guenther, *op. cit.*, p. 57. See also Eliade, *op. cit.*, p. 249, for a discussion of the "intentional" language *(sandhabhasha)* used in tantric texts.

13.   Guenther, *op. cit.*, p. 118.

14.   *Guhyasamaja-tantra*, cited in Guenther, *op. cit.*, p. 119. Another tantric text, *Prajnopayaviniscayasiddhi*, similarly states, "The adept who has sexual intercourse with his mother, his sister, his daughter, and his sister's daughter, will easily succeed in his striving for the ultimate goal *(Tattvayoga)*"; see Guenther, *op. cit.*, p. 119.

15. *Jnanasiddhi*, I.80–81, cited in Guenther, *op. cit.*, p. 59.

16. Personal communication from Amritananda Das, who is referred to as A. in the rest of the chapter.

17. Swami Yogeshananda, *The Visions of Ramakrishna* (Madras: Sri Rama-krishna Math, 1973), pp. 41–42. Sri Ramakrishna was, of course, a visionary mystic *par excellence* who had a number of visions throughout his life. It should be noted that in his tantric phase the visions had an explicitly sexual content.

18. Yogeshananda, *op. cit.*, p. 43.

19. See, for instance, Lawrence Kubie, "The Drive to Become Both Sexes," *Psychoanalytic Quarterly*, 43, 1974, pp. 349–426.

20. The evidence has been carefully marshaled as well as decisively contributed to by Robert Stoller's work: see R. Stoller, *Sex and Gender*, vol. 1 (New York: Science House, 1968); vol. 2 (New York: Jason Aronson, 1975); *Perversion: The Erotic Form of Hatred* (New York: Pantheon Books, 1975). See also J. Kestenberg, "Outside and Inside, Male and Female," *Journal of the American Psychoanalytic Association*, 16, 1968, pp. 457–520; J. Morey and A. Ehrhardt, *Man and Woman, Boy and Girl* (Baltimore: John Hopkins University Press, 1972); I. Fast, "Develop-ments in Gender Identity: The Original Matrix," *International Review of Psychoa-nalysis*, 5, 1978, pp. 443–53.

21. For an earlier view of femininity in men, see R. Boehm, "The Femininity Complex in Men," *International Journal of Psychoanalysis*, 11, 1930, pp. 444–69.

22. Sudhir Kakar, *The Inner World: A Psychoanalytic Study of Childhood and Society in India* (Delhi and New York: Oxford University Press, 1978), chapter 3.

23. For a brilliant and provocative discussion of this issue, see Ramchandra Gandhi, *Brahmacharya* (Department of Philosophy: University of Hyderabad, 1981). Personally, I tend to agree more with Thomas Mann who, in *Joseph and His Brothers* (London: Secker & Warburg, 1959, p. 719), writes:

> It is undeniable that human dignity realizes itself in the two sexes, male and female; so that when one is neither one nor the other, one stands outside the human pale and whence then can human dignity come? Efforts to sustain it are worthy of respect, for they deal with the spiritual, and thus, let us admit in honour, with the pre-eminently human. But truth demands the hard confes-sion that thought and the spirit come badly off, in the long run, against nature. How little can the precepts of civilization avail against the dark, deep, silent knowledge of the flesh! How little it lets itself be taken in by the spirit!

24. *Ibid.*

25. See Wendy O'Flaherty, *Women, Androgynes and Other Mythical Beasts* (Chicago: University of Chicago Press, 1980), pp. 310–34. See also David Shulman, "Imperfect Paradise: Some Uses of the Androgyne," unpublished ms., 1981, for a discussion of the androgyne in southern Indian temple myths.

26. O'Flaherty, *op. cit.*, p. 331.

27. Gopikrishna, *Secrets of Kundalini in Panchastavi* (New Delhi: Kundalini Research and Publication Trust, 1978), p. 203.

28.   John Woodroffe quotes from the *Kubjika-tantra, Nitya-tantra, Pichchhila-tantra* in support of this hierarchy: see his *Tantra of the Great Liberation, op. cit.,* pp. lxvi–lxvii; see also *Kalitatvamrita* in *Tantrik Sahitya, op. cit.,* p. 125, and Bharati, *op. cit.,* p. 231, who cites a verse from the *Bhavachudamani* supporting this position.

29.   *Tantra Sidhanta aur Sadhana, op. cit.,* p. 29; see also, *Tantra of the Great Liberation, op. cit.,* pp. lxxviii–lxxxiii on the *acharas.*

30.   *Kalivilasa-tantra,* 6:4–10, quoted in Bharati, *op. cit.,* p. 231.

31.   Cited in *Tantra of the Great Liberation, op. cit.,* p. 231. See also *Kulasamhita* cited in *Tantrik Sahitya, op. cit.,* p. 146, which advances the same position.

32.   Bharati, *op. cit.,* pp. 228–31.

33.   *Ibid.,* p. 231.

34.   See, for instance, the chapter "On Mantra" in Bharati, *op. cit.,* pp. 101–63; Karl G. Diehl, *Instrument and Purpose: Studies on Rites and Rituals in South India* (Lund: Gleerups, 1956); Eliade, *op. cit.,* pp. 212–16; Gopinath Kaviraj, *Tantrik Vadmaya main Shakta-drishti, op. cit.,* pp. 300–35.

35.   Bharati, *op. cit.,* p. 231.

36.   To give an example of a *prastara* (see figure): Decoded, this particular *prastara* reads: In a place surrounded by water (unconsciousness), there is an island city with four gates—mantra repetition *(japa),* ascetic austerities *(tapa),* discrimination *(vichara)* and intelligence *(buddhi).* In the center of the island is an effulgent sun wheel containing the *yantra* of the goddess of knowledge and wisdom; the lotus of the *yantra* indicates opening out to the world, the hexagon formed of superimposed

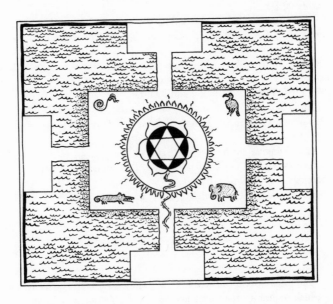

triangles symbolizes the "union of opposites." The wheel cuts the uninitiated person into pieces and there are also the four threats—vulture (aging and death), snake (hidden impulses), crocodile (hidden weaknesses) and elephant (egoism)— which can prevent the tantrik from uniting with the goddess of wisdom. After a period of contemplation of the diagram and the appropriate mantra-*japa*, the adept has the "actual" feeling of crossing the waters, entering the city, fighting off the threats and leaping over the spinning wheel to unite with the goddess of wisdom.

37. For a psychoanalytic statement on this view of dreams, see Charles Rycroft, *The Innocence of Dreams* (New York: Pantheon Books, 1979).

38. Eliade, *op. cit.*, p. 208, citing a passage from the *Satantra-tantra* which expounds the visualization of Durga, writes: "The goddess is like a black mountain, her face is terrifying, she is embraced by Siva and wears several wreaths of skulls around her neck; her hair hangs loose and she is smiling. Not a single detail is omitted—neither the snake *(naga)* that serves her as sacred thread, nor the moon on her forehead, the thousands of dead hands about her lips, the bleeding mouth and bloodstained body, the two infant corpses in place of earrings, etc."

39. Cited in Rycroft, *op. cit.*, p. 50.

40. This is the position taken by the psychoanalyst and Sanskritist J. M. Masson in *The Oceanic Feeling: The Origins of Religious Sentiment in Ancient India* (Dordrecht: D. Reidel, 1980).

41. Rycroft, *op. cit.*, p. 166.

42. Some of these texts are the *Kakshaputa, Kamaratna, Kothulvidya* and *Kotukrahasya, Dattareyatantra,* and *Bhutadamaratantra,* whose contents have been summarized on pp. 87, 105, 115, 293 and 444 respectively in Gopinath Kaviraj, *Tantrik Sahitya, op. cit.*

43. C. G. Jung, "Psychological Commentary" in W. Y. Evan-Wentz (ed.), *The Tibetan Book of Great Liberation* (London: Oxford University Press, 1977), p. xxxiv.

44. Stephan Beyer, *The Cult of Tara: Magic and Ritual in Tibet* (Berkeley: University of California Press, 1973), p. 92.

45. Wendy O'Flaherty, "Illusion and Reality in the *Yogavashistha,*" in *Journal of the Royal Society of Art,* 129:5294, January 1981, pp. 104–23.

46. Narayandutt Shirmali, *Tantrik Siddhian* (Delhi: Hind Pustak Bhandar, 1980), pp. 150–56.

47. *Tantra Sidhanta aur Sadhana, op. cit.,* pp. 52–53.

48. Coomaraswamy, "On the Indian and Traditional Psychology, or Rather Pneumatology," *op. cit.,* pp. 365–66.

49. Samaresh Bose, "The Tantrik Quest," in *Sunday,* January 25, 1981, p. 17.

CHAPTER 7 COOLING BREEZES:
THE CULT OF MATAJI

1. Mataji's description of the model is scattered through her many talks and letters which appear in the cult's journal *Ananta Jeevan* as well in its various

pamphlets, *Sahaja Yoga and Its Practice, The Life Eternal, Sahaja Yoga: A Unique Discovery*, all published by the Life Eternal Trust, Bombay.

2. Vasant Rele, *Mysterious Kundalini* (Bombay: Taraporevala, 1931).

3. Paul Watzlawick, *How Real Is Real?* (New York: Vintage Books, 1977), pp. 81–82; Leon Festinger *et al., When Prophecy Fails* (Minneapolis: University of Minnesota Press, 1956).

4. T. C. Everson, "Spontaneous Regression of Cancer," in *Connecticut Medical Journal*, 22, 1958, pp. 637–43, cited in Jerome D. Frank, *Persuasion and Healing* (Baltimore: Johns Hopkins Press, 1961), p. 57.

5. Frank, *op. cit.*, p. 58.

6. This has been experimentally demonstrated a number of times, perhaps most strikingly in the experiment reported by Rehder. Three severely ill, bedridden patients, one with a chronic inflammation of the gall bladder with stones, the other with widespread cancer and the third who had failed to recover from a major abdominal surgery and was reduced to a skeleton, were first treated by a faith healer without their knowledge. Nothing happened. The physician then built up their expectations and belief over several days that a faith healer would be treating them on a particular day from a distance. On that day, all three patients showed dramatic improvement, and the third one was cured permanently, testifying to the power of belief even when it is objectively false. See H. Rehder, "Wunderheilungen, ein Experiment," *Hippokrates*, 26, 1955, cited in Frank, *op. cit.*, pp. 60–61.

7. Lewis Thomas, *The Medusa and the Snail: More Notes of a Biology Watcher* (New York: Viking Press, 1979), pp. 76–81.

8. G. De Kalbermattern, *The Advent* (Bombay: Life Eternal Trust Publishers, 1979), p. 197.

9. *Ibid.*, p. 213.

10. *Ibid.*, p. 201.

11. *Ibid.*, p. 201.

12. *Ibid.*, p. 222.

13. *Ibid.*, p. 224.

14. *Ibid.*, p. 224.

15. *Ibid.*, p. 218.

16. Robert Waelder, "Characteristics of Totalitarianism," in W. Muensterberger and S. Axelrad (eds.), *The Psychoanalytic Study of Society*, vol. 1 (New York: International Universities Press, 1960).

17. This incident is from a meeting held on February 8, 1980, at the Constitution Club in New Delhi.

18. Kalbermattern, *op. cit.*, p. 221.

CHAPTER 8 INDIAN MEDICINE AND PSYCHIATRY:
CULTURAL AND THEORETICAL PERSPECTIVES ON AYURVEDA

1. *Caraka Samhita*, I. v. 74–75. The English translation of these verses is from the edition by Ram Karan Sharma and Vaidya Bhagwan Dash (trs.) (Varanasi: Chowkhamba Sanskrit Series Office, 1976).

2.   Gananath Obeyesekere, "The Theory and Practice of Psychological Medicine in the Ayurvedic Tradition," in *Culture, Medicine and Psychiatry*, 1, 1977, p. 155.

3.   See David McQueen, "The History of Science and Medicine as Theoretical Sources for the Comparative Study of Contemporary Medical Systems," *Social Science and Medicine*, 12, 1978, pp. 70–71.

4.   This view is admirably conveyed in the injured astonishment of Ayurvedic doctors who were asked to reply to a questionnaire distributed by a government committee set up in the nineteen twenties to examine the status of indigenous systems of medicine. "In reply to your questionnaire . . . the wording of the second question is enough to show that the Committee is not prepared to accept the third instrument of right knowledge (the teachings of authorities) . . . but would accept only two, *i.e.*, perception and inference—we are very much grieved at your words 'How far your theory or theories stand the tests of modern scientific criticism'; we beg to say very modestly that the moderners cannot even comprehend our theories of causation and the modes of treatment. They are changing their ground almost every year by refuting old theories, and experimenting, each according to his own whims, upon poor creatures, without any proportionate gain to anybody. Is this what deserves the name of science? Our idea of science is that it should be a storehouse of incontrovertible, universal knowledge which holds good for all times —past, present and future—The facts well-ascertained in our ancient books thousands of years ago have never been disputed, and can never lose their ground, being nothing short of absolute and universal truths." Cited in Charles Leslie, "Modern India's Ancient Medicine," in *Trans-Action*, June 1969, p. 54.

5.   See, for instance, Sayta Pal Gupta, *Psychopathology in Indian Medicine* (Aligarh: Ajaya Publishers, 1977), and Balkrishna Amarji Pathak, *Manasrog Vigyan* (Calcutta: Baidnath Ayurveda Bhavan, 1955). Freud seems to have a fatal fascination for both authors even though they consistently misunderstand his theories. The former author tries to equate the *sattva, rajas* and *tamas* parts *(ansha)* of the mind with the superego, ego and id of the topographical model. Superego then (p. 132) becomes "highest consciousness," "enlightenment," which "must also spread to the other segments of preconscious and unconscious."

6.   Lewis Thomas, *The Medusa and the Snail: More Notes of a Biology Watcher* (New York: The Viking Press, 1979), pp. 19–26.

7.   *Caraka Samhita, op. cit.*, I.xii. 39–43.

8.   *Ibid.*, I.xii.49.

9.   Debiprasad Chattopadhyaya, *Science and Society in Ancient India* (Calcutta: Research India Publications, 1977).

10. *Caraka Samhita*, I. i. 15–17.

11. *Ibid.*, I.i.43.

12. *Ibid.*, I. xi.3.

13. *Ibid.*, I.xi.4.

14. *Ibid.*, xi.5.

15. *Ibid.*, xi.6.

16. Chattopadhyaya, *op. cit.*, pp. 175–88.

17. *Caraka Samhita,* I. ix.
18. *Ibid.,* I.ix.5.
19. *Ibid.,* I.xxvii.79.
20. Gautama, Apastamba, Vasistha, Manu, Vishnu and others declare the drinking of alcohol to be a grave sin *(mahapataka).* See Chattopadhyaya, *op. cit.,* p. 392.
21. *Caraka Samhita,* VI.xxiv.134. Translation from Chattopadhyaya, *op. cit.,* p. 394.
22. *Caraka Samhita,* I.xxvi.194.
23. *Caraka Samhita,* I.i.47.
24. See Chattopadhyaya, *op. cit.,* p. 98. The Ayurvedic view of the whole person as focus of the healing sciences is not unique. Mesopotamian medicine was at least psychosomatic, as was Greek medicine. Hippocrates maintained that "In order to cure the human body, it is necessary to have a knowledge of the whole of things"; and Socrates stated, "As it is not proper to cure the eyes without the head, nor the head without the body, so neither is it proper to cure the body without the soul." What is unique about Ayurveda is the detailed elaboration of this view in practical therapeutics so that it becomes the very essence of Indian medicine.

The perspective of the whole person as the subject matter of medicine seems unfamiliar to modern Western consciousness only because of the rise of mind-body dualism, especially during the Renaissance period, and the laboratory-based medicine of Pasteur and Virchow in the nineteenth century, when the definition of disease was narrowed down to structural cell change. Disease now became only the disease of the cell and took the mind-body schism to its furthest point. For a short historical account of this problem in Western medicine, see "History of Psychophysiologic Medicine," in Alfred M. Freedman, H. I. Kaplan and B. J. Sadock (eds.), *Modern Synopsis of Comprehensive Textbook of Psychiatry* II (Baltimore: Williams and Wilkins, 1976), pp. 792–96. The quotes from Hippocrates and Socrates are on p. 793.
25. *Caraka Samhita,* III.viii.103. My translation.
26. The *Caraka Samhita* states this clearly: "The person is comparable to the cosmos. So said Lord Punarvasu Atreya. That is, the person is a minuscule image of the great cosmos. All the features [*bhava*] that are present in the cosmos are present in the person. All that are in the person are in the cosmos. . . . Here are only few of the main equivalents. Listen with concentration.

"The cosmos is constituted of six elements. These six elements are earth, water, fire, wind, ether and the unmanifested Brahman. These elements also constitute the person. . . . As the cosmos is pervaded by the creative capacity [*vibhuti*] of Brahma, so is the indwelling *atman* the *vibhuti* of the person. As Prajapati [Lord of Creatures] is the *vibhuti* of Brahma in the cosmos, so is the mind the *vibhuti* of the *atman* in the person. What is Indra (king of gods) to the cosmos is *ahankara* ['I-ness'] to the person. As is sun in the cosmos, so is *adana* [absorption power] in the person. What is Rudra [Vedic form of Shiva] in the cosmos, is anger in the person. Moon in the cosmos is happiness in the person. Vasu in the cosmos is contentment in the person. Ashwins [divine physicians] in the cosmos is effulgence of the body. The Marut-host [companions of Indra] in the cosmos is enthusiasm in the person. The gods [deva] in the firmament are the sense-organs and the sense-faculties. Darkness in the cosmos is infatuation in the person. Light in the cosmos is knowledge in the person. The beginning of creation is the conception of man. Sat-yuga [the first, 'golden' world age] is childhood: *treta-yuga* is youth, *dvapara-yuga* is old age. As is the end of a cycle of creation, so is death." Cf. *Caraka Samhita*, IV.v.2–5.

27.   *Ibid.*, I.xxvii.349–50.
28.   *Ibid.*, IV.i.45–46.
29.   Quoted in Ashis Nandy, *Alternative Sciences* (New Delhi: Allied Publishers, 1980), p. 47.
30.   To elaborate on these: 1. *The objects of the senses:* Looking at highly luminous objects too much would be the excessive use of vision. Not looking at anything at all would be nonuse, while looking at things from too close or too far, or looking at things that are alarming or terrifying, would be the misuse of the objects of vision. Similarly, smelling exceedingly sharp and acute odors is excessive utilization of the olfactory sense, not to smell at all is nonuse, while the smelling of putrid, unpleasant and dirty objects is misuse. These examples can be multiplied for the other senses.

   2. *Action:* Here action means mental, physical and "vocal" action. Excessive indulgence in any bodily, mental or speech activity as well as refraining from these activities may cause disease. An example of the misuse of the body is the forceful suppression of natural urges relating to urine, feces, semen, flatus, vomiting, sneezing, yawning, hunger, thirst, tears, sleep and breathing caused by overexertion. Examples of the misuse of speech are lying, backbiting, unpleasant and harsh utterances. Examples of misuse of mind are giving way to fear, anxiety, anger, greed, vanity, envy and delusions. The whole complex of the improper use of the body-mind-speech entity is also called "intellectual blasphemy" *(prajnapradha)* and is assigned a prime role in disease causation.

   3. *Time:* Diseases are also caused when the characteristics of a particular season manifest themselves in an excessive measure or when the season is marked by a deficiency of its traits or when it is marked by characteristics that are contrary to its true nature.
31.   For a psychoanalytic discussion of the body image see Paul Schilder, *The Image and Appearance of the Human Body* (New York: International Universities Press, 1950); see further Phyllis Greenacre, *Emotional Growth*, vol. 1 (New York: International Universities Press, 1971), pp. 22–25, and pp. 113–27; W. Hoffer, "The Development of the Body Ego," *The Psychoanalytic Study of the Child*, 5, 1950, pp. 18–24; G. J. Rose, "Body Ego and Reality," *International Journal of Psychoanalysis*, 47, pp. 502–09.
32.   Phyllis Greenacre, *Emotional Growth*, vol. 1 (New York: International Universities Press, 1971), p. 118.
33.   Krsna-dhan Cattopadyaya, *The Doctrine of the Body* (1878), Adati Nath Sarkar (tr.), Ralph Nicholas (ed.), Department of Anthropology, University of Chicago, unpublished ms., p. 31.

34. Francis Zimmermann, "Remarks on the Conception of the Body in Ayurvedic Medicine," paper presented at the ACLS-SSRC Seminar on the Person and Interpersonal Relations in South Asia, University of Chicago, 1979, p. 7.

35. Wendy O'Flaherty, *Women, Androgynes and Other Mythical Beasts, op. cit.,* chapter 2.

36. *Caraka Samhita,* I.v.15–19.

37. *Ibid.,* I.v.57–62.

38. *Ibid.,* I.v.78.

39. *Ibid.,* I.v.68–89.

40. *Ibid.,* I.v.96–97.

41. *Ibid.,* I.vi.17 and 32.

42. Lawrence Kubie, "The Fantasy of Dirt," *Psychoanalytic Quarterly,* 6, 1937, p. 391.

43. For a recent statement on the methodological usefulness of interactionism see Karl R. Popper and John C. Eccles, *The Self and Its Brain* (New York: Springer International, 1979).

44. For a short discussion of the identity thesis in current Western philosophical thought see Robert C. Solomon, "Freud's Neurological Theory of Mind," in R. Wolheim (ed.), *Philosophers on Freud* (New York: Jason Aronson, 1977), pp. 25–52. It must be pointed out that there is no more evidence for the identity thesis than there is for psychophysical parallelism or for interactionism; the difference between the three hypotheses lies purely in their ontological and heuristic appeal.

45. In this connection, see also C. G. Jung, *Analytical Psychology* (New York: Pantheon Books, 1968), pp. 8–9.

46. Joyce McDougall, "The Psycho-soma and the Psychoanalytic Process," *The International Review of Psycho-Analysis,* 1(4), 1974, p. 441.

47. Franz Alexander, *Psychosomatic Medicine: Its Principles and Application* (New York: W. W. Norton, 1950).

48. Quoted in Jyotimitra Acharya, "Mano Nirupan," in *Indraprastha Ayurveda Sammelan Patrika: Manasroga Samarika* (Delhi: Shri Indraprastha Vaid Sabha, 1979), pp. 17–24.

49. For the Ayurvedic dream typology, see *Caraka Samhita, op. cit.,* V.v.42.

50. Kaviraj Nanakchandra Sharma, "Manasrog aur Abhichar," in *Indraprastha Ayurveda Sammelan Patrika, op. cit.,* p. 94.

51. Kailashnath Jaitley Vaid, "Trigunatamak mana aur nadi," in *Indraprastha Ayurveda Sammelan Patrika, op. cit.,* p. 73.

52. Mahavir Prasad Pandey, "Manas rogon ki Pristhbhumi," in *Indraprastha, op. cit.,* p. 39.

53. *Caraka Samhita,* I.viii,17–35.

54. *Ibid.,* I.viii,25–28.

55. For a detailed discussion see Sudhir Kakar, "Relative Realities: Images of Adulthood in Psychoanalysis and the Yogas," in S. Kakar (ed.), *Identity and Adulthood* (Delhi and New York: Oxford University Press, 1979), pp. 118–30.

56. *Caraka Samhita,* I.xi.54.

57.   See Zimmermann, *op. cit.*, p. 20.

58.   For a short list and description of Ayurvedic medicines used in mental disorders see Jageram Gupta, "Manasikrogon par vishesh prahbavkari aushadion ka sankshipt vargikaran tatha sangraha" in *Indraprastha, op. cit.*, pp. 102–06.

CHAPTER 9 THE GOOD DOCTOR OF JHARSETLI

1.   See Thomas Szasz, *The Ethics of Psychoanalysis* (London: Routledge, Kegan and Paul, 1974), p. 25.

2.   *Ibid.*, pp. 35–37.

3.   See Paul Watzlawick *et al.*, *Lösungen: Zur Theorie und Praxis menschlichen Wandels* (Bern: Hans Huber, 1975).

4.   *Ibid.*, p. 129.

5.   R. H. Prince, "The Use of Rauwolfia for the Treatment of Psychoses by Nigerian Native Doctors," *American Journal of Psychiatry*, 118, 1960, pp. 147–49.

6.   For descriptions of these systems, see R. D. Walter, *Weir Mitchell, M.D.—Neurologist* (Springfield, Ill.: Thomas, 1970), and T. Kora, "Morita Therapy," *International Journal of Psychiatry*, 1, 1965, pp. 611–40.

7.   Indradev Tripathi (ed.), *Nadi-Vijana of Maharsi Kanada* (Varanasi: Chowkhambha Orientalia, 1976).

8.   *Nadi-Vijana, op. cit.*, pp. 12–17.

9.   See Eugene Anderson, "Folk Dietetics in Two Chinese Communities and Their Implications for the Study of Chinese Medicine," and A. Harwood, "The Hot-Cold Theory of Disease: Implications for Treatment of Puerto-Rican Patients," cited in A. Kleinman, "The Symbolic Context of Chinese Medicine: A Comparative Approach to the Study of Traditional Medical and Psychiatric Forms of Care in Chinese Culture," in *American Journal of Chinese Medicine*, 3(2), 1975, p. 114.

10.   Margaret T. Egnor, *The Sacred Spell and Other Conceptions of Life in Tamil Culture*, unpublished Ph.D. thesis, Department of Anthropology, University of Chicago, 1978, p. 52.

11.   D. W. Winnicott, "Appetite and Emotional Disorder," in *Collected Papers* (London: Tavistock Publications, 1958), p. 34.

CHAPTER 10 EPILOGUE: HEALING AND CULTURE

1.   Heinz Kohut, "The Two Analyses of Mr. Z.," *International Journal of Psychoanalysis*, 60, 1979, p. 12.

2.   See Sudhir Kakar, *The Inner World: A Psychoanalytic Study of Childhood and Society in India* (New York and Delhi: Oxford University Press, 1978), p. 124.

3.   For a description and analysis of these myths see Kakar, *The Inner World, op. cit.*, pp. 100–02.

4. Stephen A. Mitchell, "The Psychoanalytic Treatment of Homosexuality: Some Technical Considerations," *International Review of Psychoanalysis*, 8(1), 1981, p. 78.

5. For a representative statement of Marriott's views see McKim Marriott, "The Open Hindu Person and Interpersonal Fluidity," unpublished paper read at the session on "The Indian Self" at the meetings of Association for Asian Studies, Washington, D.C., March 1980.

6. McKim Marriott, personal communication.

7. Sigmund Freud, "On Psychotherapy" (1905), in *The Standard Edition of the Complete Psychological Works of Sigmund Freud* (ed. J. Strachey), vol. 7 (London: Hogarth Press, 1953), pp. 257–70.

8. See, for instance, Franz Alexander, "Psychoanalysis and Psychotherapy," *Journal of American Psychoanalytic Association*, 2, 1954, pp. 722–33. Of course, a section of psychiatrists believes that the therapeutic force in all psychotherapies, including the "uncovering" of psychoanalysis, is fundamentally the same, *i.e.*, suggestion. For representative views of this position, see Jerome D. Frank, *Persuasion and Healing* (Baltimore: Johns Hopkins Press, 1953); K. M. Calestro, "Psychotherapy, Faith Healing and Suggestions," *International Journal of Psychiatry*, 10, 1972, pp. 83–113; E. F. Torrey, *The Mind Game* (New York: Emerson Hall, 1972).

9. Jerome D. Oremland, "Transference Cure and Flight into Health," *International Journal of Psychoanalytic Psychotherapy*, 1(1), 1972, pp. 61–75.

10. See Sudhir Kakar, *The Inner World, op. cit.*, pp. 34–36 and 85–87.

11. See J. S. Neki, "Guru-Chela Relationship: The Possibility of a Psychotherapeutic Paradigm," in *American Journal of Orthopsychiatry*, 1973, pp. 755–66; see also G. M. Carstairs, "Cultural Elements in Response to Treatment," in *CIBA Symposium on Transcultural Psychiatry* (A.V.S. de Rueck and P. Porter, eds.) (London: J. & A. Churchill, 1965).

INDEX

Sudhir Kakar was educated in India, the United States, West Germany and Austria. He is a practicing psychoanalyst, a senior fellow of the Centre for the Study of Developing Societies and the author of several books, including *The Inner World: A Psychoanalytic Study of Childhood and Society in India*. He lives in New Delhi.

A NOTE ON THE TYPE

The text of this book was set via computer-driven
cathode-ray tube, in Electra, a typeface designed by W. A.
Dwiggins (1880–1956). This face cannot be classified as
either modern or old style. It is not based on any historical
model; nor does it echo any particular period or style. It
avoids the extreme contrasts between thick and thin
elements that mark most modern faces and attempts to give
a feeling of fluidity, power, and speed.

Composed, printed, and bound by
The Haddon Craftsmen, Inc.,
Scranton, Pennsylvania.

Designed by Judith Henry.